Queer-Contextualized Family Therapy

Queer-Contextualized Family Therapy: Toward Radically Inclusive Theory and Practice offers a groundbreaking reimagining of foundational family therapy models through an intersectional queer lens. In this essential volume, the authors chart a transformative path forward for relational and systemic therapy that affirms, honors, and centers queer and trans lives.

More than critique, this book introduces an innovative approach to update and revise any therapeutic theory. This new framework—queer-contextualizing—is applied to specific family therapy models, providing a compelling blend of scholarly insight and practical, tangible strategies for real-world application.

Designed for experienced therapists, students in training, and educators shaping the future of the field, this book stands as both an essential resource and an inspirational call to action. With its bold, expansive vision, *Queer-Contextualized Family Therapy* redefines what it means to do ethical, inclusive, and culturally attuned clinical work in the 21st century.

Erica E. Hartwell, PhD, LMFT, is an Associate Professor of Marriage, Couple, and Family Therapy at Lewis and Clark Graduate School, Portland, Oregon, USA. She served as the first chair of American Association of Marriage and Family Therapy's Queer and Trans Advocacy Network and led the development of AAMFT's Clinical Guidelines for LGBTQIA Affirming Marriage and Family Therapy.

Lindsay L. Edwards, PhD, LMFT, works for Colorado's Behavioral Health Administration, Denver, Colorado, USA. She specializes in LGBTQ+ inclusive family therapy and currently provides private practice supervision.

"This compelling book brilliantly accomplishes what it sets out to do: address the gap between foundational systemic theories and affirmative therapy. By 'queer contextualizing' esteemed therapeutic theories, the authors skillfully address intersectionality and re-imagine the wisdom each theoretical perspective might offer when queer and trans people are intentionally included, respected and honored. The overall work is both practical and inspirationally transformative. It should be required reading for anyone seeing clients in the 21st century."

Rebecca Harvey, PhD, professor of marriage and family
therapy at Southern Connecticut State University,
author of *Nurturing Queer Youth*

"A must-read for any clinician dedicated to inclusivity and equity, *Queer-Contextualized Family Therapy: Toward Radically Inclusive Theory and Practice* is a groundbreaking work that revolutionizes our understanding of family therapy approaches through an intersectional queer lens. Drs. Erica Hartwell, Lindsay Edwards, and a team of leading voices in the field reimagine traditional models, providing tangible, practical strategies for evolving clinical theory to better serve all of your clients. This book is guaranteed to be an essential resource for contemporary practitioners."

Diane R. Gehart, PhD, founder and CEO of Therapy
that Works Institute and Professor Emerita at
California State University, Northridge

"This thought-provoking book re-imagines family therapy by centering queerness and other marginalized identities rather than mainstream White heterosexuality. It will challenge your most precious notions about healthy family functioning and persuade you to reconsider your implicit promotion of mainstream conformity. I highly recommend it for those who already are familiar with one or more traditional approaches to systems therapy and seek to expand their capacity to work more creatively with all couples and families!"

Robert-Jay Green, PhD, Distinguished Professor Emeritus, Clinical
Psychology PhD Program, Alliant International University, San
Francisco; Co-editor, *Lesbians and Gays in Couples and Families: A
Handbook for Therapists*; Recipient, 2024 AAMFT Outstanding
Contribution to Marriage & Family Therapy Award

"This book provides a reimagined family therapy for the 21st century that centers the lives of queer individuals in reworking theories at the core of relational and systemic work—updating what feels outdated. The editors and authors are current and emerging leaders who place these models within a queer-contextualized framework. One of the things I love about this book is that it goes beyond just critique by creating useful and applicable queer recontextualizations of our models. Importantly, the authors use an intersectional framework, allowing for attention to multiple layers of oppression. The editors and authors have created a recontextualizing framework that guides this work and can also be usefully applied in other ways, where one can 'reimagine … theor[ies] for radically inclusive practice' (p. 9). One of the strengths is that this reimagining broadens the applicability of these models to all those on the margins in multiple ways. These reimagined models are expanded in ways that make them more useful in all clinical work, not just in work with queer individuals and families. Importantly, this book is also about practice and not just theory—examples make clear the utility of these queer-contextualized models. This vital book provides a much-needed resource for teaching and learning about family therapy models in contemporary society and will be required reading in many MFT programs!"

Kevin Lyness, PhD, professor and director of the couple
and family therapy PhD program at Antioch University,
New England

"Brilliant! Hartwell and Edwards' concept of 'queer-contextualized' couple and family therapy is an innovative and necessary framework that will advance the field of family therapy, not only for practitioners but for the field of family science in general. This book is scholarly and theoretically rich, and the case examples for each reimagined systemic model of therapy bring their framework to life. For all couple and family therapy enthusiasts, this book will be a joy to read, and it is essential for the practice of ethical and equitable systemic psychotherapy."

J. Maria Bermudez, PhD, is an associate professor of couple and
family therapy and human development and family science at
the University of Georgia, co-author of *Socioculturally Attuned
Family Therapy: Guidelines for Equitable Theory and Practice*
and author/editor of *Intersectionality and Context Across the
Lifespan: Readings for Human Development*

Queer-Contextualized Family Therapy

Toward Radically Inclusive Theory and Practice

Edited by Erica E. Hartwell and Lindsay L. Edwards

Routledge
Taylor & Francis Group

NEW YORK AND LONDON

This book is dedicated to those who see the potential for a better world—one where *all* people are treated with respect and dignity—and have invested their whole radical selves in pursuit of this endeavor.

Contents

Contributors

Sheila M. Addison, PhD, is an AAMFT Approved Supervisor, Certified Gottman Therapist, and AASECT Certified Sex Therapist in Seattle, Washington, who has worked with couples for more than 25 years, specializing in LGBTQ+, BIPOC, and nonmonogamous relationships.

Pia Alexander, MA, is a licensed marriage and family therapist and clinical supervisor in Brooklyn, New York, and a member of core faculty in the Couple and Family Therapy Program at Antioch University, New England.

Robert Allan, PhD, is an Associate Professor in the Couple and Family Therapy Program, University of Colorado, Denver.

Christopher K. Belous, PhD, is an Associate Professor and Director of the Couple and Family Therapy Graduate Program at Purdue University Northwest, specializing in sex therapy, sex education, and work with queer folx.

Brooks Bull, PhD, is a family therapist in private practice in Northampton, Massachusetts. They primarily see trans and queer clients, and research and write about families with transgender members.

Justine D'Arrigo, PhD, is an Associate Professor in the MS in Counseling Program at California State University, San Bernardino, where they also serve as the faculty coordinator for the Undergraduate Minor in Counseling and Social Change.

Becky A. Diaz, MA, is a licensed marriage and family therapist and clinical supervisor based in New Jersey and New York. She is a core faculty member in the Marriage and Family Therapy Program at Kean University. Her clinical and teaching work emphasize systemic practice with an intersectional lens.

Caitlin Edwards, PhD, is a postdoctoral research fellow at Colorado State University, a certified Emotionally Focused Therapist, and enthusiastic researcher of community-engaged mental health interventions for the LGBTQIA + communities.

Lindsay L. Edwards, PhD, works in the Children, Youth, and Family Division of Colorado's Behavioral Health Administration (BHA). Dr. Edwards specializes in LGBTQ+ inclusive family therapy and provides private practice supervision as an AAMFT Approved Supervisor. She has also worked as an Associate Professor of marriage and family therapy.

Benjamin T. Finlayson, PhD, is an Assistant Professor of Marriage and Family Therapy at Regis University in Denver, Colorado. Dr. Finlayson uses his identity as a queer professional to ground his writing and advocacy. His research centers on queer experiences and solution-focused brief therapy.

Rashmi Gangamma, PhD, is an Associate Professor and Program Director in the Couple and Family Therapy Program at the University of Colorado, Denver.

Kristi Harrison, PhD, is a licensed marriage and family therapist, supervisor, and Core Faculty and Program Director in the Couple and Family Therapy Program at Antioch University, New England.

Erica E. Hartwell, PhD, is an Associate Professor of Marriage, Couple, and Family Therapy at Lewis & Clark College, Portland, Oregon.

Tomoyo Kawano, PhD, is an Associate Professor and Director of the Master's Program in Dance/Movement Therapy with a Concentration in Couple and Family Therapy Program at Antioch University, New England.

Le Nguyen Anh Khoi (Anh-Khoi Le), MA, is a doctoral student in the Department of Marriage and Family Therapy at Syracuse University, and an affiliate at the Center for Population Sciences and Health Equity in Tallahassee, Florida.

Logan Parrott, MA, is a graduate from Antioch University, New England, with a master's degree in dance/movement therapy with a concentration in couple and family therapy.

Sara Smock Jordan, PhD, is a Professor of Marriage and Family Therapy and Program Director of University of Nevada, Las Vegas' Couple and Family Therapy Program. In her scholarship, Dr. Jordan focuses on applying solution-focused brief therapy (SFBT) to marginalized groups, such as the LGBTQ community.

Carla Vitola, MA, is a licensed marriage and family therapist and clinical supervisor at Tri-Meta Counseling & Associates private practice and adjunct professor in Marriage and Family Therapy Program and Community Care Coordinator at Kean University.

Andrea K. Wittenborn, PhD, is Professor and Director of the Couple and Family Therapy Doctoral Program in the Department of Human Development and Family Studies at Michigan State University.

Foreword

The field has needed this book for years.

In 1996, I published my first family therapy journal article in *Family Process*, addressing the exclusion of queer issues in family therapy models and theories, and thus from the practice of clinical supervision. I remember the fear and trepidation I experienced submitting that article and wondering if it would ever get published. Why did I have those fears? When I entered the marriage and family therapy (MFT) field in the early 1990s and began writing, I knew no other academic LGBTQ+ folk who could serve as role models or mentors. As I reviewed the literature, I discovered others who were writing about and researching queer relationships and families outside of MFT, including Joan Laird and Ann Hartman from social work, Robert-Jay Green from psychology, and Nanette Gartrell in psychiatry, to mention a few. Within MFT, I had the good fortune to enter academic life at the same time as Julie Serovich. We coauthored my second queer article for *The Journal of Marital and Family Therapy* focused on training issues in MFT related to working with same-sex couples and families and addressing the fact that reparative therapy was being taught in some COAMFTE-accredited programs.

It is important to remember that there was a time into the mid-2000s when the American Association for Marriage and Family Therapy (AAMFT) did not openly support same-sex marriage and had not openly stated that "homosexuality" was not a mental illness. I served on the board of directors of AAMFT at the time and advocated that we make a strong statement making our stances clear that sexual orientation was not a mental illness, and that we support same-sex marriage. These stances on my part were not popular ones at that time. I received hundreds of emails and messages from AAMFT members who were opposed to my efforts and many who held me personally responsible for the ruin of MFT because I was encouraging people to adopt a sinful "lifestyle".

Historically, there were strong ties between the professions of MFT and pastoral counseling. Many MFT training programs were housed within religiously affiliated academic institutions. Even most early programs in nonreligious institutions were housed within traditional colleges of home economics. These predominantly cishetmononormative systems held a lot of power in determining what was taught, who should teach and supervise, what was considered ethical, and what was published.

Despite this pushback, I continued the call for LGBTQ+ inclusive revisions throughout the rest of my career in MFT, and every year I hoped the primary authors of family therapy theories and models would take up my challenge to recontextualize those foundational theories. Nearly 30 years later, the authors in this book have answered that call.

Reading the chapters of this book and writing this foreword took me back in history in a way that really surprised me. The strong pushback I received from being out and advocating for queer inclusion in MFT came flooding back to me in a way I would not have expected. From being told not to research or "write about gays" again by my department chair; being told that I had turned all the grad students in the department to a "bunch of queers" by colleagues; being told never to publish in a family therapy or a feminist journal again by another department chair; being told that I was recruiting too many minority students to our program and that I should quit mentoring Black, gay, and international students by a department chair.

These sentiments reflected the larger academic system at the time. However, I would be remiss if I did not mention that I had many colleagues who were wonderful allies and who supported me during my academic journey: Jerry Gale, Charles Cole, Rachel Hare Mustin, Julie Serovich, Cheryl Storm, John Lawless, Elizabeth Lindsey, Karen Rosen, Sandra Stith, Jenny Simons, Mike Fitzpatrick, Kevin Lyness, and Anne Prouty, to name a few.

In these days of extreme transphobia and regression from support for same-sex marriage, the erasure of our history, and a return to increased support for reparative therapies in the larger American culture, it is essential for the work of these editors and authors to finally surface in the MFT literature.

Erica Hartwell and Lindsay Edwards have bravely and responsibly provided a socially conscious and intersectional framework for such a recontextualization and have selected a diverse group of authors to join them. They outline the limitations and strengths of each approach and offer us new creative ways to think about how those approaches can honor and be centered in ways that support queer individuals, relationships, and families. They invite the reader to imagine new inclusive versions of the models based on evolving theory that deconstructs the heteronormative power imbalances upon which the foundational models were built. Clinical case examples and a set of relevant questions for the reader to examine themselves in the context of the newly imaged models help to make this a highly effective and useful book for clinicians at all stages of development. For readers who have long been struggling with outdated, heteronormatively biased, and non-inclusive theories and models, the editors and authors provide a starting point and invite us all to join them in their journey toward radically inclusive theory and practice. May the reader be inspired to take their writing to heart and use it to work in ways that do no further harm to those we have previously failed.

Janie K. Long, PhD
Faculty Emerita, Duke University

Acknowledgments

We want to start by expressing our sincere gratitude to the marriage and family therapy scholars, educators, and clinicians who have come before us and made this book possible. Those who challenged the status quo of our field when it wasn't safe to do so. Those who stood up at conferences and in meetings knowing there would be a cost. Those who gathered in hallways and bars. We know that we are only able to publish this book— a book that not only critiques our foundational theories but reimagines them with queer folks at the center—because of the courage and determination of queer, trans, BIPOC, and allied MFTs who cleared the path.

When we thought about those who paved the way for this book, Janie Long came quickly to mind. In the nineties, she was among the first to openly advocate for LGBTQ+ inclusion in MFT graduate programs, conferences, and scholarship. She went on to advocate for LGBTQ+ young people at Duke University, where she led the Center for Gender and Sexual Diversity and eventually retired as an associate vice provost with a library space and a speaker series named in her honor. Janie's career has always centered the well-being of queer people, which is why we are so grateful to have her write the foreword for this book.

We also want to thank Julia Giordano and Heather Evans, the two wonderful editors we worked with at Routledge. Thank you to the students who donated their precious time to make this book come to life: Anne Boatman, Sean Douglas, Benjamin Griffiths, Lauren Meyers, Rinny Newell, and Atlas Willow. Thank you to Kate Greenen for her wit and intellect, as always. Thank you to everyone who submitted a proposal for a chapter or attended presentations and helped us think through our ideas. Thank you to the authors who shared their compassionate wisdom in these pages, and who graciously allowed us to shape their chapters to fit our vision for this book. Thank you to our students who demand more from the field, from the theories, and from us. Thank you to everyone who said, *we need this book*. We know it isn't the answer to all of your questions, but we hope it's a start.

Erica: I am incredibly proud of this book, and I am keenly aware that I could not have done this without the love and support of many people along the way. I am grateful to have grown up in an expansive family of origin that was defined by care and commitment over blood and marriage. Three of my most treasured possessions are quilts made by three different grandmothers. These quilts not only remind me of days spent crafting, cooking, and creating with the women in my family, they are also symbols of the traditions and wisdom I received from multiple generations and cultures that have been stitched together like a patchwork quilt—creating a one-of-a-kind source of warmth and comfort. To my family, thank you for providing the tools and the fabric and encouraging me to craft my own way.

I have been very lucky in my life to have incredible mentors who saw what I was capable of, who I could become, and empowered me to step outside of my comfort zone. Thank you to Chip Schneider for guiding me toward a future I didn't know was in my reach. To Reba McCutcheon, thank you for showing me what it means to lead with your whole heart. Thank you to Amy Blanchard and Walter Lowe for pushing me to go further. To Suzanne Bartle-Haring, you are brilliant and caring and a person of deep integrity. Thank you for showing me that being an academic doesn't mean choosing between the three. To Rona, Nicole, and Maryann, thank you for making a job feel like a family.

I am grateful for the time I was granted to work on this book while at Fairfield University, and for receiving the honor of the Robert E. Wall Award. Thank you to everyone—friends, family members, colleagues, and students—who asked me how the book was coming along, who wrote with me, who talked through my imposter syndrome, and who harassed me to just get it done already. Thank you to Lindsay, for your unwavering enthusiasm and belief in what we were doing long before there was a book contract, for your thought-provoking questions and analytical mind, and for becoming a friend.

And, finally, my deepest gratitude is for my chosen family, my squad, thank you for the gift of belonging. Thank you for reminding me who I am when I lose my way. Thank you for doing the hard work of cultivating our community—these sacred constellations of relationships. We are made of stars, and we are here to light the world.

Lindsay: Relationships are what I live for, and I am fortunate to be in relationship with some of the most loving, considerate, smart, and funny people in the world. It is difficult to express in words how grateful I am for my partner Matt, who I have grown alongside of for 19 years. Matt, thank you for being my best friend, for continuing to experience life with me, for stretching me, and for still trying to make me laugh. My life is beautiful because of you. Thank you to my daughter Evie for sharing her wisdom with me and helping to spark new ideas and thoughts during our many deep conversations. Thank you to my son Emmet for showing me what it means to be genuine and enthusiastic, and connecting me with these parts of myself that are so hard to hold on to as an adult. Thank you to my parents for making sure that I know, above all else, that I am loved and always have someone in my corner. To my sister Kim, I am so glad that I got you as a sister. Sibling relationships are the longest relationships we have, and I am so lucky that I have such a considerate, encouraging, and fun partner in life. Thank you to Kristi, my friend of 17 years, for being someone who leads by example and who is the most caring person I have ever known. Thank you to my friend Luis, for showing me what it means to live in integrity, to center connection and ethics in relationships, and for always having my back. Finally, thank you to my friend and coeditor Erica for thinking big with me. I have thoroughly enjoyed every hour we spent discussing, generating, and editing the ideas we have included in this book. This was a labor of love, and I am so grateful for the opportunity to do this with you.

Let me end by expressing my gratitude for Drs. Tony Jurich and Candyce Russell, who taught me what it means to think and live systemically. Tony, in particular, taught me the importance of living life on my own terms. I can still remember what it felt like to wait outside of his office for supervision and hear him walking down the hallway singing at the top of his lungs. He sang because he liked signing, I dance because I like dancing. Candy helped me realize that I could be an academic, and that writing and research are experiences to be enjoyed. Candy, thank you for this gift. Similarly, I feel deep gratitude to Virginia Satir for putting her masterful ideas in writing. Reading her books felt like a warm hug, and learning from her ideas changed the trajectory of my life. Understanding systems theory, our interconnectedness, the importance of congruence, and the power of process have helped me live relationally and with greater connection to my essential self. Learning from these masters has made me a better partner, parent, daughter, sibling, friend, and citizen. For that, I am eternally grateful.

Chapter 1

Queer-Contextualized Family Therapy

Erica E. Hartwell and Lindsay L. Edwards

The first two classes I (Erica) took in my marriage and family therapy (MFT) master's degree program were on ethics and foundational theories. I remember feeling overwhelmed trying to understand what it meant to think systemically. Looking back, I can see why these courses are scheduled early in a training program. They say a lot about what we think is essential to the practice of MFT. We think it is important that a student learns the ethical code before they ever meet with a client, because our most crucial responsibility is to do no harm. Of course, we hope for more than just doing no harm—we aspire to do good, to be helpful. Since that first semester I have asked myself, what does it mean to do good? Who decides what is good? Where is the line between respecting client autonomy and exercising clinical judgment? When do we need to make a report, and when do we need to learn more about parenting in our client's culture? What is the difference between practicing within our scope and making a referral because we are uncomfortable? These questions, which weigh on the most experienced MFTs, were terrifying to a first-semester therapist.

Equally terrifying was my foundational theory course, in which I learned about communication theory, structural family therapy, and Bowen family systems theory. I struggled through the assigned texts—all of which were older than me—dutifully highlighting the pages and taking notes on the key concepts. I learned more from class discussions, though. My professor had a deep understanding of these theories and was patient as we slowly loosened our grasp on linear thinking. I noticed that, while he was very knowledgeable, the professor did not seem to have much enthusiasm for these theories. He had a dry sense of humor and often smirked to himself while we wrestled with the concepts out loud. At the time, I found this intimidating. I took it to mean that we weren't getting it. Years later, my interpretation has changed. Like many MFT students, we were a group of anxious overachievers beginning the messy process of changing our worldview, all the while hating the mess. He had no doubt witnessed this before, and the

DOI: 10.4324/9781003308188-1

smile probably came from a place of recognition. It has also occurred to me that the smile may have had nothing to do with the students, and everything to do with the content of the course. Maybe he found it absurd that we were expected to learn and use these sixty-year-old theories, which had never been revised or updated, in our twenty-first century clinical work.

The first edition of the *Handbook of LGBTQ-Affirmative Couple and Family Therapy* (Giammattei & Green, 2012) opens with direct quotes from two theories I studied that first semester, communication theory and Bowen theory, reprinted here:

> This is also the problem of the homosexual who longs for an intense relationship with a "real" male, only to find that the latter is always, must always be, another homosexual.
>
> (Watzlawick, Helmick Beavin, & Jackson, 1967, p. 200)

> All psychiatric diagnosis, in fact, can be conceptualized on this continuum of adaptiveness or differentiation. The age of onset, severity, and impairment of life functioning associated with all psychiatric diagnoses can be understood in the context of the multigenerational emotional process. The most extreme forms of manic-depression, alcoholism, obsessive compulsive neurosis, and homosexuality, for example, develop over the course of at least several generations.
>
> (Kerr & Bowen, 1988, p. 241)

These statements are not surprising, given they were created at a time when the gender binary was being enforced through stigmatization, pathologization, and criminalization. It is also not surprising, given the writers' identities and sociocultural context, that race and class are not meaningfully considered in these theories either. In fact, the founders of family therapy intentionally ignored the impact of power, insisting instead on neutrality. They believed that all parts of a system played an equal role. While this would be true if we lived in an egalitarian society, we do not. We exist within systems of power that play out in our families and relationships. In this context, neutrality is never equal. Neutrality serves the status quo.

The conversation about power in the family therapy field has been going on for decades, beginning with the feminist critique in the 1980s (e.g., Walters et al., 1988), followed by a multicultural and critical race critique (e.g., Hardy & Laszloffy, 1994), and eventually addressing the exclusion of lesbian, gay, bisexual, transgender, and queer (LGBTQ) issues (Long, 1996; Long & Serovich, 2003). Over time, the literature moved from a pathological and negative view of queer folks to a more affirming and normalizing stance (Hartwell et al., 2012). The affirmative therapy approach arose in response to the continued unethical and traumatic practice of sexual orientation and gender identity change efforts. To be affirmative, a therapist must, at a minimum, view the diverse range of sexual orientations and gender identities and expressions as normal and natural, have a basic understanding of the lives and contexts of their queer clients, and be continually monitoring their own biases and misconceptions (Ritter & Terndrup, 2002). Harvey, Murphy, and Laszloffy (2022) encourage therapists to go beyond these minimum requirements and give six recommendations for deepening and furthering affirmative practice: (1) center ethics and intersectionality; (2) recognize that there is no universal LGBTQ experience; (3) challenge the gender binary; (4) fully explore the singularity of each identity and each person's unique experience of that identity; (5) focus on training; (6) self-examination. Even with this deepening of affirmative practice, affirmative therapy is still just an approach, not a theory of clinical change (Harvey et al., 2022). In fact, none of the cultural critiques of family therapy—feminist, multicultural, or affirmative—help clinicians conceptualize problems or change, which is the essential purpose of a theory. They are layers added on top of a traditional model, requiring the clinician to be continually monitoring for bias inherent in the models, and revising or discarding the parts that don't fit. This is a considerable amount of work that leaves many therapists feeling they have to choose between theory and inclusive practice. In an effort to do good, we abandon our theories because most were created without regard for privilege, power, and oppression, so there will always be components that don't work for our clients and, at worst, harm them.

We need to suck the poison of racism, classism, and heterosexism out of our theories for the good of our clients. Family therapists have been calling for this for years (Addison & Coolhart, 2015; Harvey et al., 2022; Long et al., 2006), and it hasn't been done yet—although some have come close. In 2005, Harvey and Stone Fish created a model for working with queer youth and their families that integrates elements of systems theory, queer theory, and youth development. It focuses on deconstructing parents' fears or misconceptions and moving them past mere acceptance to embracing their child's queer identity. It addresses the gaps in most family therapy theories when it comes to working with families of queer youth by creating a new model. The following year, Long et al. (2006) applied several foundational models to clinical work with queer families but did not adapt or reimagine the models. The authors did, however, issue a direct call for clinicians who are well trained in these models to dig deeper in their work with queer clients, determine how the models do or do not fit, and to publish what they find. No one has answered that call—until now. The book in your hands adds a new level to affirmative practice by not only critiquing the way family therapy theories maintain the status quo, but also recognizing their potential for radical and systemic conceptualization and treatment. In this book, we reimagine these theories in a way that centers those on the margins, honors their diversity and uniqueness, and improves the theories in ways that benefit all clients and clinicians.

From Queering to Recontextualizing to Queer-Contextualizing

In order to describe the strategy that we used to reimagine the theories in this book, we must first orient you to our frame of reference. You might be wondering "What's with the long, complicated book title? Wouldn't *Queering Family Therapy* have been better?" Indeed, this title would have been more compelling, and certainly easier to say, but such a title would have obscured the intent and focus of the book. This book does *not* queer MFT theory and practice. As Tilsen (2021) explains, queering—or rather implementing the critical practices of queer theory—is a strategy for challenging the structural and essentialist assumptions that underpin a modern and individualistic view of reality. Such a strategy is rooted in social constructionism and post-structuralism, which assume that there is no interior "self" separate from culture, nor is there a "truth" that exists independent of human interpretation. The critical practices of queer theory not only call into question essentialist binary assumptions of gender and sexuality but also dismantle the entire notion that there is a reality which we can accurately represent using language. From a post-structuralist view of the world, there are no family dynamics, only language with which we use to co-construct family dynamics. Rather than viewing language as a way to describe reality, post-structuralists view language as reality. Correspondingly, if we were to "queer" our foundational theories, many of which are rooted in modernist assumptions of reality, they would all but disappear. As radical pragmatists, we do not believe that this would be helpful for practicing systemic therapists who use our foundational theories to organize their thinking. Accordingly, our goal for this book is to implement a critical evaluation of our MFT foundational theories using a strategy that lands somewhere between the "layer cake" version of cultural critique and queering our foundational theories into oblivion.

To conceptualize these efforts, we borrowed from a vocation with a long history of documenting, questioning, and critiquing truth about the human experience—the arts. Art in all of its forms offers a medium through which we can "reorient the way we attend to things and evaluate them" (Makkreel, 2022, p. 342). In particular, principles of contemporary art like appropriation and recontextualization offer effective strategies for activism, cultural analysis, and liberation from colonialism (Gude, 2004; Mix, 2015). For our purposes, the strategy of recontextualization is especially useful since it allows us to play with and manipulate cultural frames of reference (Makkreel, 2022). In art, to recontextualize is to position something familiar, often an image or sound, in a new context where there is an unexpected relationship between the familiar thing and its new context (Barrett, 2006, 2011). Doing so constructs new meaning for the viewer and allows often unnoticed cultural frames of reference to become visible (Gude, 2004).

As a theoretical strategy, recontextualization means moving a construct from its original context to a new one in order to explore its cultural frame and reconceptualize and expand the construct. For our part, we use recontextualization to move our family therapy theories from their original context to a context that centers queer identities, lives, and relationships across race, ethnicity, gender, and class. This "new" context is distinctly different from the contexts in which many of these theories were developed and in which they are often taught and practiced, which center and privilege heterosexual, cisgender, and white identities, lives, and relationships. Thus, our use of "queer-contextualized" in the title of this book denotes the queer and trans-centered context in which we (and the contributing chapter authors) positioned each MFT theory, so that we could explore their invisible frames of reference—thereby making the implicit explicit. Doing so fostered new meaning within our theories and effectively overhauled their theoretical assumptions, which were rooted in a white, middle-class, and heterosexual frame of reference.

It is also important to note that our recontextualization efforts are rooted in the framework of intersectionality—a concept created to illustrate the unique oppression experienced by Black women at the intersection of racism and sexism (Crenshaw, 1989, 1991, 2016). More recently, this frame is used to see how oppressive forces like racism, sexism, classism, ableism, homophobia, and cissexism come together to differentially impact the lives and welfare of people with nondominant social identities. The extension of Crenshaw's original work to other systems of oppression was possible in large part because intersectionality is focused on process-level power dynamics as they exist in institutionalized systems rather than on characteristics of individuals. Given its process-level focus, it is a mistaken application of Crenshaw's ideas to reduce intersectionality to a list of identity categories (Cho et al., 2013). Throughout this book, our efforts to recontextualize MFT theories will attend to the effects of intersectional oppression on the lives of queer people, but especially queer people who are multiply marginalized by additional power structures. You might ask, "If we hope to make these theories more inclusive of all people, then why are we centering it around queerness?" Because queerness can and does encompass all other identities (Gokhale, 2005). Queerness intersects with all other social locations and lived experiences. So, if we bring queerness to the center, we can bring the margins with it, as well as the opportunity to diffuse racism, sexism, classism, ableism, and more.

What Is the Original Context?

Before we can recontextualize the foundational models in a way that centers queer and trans lives and relationships, we must first define the original (i.e., current) sociocultural context in which queer and trans folks live. It is the same context in which MFTs practice, although the more dominant identities you hold, the less aware you might be of it. For the purposes of this book, we focus on the U.S. context, although the process of recontextualizing can occur anywhere. There are many interlocking systems of power in the U.S. that influence our lives and our theories; here we highlight two: white supremacy and patriarchy.

White supremacy is a system of dominance that privileges those who are socialized and perceived as white and oppresses those who are socialized and perceived as other-than-white (Flint, 2004). The system itself defines whiteness and who gets to claim it and benefit from it. White supremacy is closely tied with imperialism, colonialism, and capitalism. Whiteness (as a race) was created in the seventeenth century as a means of justifying the violent expansion and intrusion of primarily English settler-colonizers onto what is now known as the North American continent (Menakem, 2017). English landowners began amassing significant wealth as a result of the resources, goods, and labor stolen from African, indigenous, and poor white bodies. By creating a false hierarchy between white bodies and black and brown bodies, these landowners justified and institutionalized inhumane treatment of those labeled not white and ameliorated unrest among the poor labeled as white. In addition to stealing what they deemed valuable, colonizers (around the world) also attempted to eradicate what they deemed to be a threat to their power—including the vast sexual and gender diversity and expansive relationship networks of many indigenous cultures (Morgensen, 2011). Through extreme violence, the same people who created whiteness also enforced heterosexuality, monogamy, and a strict gender binary across all cultures and ethnicities. In this way, white supremacy and patriarchy are inextricably linked.

Patriarchy is a system of dominance that privileges men, boys, and masculinity and oppresses women, girls, and femininity. It relies on the socially constructed gender binary system to define who has power. This system divides sex, gender identity, gender expression, and attraction into two mutually exclusive categories (Hartwell et al., 2022; Vaid-Menon, 2020). It is rooted in gender essentialism, which assumes that a person's gender develops from their chromosomal makeup and only exists in two discrete manifestations—male and female. Once a person has been assigned a sex at birth, gender identity, gender expression, and sexual orientation are assumed and reinforced. That is, someone who is assigned a male sex is presumed to identify as a man, express that gender in (socially sanctioned) masculine ways, and be exclusively attracted to and partnered with their "opposites" on the gender binary—meaning heterosexual, appropriately feminine, cisgender women.

The gender binary requires everyone to fit neatly into one of these two gender categories, and movement between or beyond them is discouraged, punished, or prevented. People who are attracted to those on their "same side" of the gender binary —who might label that attraction as gay, lesbian, queer, bisexual, etc. —face ostracization, oppressive legislation, and violence. People whose gender identity or expression does not conform to the binary are often subjected to questioning, with others demanding to know which category they are to be placed in. Intersex people—those born with a combination of what we refer to as male and female chromosome patterns, gonads, and/or genitalia—are subjected to medical trauma like genital surgeries when they are very young (Sanz, 2017). These surgeries are attempts to fit natural biological variation into socially constructed categories.

As we mentioned above, the gender binary functions to delineate who has power in a patriarchal system. Relegating people to one of two boxes makes it easier to determine who is in the dominant group and who is not. As you can imagine, the criteria for membership in the dominant group—the masculine group—is much stricter, and violation of that membership is often met with more severe punishment. Young girls might be discouraged from joining in so-called boys' activities, but they are often praised when they are successful. On the other hand, young boys are often met with disgust or anger if they partake in so-called girls' activities and must prove their membership in the dominant group with overt displays of socially sanctioned masculinity. We see a similar phenomenon, but with much higher stakes, when it comes to transgender individuals. While trans men experience social and physical consequences for defying the gender binary, trans women—especially trans women of color—are victimized and murdered at higher rates than any other group (Griffin, 2016). Trans women of color challenge the supremacy of whiteness, masculinity, and heterosexuality in a society that worships these three as ideals.

White supremacy and patriarchy create many other oppressive and restrictive discourses, such as heteronormativity, cisnormativity, and compulsory monogamy. Heteronormativity is the assumption, in individuals or institutions, that everyone is heterosexual and that heterosexuality is the only natural, normal, and healthy sexual orientation (Warner, 1991).

Because heteronormativity reinforces the idea of opposite sexes, it also promotes gender essentialism and cisnormativity—the beliefs that a person's chromosomal makeup is the sole determinant of their gender identity and expression, and that there are only two natural, normal, and preferred alignments of chromosomes, identity, and expression (Worthen, 2016). Mononormativity (also referred to as compulsory monogamy) is the cultural expectation that monogamy is the natural, preferred, and universal structure for adult relationships (Conley et al., 2012a, 2013; Perel, 2006). Homonormativity (Duggan, 2002) reflects the influence of all of these discourses by imposing heteronormative ideals onto queer people and their relationships as a way of legitimizing them in larger society. For example, queer relationships are seen as valid only when they are monogamous, married, raising children (or desiring to do so), and contributing to and participating in capitalism through paid labor and consumerism.

These socially constructed and systemically reinforced power structures, and all the discourses they create, are the context in which MFT theories were created and in which we all currently practice (Harvey et al., 2022). Our foundational theories were created in a homophobic, transphobic, misogynist, racist, and pathologizing context that cannot simply be edited out. Therefore, our theories must be placed in a new context and reimagined. As long as these power structures and discourses underpin our theories and practice, people who represent threats to the patriarchy, the gender binary, and the supremacy of whiteness (and there are quite a few of us) will continue to be pathologized and marginalized.

How Can We Queer-Contextualize Our Theories?

In order to queer-contextualize our foundational MFT theories, we developed a framework to systematically investigate the theoretical assumptions of each model in order to reimagine them for a more inclusive and expansive clinical practice. The first step in this framework is to *identify* the assumptions that underpin a theory. An important assumption to consider in this regard is how the theory views health and dysfunction in a systemic context. This view includes a definition of health from the model perspective, beliefs about what contributes to healthy family functioning, and thoughts on how problems emerge in families. Relatedly, it is important to consider theoretical assumptions about family structure, including who is commonly recognized as a part of a family system, what are the various roles of family members, how a family system should be organized, and how power is best distributed. Another important theoretical assumption to identify is how the theory talks about change—both the mechanism of change and the role of the therapist in carrying out this change.

After identifying the assumptions of a theory, the next step in the recon-textualization framework is to *evaluate* them for how they marginalize and exclude queer people and relationships. This includes asking "*What and whose experiences do these assumptions reflect?* as well as "*What norms are used to anchor the ideas of this theory?*" Furthermore, these questions should be asked intersectionally—meaning that as we consider who a theory overlooks, we need to simultaneously "ask the other question" (Matsuda, 1991, p. 6). Asking the other question is a strategy for considering the interconnectedness of all forms of oppression. Matsuda (1991) writes, "When I see something that looks racist, I ask 'Where is the patriarchy in this?' When I see something that looks sexist, I ask 'Where is the heterosexism in this?' When I see something that looks homophobic, I ask, 'Where is the classism in this?'" (p. 6). This means that when we evaluate a theory for who it overlooks, we must also ask ourselves "*Who is centered in my evaluation of this theory?* and "*Who have I forgotten as I have asked these questions?*" Doing so interrogates a theory for how its assumptions and norms reinforce interconnected systems of dominance like patriarchy and white supremacy. A final circumstance to consider in the evaluation step of this framework is how the norms and assumptions of a theory might account for—even if it is unintentional—the relation-ships and experiences of queer people. The systemic roots of our various MFT theories make them *all* process-oriented theories of change. Given this disposition toward process, it makes sense that aspects of these the-ories would be content-neutral and account for the experiences of *any* prospective client, including queer and trans people. Correspondingly, this evaluation is not just a process of deletion, but one of determining (a) what should be fully retained in a model, (b) what should be kept but reimag-ined, and (c) what should be discarded entirely.

The final step in our queer-contextualization framework is to *reimagine* a theory for radically inclusive practice. To do this, we ask "*If this theory had been created around queer and trans people, lives, and relationships, what might the theory have assumed about health and dysfunction, family structure, and change in therapy?*" Fully reimagining our theories requires that this question be answered from within two distinct queer and trans-centering contexts. The first context is our existing context, where oppressive systems shape the lives of queer and trans people. This means considering how we would answer the question in light of racism, sex-ism, classism, and so on that exists. Answering this first question begins to center queer and trans people but is limited since the insights we can cull from this context are still shaped by existing hierarchical systems. Therefore, the second context we need to consider is one that is outside the influence of oppression. Such a context would assume that queer and trans people and relationships are natural, normal, and valuable. This context is one of liberation and requires that we think flexibly and creatively. We might ask, *"In a world where queer and trans people are respected, valued, and considered the norm, what might the theory assume about health and dysfunction, family structure, and change?"* By considering this question from both contexts, we hold the tension of seeing queer and trans people as natural, normal, and valued, while also acknowledging that we still exist in a society that does not see queer and trans people in this way.

The Family Life Cycle

To illustrate the steps of recontextualization, we will use a foundational model that has been critiqued, revised, and expanded four times since its first publication: the family life cycle (Carter & McGoldrick, 1980, 1988, 1998; McGoldrick et al., 2010, 2016). The fact that this model has been critiqued and expanded multiple times (and by one or more of the original authors) to make it fit the changing context of families makes it unique in the family therapy field. There are many examples of recontextualization among the five editions, and we will point to some of the ways the life cycle was revised from 1980 to 2016. We will also include some of our critique of the central assumptions of the model, and finally provide a reimagination of the model that includes some of the authors' (2016) own revisions, as well as our own reimagining from a queer and trans-centered context (see Figure 1.1).

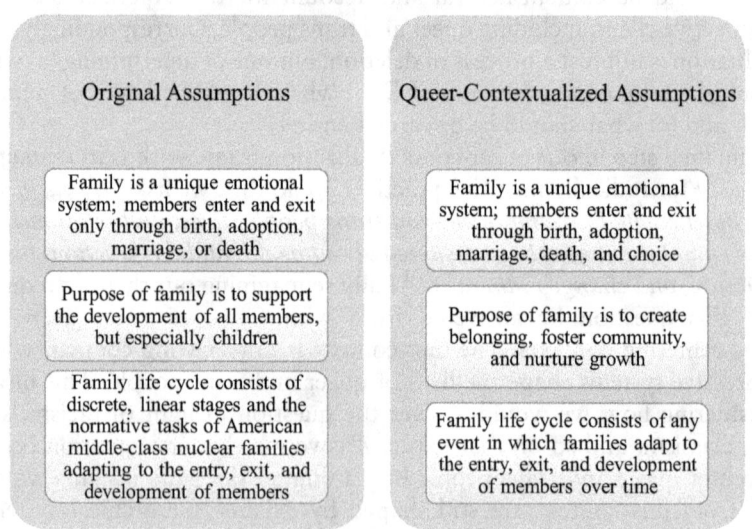

Figure 1.1 Comparison of Assumptions in the Original and the Queer-Contextualized Versions of the Family Life Cycle Model.

Identify

The queer-contextualization process begins with identifying core assumptions of the family life cycle. When we say assumptions, we are referring to basic truths of the theory that must be accepted in order to apply the concepts. Sometimes these are explicitly stated in theoretical writings, and sometimes they are only inferred. For our purposes, we focus on three central assumptions of the family life cycle: the definition of family, the purpose of a family, and the trajectory of development.

Definition of family. In their 1980 text, Carter and McGoldrick define the "operative emotional field" as "the entire family emotional system of at least three generations" (p. 9). The authors assert that families are unique among systems because members can enter and exit in only a few ways—namely, birth, adoption, marriage, and death—and that intergenerational connections are one of our greatest human resources while also being a source of stress.

Purpose of family. The purpose of a family, according to the original text, is to "provide a context that supports need attainment for all its individual members," although the primary focus seems to be on children (1980, p. 25). The family life cycle consists of stages of development for individuals within family systems that center around the birthing, raising, and launching of children. The cycle comes full circle when adult children form intimate partnerships in which they raise their own children. Although the model does include human development over the course of a lifetime, the developmental stages of adults are largely focused on the raising of children. Thus, we infer that an assumption of the family life cycle theory is that the purpose of a family is to support the development of children.

Developmental trajectory. The original family life cycle presented "the predictable developmental stages of American middle-class families" (Carter & McGoldrick, 1980, p. 13). These stages are presented in the following sequence: (1) the unattached young adult, (2) the newly married couple, (3) the family with young children, (4) the family with adolescents; (5) launching children and moving on; (6) the family in later life. Events such as untimely deaths, divorce, remarriage, and single-parent families are believed to interrupt the normal course of family development and require additional stages. In addition, the development of "multiproblem poor" families are considered separately from middle-class family development (p. 15). Regardless of the family structure or context, the authors assert that the underlying process of all stages is the negotiation of "expansion, contraction, and realignment of the relationship system to support the entry, exit, and development of family members in a functional way" (p. 16).

Evaluate

Definition of family. Upon evaluating the assumption that families consist of multiple generations of members who enter and exit through birth, death, and marriage only, it is evident that this definition is too narrow. In fact, Carter and McGoldrick (1980) are clear in the preface of their first edition that this model does not account for the effects of immigration, socioeconomic stress, or other cultural factors. They state that their model "is about the predictable developmental stages of American middle-class families in the second half of the twentieth century" (p. xxi). In the most recent revision (2016), they clarify that the traditional nuclear family structure is a creation of the industrial era. This structure—in which men earn wages, women raise children, and the household consists only of the marital couple and their offspring—is ideal for producing workers in a capitalist system that relies on an abundance of wage-dependent labor (McDowell, 2015). While it may be ideal for capitalism, the nuclear family is not ideal for a growing number of people. Black, indigenous, immigrant, and lower to working-class women have long had to engage in paid and unpaid labor outside of their homes to sustain their families. In the last several decades, white middle-class women have also needed to work for wages for their family's economic survival. And while multigenerational households and extended communities of care have long been the preferred family form in many indigenous, Eastern, and African cultures, they have increased across ethnic groups in the U.S. in the last decade, largely due to the economic stressors of COVID-19 (Generations United, 2021). Marriage rates have decreased steadily since the 1980s (Curton & Sutton, 2020). Without assets or sufficient income, the tax benefits and legal protections of marriage becomes a less attractive or even necessary option. The nuclear family was never desired by nor possible for all families, and it is increasingly undesirable and unattainable for the people it was designed for—white middle-class Americans.

In addition to being centered around white European-American middle-class families, we would add that the original definition of family does not account for those who choose not to partner, marry, or have children, who are not monogamous or have more than one partner, who have multiple generations and family units living within one household, who are in queer relationships, and who raise children that they are not genetically related to. Likely, such experiences were overlooked because they upend the "predictable" nature of developmental stages, which was an anchor for the original theory. Although it might have been necessary to anchor the life cycle using a homogenous definition of family, we argue that omitting such experiences from the definition of family has the effect of implying that families who do not fit this original definition are, in fact, not families at all. This is, of course, not the case but it has the effect of delegitimizing families that form under circumstances other than those specified in the original family life cycle.

Purpose of family. According to the family life cycle, the purpose of families is to oversee the development of all of its members, but the focus of the model is primarily on the development of children. While many queer and trans folk do raise children, many do not, and for a variety of reasons. One reason is that the options for having children outside of cisheterosexual intercourse—such as fertility treatments, surrogacy, or adoption—require a significant investment of money, time, and emotions (Goldberg, 2022). While cisheterosexual people experiencing infertility face similar barriers, they do not face the same stigma or discrimination that hopeful queer parents often do. These barriers can make the road to parenthood far more difficult for those who desire it. That brings us to another reason queer folks might not raise children—they simply don't want to. Having had lived experiences that do not fit with dominant norms, queer folks have ample opportunity to question those norms and, correspondingly, may feel less confined by them. As a result, they may be more likely to choose nondominant paths in life, such as nonmonogamy, partnering without marriage, or childlessness. Although these same paths might resonate for cisheterosexual people, they may be less accustomed to questioning dominant norms and less inclined to redefine norms. For this reason, centering a queer purpose of family has the potential to be liberating for non-queer people as well.

When conceptualizing through the family life cycle model, the nuclear family is often thought of as an island that exists by itself—without extended family, neighborhoods, or community. There is little discussion of how larger sociocultural context and norms impact the family and the development of children. This narrow view of families—divorced from their larger environment—separates families from the resources of extended family, community, and culture. It pathologizes families that are unable to be financially independent under capitalism. And it creates an expectation that the white, middle-class family structure is not only normal and natural, but preferable.

Developmental trajectory. In the fifth edition, McGoldrick et al. (2016) suggest that the "phases of the life cycle themselves are arbitrary breakdowns" since they relate to change over the course of time and according to race, gender, class, sexual orientation, etc. (p. 3). Although this statement provides some acknowledgment of the subjective nature of the defined stages, the authors are not always clear on how the life cycle phases may differ according to sociocultural context. A linear focus on development does not account for the life cycle phases of individuals with developmental or acquired disabilities nor does it recognize that launching is not possible nor desirable for all individuals, families, and cultures. Additionally, the presumed goal of autonomy and independence from one's family of origin reflects white, Western, and capitalist values and does not account for collective, indigenous, and Eastern values that center connection and interdependence.

The purpose of families—essentially the raising of children—is reflected in the developmental trajectory of the family. More specifically, the tasks of most family life cycle stages are centered on raising children to become autonomous adults, who then go on to raise children who become adults that raise more children, and so on and so forth. The ultimate outcome of the family life cycle's developmental trajectory is the propagation of workers who can meet the demands of capitalism. Given the capitalist underpinnings of the family life cycle, the developmental needs of adults who do not raise children are sidelined in the theory. In particular, the cultural invisibility of adults who do not bear and raise children is evident in McGoldrick et al. (2016), where the authors suggest that adults who do not partner and raise children will move through life caring for the children of their friends and siblings. Although this is an acknowledgment that such adults exist and still have a role in the family life cycle, it reinforces that the only purpose of a family is to raise children. The role of childless individuals is not fleshed out in the theory, indicating that these stages are not actually about the development of families but about the development of children.

The life cycle model does include aspects of vertical and horizontal identity. Vertical identity is anything that is passed down from generation to generation, such as class background, family history, ethnicity, or culture. Horizontal identity is anything that happens within an individual's lifetime that is unique to their identity and experience, including anything that is not predicted by the vertical identity. McGoldrick et al. (2016) include being queer or trans in their list of unpredictable life events that form horizontal identity. The idea that a queer or trans gender identity is unexpected is distinctly heteronormative. Cisheterosexual parents often assume—consciously or not—that all of their children will also be heterosexual and cisgender. Not only that, but parents (and McGoldrick et al., 2016) assume the same of their ancestors, thereby erasing queerness from their vertical identity entirely. For this reason, including queerness as an unpredictable part of horizontal identity, while leaving it entirely out of the vertical identity, reinforces heteronormativity and the belief that being queer or trans is not a normal or natural part of our families and our family history.

Reimagine

Definition of family. When we place the family life cycle in a queer and trans-centered context, the definition of family expands. It now includes members who enter and exit through birth, death, marriage, and *choice*. People may choose to leave families for a number of reasons and in a number of ways, and they may choose to enter or form families in new ways, such as adoption and other formal and informal ways of parenting and caregiving, building multiple partner relationships, and creating chosen family. Chosen families are support systems that are intentionally created and maintained and can include friends, current and former romantic partners, co-workers, and legal or blood relatives. When we bring the margins to the center, family is not only multigenerational but also communal and collective. It can look like grandparents raising grandchildren, platonic life partners buying a home together, ballroom houses, or extended family caring for the aging. A queer-contextualized family life cycle (QC FLC) does not demand that young people move out of their family home and become financially independent at a particular age, if ever. It does not require any particular form of partnership or child-rearing. In this queer-centered context, maturity and health are dynamic, multifaceted, and shaped by context-specific cultural norms and values.

Purpose of family. When we reimagine the purpose of family from a queer- and trans-centered context, raising children remains an important task, but it is no longer an apolitical endeavor accomplished by white middle class cisheterosexual nuclear families. In a queer context, families support identity development, belonging, and healing as a counterpoint to an oppressive cultural context. Families become the site of liberation.

The idea of family as a buffer against oppression has been studied and discussed at length in relation to racially minoritized families, who support their children in developing healthy racial identities and resilience in the face of racism (Hughes et al., 2006; Sanders, 1994; Umaña-Taylor & Hill, 2020). In the most recent revision of the family life cycle, McGoldrick et al. (2016) incorporate this type of support through bell hooks' (1999) concept of homeplace. McGoldrick and colleagues summarize homeplace as the "multilayered, nuanced individual and family processes anchored in a physical space that elicits feelings of empowerment, belonging, commitment, rootedness, ownership, safety, and renewal" (p. 8). More to the point, hooks (1999) describes homeplace as a refuge from white supremacy that Black women create for their families. She talks about family as an essential site of resistance and liberation struggles, and how continued pressure to conform to dominant norms—patriarchy in particular—has diminished the ability of Black women to create these activist spaces in their homes, which has had a negative effect on the larger liberation movement. According to hooks, liberation work must be done in the homeplace if there is to be meaningful change in society.

Queer folks are less likely to have a homeplace in their family of origin, because most are not raised by queer people. More often, queer folks are raised by cisheterosexual caregivers who, at their best, may not know how or anticipate having to protect their children from queer and trans oppression, and at their worst, may be enacting that oppression through abuse, rejection, or violence. It is more likely that queer folks will not experience homeplace until they find or create their chosen family. The fact that queer people intentionally create families to support their identity, belonging, and healing tells us that this is an essential need. Therefore, the purpose of family in a QC FLC is to create belonging, foster community, and nurture growth.

The queer-contextualized purpose of family should not be considered exclusive to queer people. Many people seek belonging because they did not get it in their family of origin. Many seek it because they do not find it within the larger culture. Belonging is an essential human need (Brown, 2010), and the QC FLC model suggests that family should provide it. Thus, part of the QC FLC developmental trajectory for all people is to find and create a family that provides belonging.

Developmental trajectory. The QC FLC retains the original assumption that the life cycle stages are about negotiating the "expansion, contraction, and realignment of the relationship system to support the entry, exit, and development of family members in a functional way" (Carter & McGoldrick, 1980, p. 16). However, the QC FLC discards the use of linear, prescriptive stages. Instead, any event that necessitates a shift or change in the family's structure, roles, or relationships is considered a stage in that family's life cycle. There are no normative and nonnormative stages or events, because anything that families do is considered normal and natural, as families are a part of nature. As an example, McGoldrick and colleagues considered untimely deaths to be nonnormative and disruptive. However, "timely" deaths can also prompt significant change and disruption in a family, particularly when the deceased was a central family figure. It could be argued further that all deaths are normal and natural, but some are unexpected, traumatic, or disruptive. In any stage, families adapt to meet the needs of its members, with special care given to the needs of those members with the least social power. This may often mean children, but it can also be aging family members, those living with chronic illness or disability, or facing racial, economic, or gender-based oppression. The QC FLC recognizes that members may leave and return to the family multiple times, and that these may represent different stages. What is constant throughout every type of family life cycle stage is that the family is called on to adapt to the entries, exits, and development of family members.

A key developmental task for all humans is to find or create belonging, which is about being accepted for who you are. Families may wrestle with this task across the life cycle. In fact, the presence or absence of belonging in a given family group may influence the entering and exiting of members. Take the story of Ceyenne Doroshow, an author, activist, and founder of a nonprofit dedicated to providing housing and health care for trans people. She was born in the 1960s to a conservative and religious Black middle-class family (Mukerjee, 2022). In her memoir-cookbook, she shares how she found belonging in her grandparents' Park Slope apartment where she learned how to cook as a child (Doroshow, 2012). Her father became increasingly abusive in response to her budding femininity, prompting her to leave home around the age of 15. She spent years sleeping on couches, in shelters, and in Central Park. She began to find community in her twenties in New York City's queer clubs, where she met Jack Doroshow, also known as Flawless Mother Sabrina, an artist, activist, and drag legend who mentored and mothered hundreds of queer and trans teens in her lifetime. Jack and Ceyenne formed a close mother–daughter relationship and when Ceyenne was eventually able to legally change her name, Jack was happy to have her take his last name (Drucker, 2018). In Ceyenne's story, we see her family of origin struggling to adapt to having a gender-expansive child. Her grandparents are more adaptable and provide support for her development, but her parents are unable to provide her with a sense of belonging. Ultimately, she leaves that family system, and though we can assume her departure changed them, we do not know how. Ceyenne spends the next several years of her life surviving and searching for belonging. She finds it in New York City's queer community and with Mother Sabrina, and goes on to create community for countless people in her work at homeless shelters, running support groups, and founding a nonprofit. Ceyenne's story is a powerful example of the reciprocal nature of belonging and the ways we both find and create belonging through forming, leaving, and reshaping family systems. As Ceyenne put it: "I have grown family where it needed to grow" (Doroshow, 2012).

Implications for Practice

The family life cycle is often used in clinical assessment to determine which stage a family is currently in, and how well they are meeting the tasks of the stage. That information is then used to inform intervention using the therapist's theory of change. Presenting problems are conceptualized as indications that the family is having trouble transitioning from one stage to another. Imagine that Alicia (40) brings her daughter, Andrea (16), to therapy saying that she has been depressed and withdrawn lately. Alicia has become increasingly concerned and been pressuring Andrea to spend more time with her and with friends. Many clinicians might view this family as struggling to adapt to the "families with adolescents" stage and hypothesize that the family needs to be more flexible as Andrea is moving through adolescence. While thinking about families and children developmentally is clinically useful, the family life cycle stages may be too prescriptive and restrictive to be useful for most families. Consider that Alicia is married to Ben (47, Anglo-American), and they both have two children from previous relationships. Alicia's daughters are both teenagers, but Ben's children are in their twenties and his son, Jake (22) lives with them. Alicia's mother, Rita (70), recently moved from Puerto Rico to live with them. The family's life cycle stage changes depending on which part of the family we focus on—adolescents, launching, or later life. Most likely, this family is working to accomplish developmental tasks of three different family life cycle stages while also combining multiple family systems. Applying the tasks of any single stage to this family would be reductive and potentially harmful.

Alternatively, a therapist using the QC FLC would ask expansive questions to understand how the family determines who is a part of the system. Assessment questions might include: *who do you belong to? Who do you depend on and who depends on you? How do you define family? How does your culture define family? If there is a difference between these definitions, how do you reconcile it?* When the therapist asked Alicia and Andrea these questions, the two talked about how their family had changed over the past few years, adding Ben and his kids, and then their grandmother. When Ben came to session, he and Alicia discussed the differences between their definitions of family and the constellation of people they feel interdependent with. Alicia's network was bigger and included her extended family in Puerto Rico. Although Ben's parents, siblings, and oldest daughter lived in the same state, he did not feel a strong sense of interdependence with them, saying they all tended to take care of themselves. The therapist noted that their respective cultures influenced who they each felt they belonged to and what that belonging looked like.

In addition to determining who is a part of the family system, the QC FLC therapist also assesses how the family is meeting its purpose to create belonging, foster community, and nurture growth. Assessment questions might include: *How does your family create belonging, foster community, and nurture growth? How are you co-creating resilience for the oppression you face outside of the family? Inside of the family?* The family agreed that they were struggling to create belonging for Andrea and Rita, who both seemed withdrawn. Andrea spent most of her time in her room and did not hang out with her friends from junior high. Rita did not go out of the house much and spent a lot of time on the phone with family back in Puerto Rico. When Rita joined the sessions, she shared that she was homesick and didn't feel hopeful she would make friends in their mostly white town. Ben worried that he was not nurturing Jake's growth, who he thought should be living on his own.

Using the QC FLC, the therapist conceptualizes the unique stage that the client family is currently in, recognizing that each family is experiencing its own intersection of individual, familial, and cultural contexts. The therapist prioritizes adaptability over linear development in their assessment. Questions might include: *What has changed in your family and how is that affecting belonging? What external forces may be getting in the way of your family creating belonging for each member? How have you successfully adapted to changes in the past?* By meeting with Andrea alone, the therapist learned that Andrea identified as a lesbian and had not told her mother or any of her friends at school. She suspected her mom knew but was choosing to ignore it. With the therapist's support, Andrea decided to tell her mom, and Alicia admitted she had a feeling, but was afraid that life would be harder for Andrea and their family if it were true. In this instance, cultural narratives like heterosexism were getting in the way of Alicia creating a sense of belonging for her daughter. Once this was brought to the surface, the entire family offered their support and acceptance to Andrea. Other cultural forces impacting the family's ability to create belonging might include white supremacy (e.g., preventing Rita from finding community in her new home) and Western individualism (e.g., preventing Ben from acknowledging Jake's value as an adult child living at home).

These assessment questions give the therapist a holistic view of the family's composition, connectedness, and adaptability. The therapist can integrate this conceptualization into a family therapy theory to work with the family to adapt to changes and increase belongingness. In this case, the therapist worked to strengthen the relationship between mother, grandmother, and granddaughter, as well as between father and son. Alicia and Ben were able to support each other as they fostered belonging with their children, drawing on their different cultural and familial backgrounds. Jake became a source of community to Andrea, celebrating her identity and introducing her to some of his queer young adult friends who served as role models to her.

The Book

Our vision for this book was for passionate and creative marriage and family therapists to write about the ways they had reimagined their favorite family therapy theories to use with queer and trans clients. Even more, we wanted to present a way to critique and revise clinical theory so that readers could follow such a process with any model they wanted. What emerged was a new way of modernizing clinical theory and practice: queer-contextualizing. This book offers a strategy for evolving clinical theory and describes reimagined versions of family therapy models that are both tangible and practical for clinicians of any experience level.

In the interest of including diverse lived experience and clinical expertise in this book, we issued an open call for chapter proposals, rather than inviting authors already known to us. Our hope was to reach a broader range of potential contributors, not only in terms of social identity but also in terms of highest degree, clinical experience, and professional setting. Said more plainly, if we had only invited authors we knew personally, the author list would be largely white, cisgender, queer-identified women who hold PhDs and work in academic settings. With an open call, we hoped to reach more BIPOC, trans or nonbinary, and male or masc authors and those who held master's degrees and/or worked in clinical settings. The authors in this book represent all of these backgrounds and more, and are still majority white, cisgender, and academic.

From the beginning, we wanted this book to include as many systemic theories as possible. In response to our open call, we received proposals for both modern and postmodern theories. Although postmodern theories seem to lend themselves more easily to the process of queer-contextualizing, modern family therapy models are also malleable—in large part because they are process oriented. Having received numerous quality proposals for each of the foundational family therapy theories, we were able to select authors who proposed the most radical and creative reimagination of any given theory and who represented newer voices in the field of MFT. At this early juncture, we also decided not to include narrative family therapy because of the comprehensive work already published on its use with queer and trans clients (Tilsen, 2013, 2021).

We believe we have nine chapters that offer new possibilities for some of the field's most beloved models. Each theory chapter follows a similar structure, beginning with a brief overview of the theory as it was origin- ally written or is commonly understood. We asked authors to be brief and succinct in this overview, and focus instead on the reimagination of their model. Correspondingly, each chapter includes references to primary sources, should readers want to know more about the original version of a model. In this brief overview, the authors highlight some of the theory's core assumptions, which are then critiqued through a critical sociocultural lens, and finally placed into a queer and trans-centered context to be reim- agined. Each chapter ends with a case study that illustrates clinical appli- cation of the queer-contextualized model. Throughout each chapter you will also find bolded key terms that are essential to understanding both the original and the reimagined versions of the theory. At the end of the book, you will find a glossary that includes the various sociocultural terms and identity labels used throughout the book.

To our knowledge, this is the first book to go beyond cultural critique to update and revise our "sacred models" (Sprenkle & Blow, 2004) for more radical and inclusive clinical practice. It feels like a big responsibility, and as with any first attempt at something new, our efforts are imperfect. We see this book as a tool for a larger conversation, one that we hope extends far beyond ourselves and these pages. We hope that you will have ques- tions, challenges, and a-ha moments as you read these chapters and that

> What steps have you already taken to bridge the gap between foundational MFT theories and your contemporary clinical practice?

> Think about your preferred clinical theory(ies). Who developed this theory? When and where? How does this context show up in the assumptions of the theory? (If your theory is in this book, answer this question before you read the chapter!)

> What would you add to the section on "original context"? What systems or discourses are important as you critique and reimagine therapy theories?

> What resonates for you about the QC FLC definition and purpose of family? What about it challenges you?

> Where in your life have you found belonging? Where have you created it?

Figure 1.2 Questions for Reflection.

you will share them with your classmates, colleagues, and with us. We hope you present and publish work that builds upon what we have started here. We are grateful to be with you on this lifelong journey toward radically inclusive theory and practice.

References

Addison, S. M., & Coolhart, D. (2015). Expanding the therapy paradigm with queer couples: A relational intersectional lens. *Family Process, 54,* 435–453.

Barrett, T. (2006). Approaches to postmodern art-making. *FATE in Review, 28,* 2–15.

Barrett, T. (2011). *Making art: Form and meaning* (pp. 202–228). McGraw Hill.

Brown, B. (2010). *The gifts of imperfection: Let go of who you think you're supposed to be and embrace who you are.* Hazelden.

Carter, B. E., & McGoldrick, M. E. (1980). *The family life cycle: A framework for family therapy.* Gardner Press.

Carter, B., & McGoldrick, M. (Eds.). (1988). *The changing family life cycle: A framework for family therapy* (2nd ed.). Gardner Press.

Carter, B., & McGoldrick, M. (Eds.). (1998). *The expanded family life cycle: Individual, family, and social perspectives* (3rd ed.). Allyn & Bacon.

Cho, S., Crenshaw, K. W., & McCall, L. (2013). Toward a field of intersectionality studies: Theory, applications, and praxis. *Journal of Women in Culture and Society, 38*(4), 78–810. https://doi.org/10.1086/669608

Conley, T. D., Ziegler, A., Moors, A. C., Matsick, J. L., & Valentine, B. (2013). A critical examination of popular assumptions about the benefits and outcomes of monogamous relationships. *Personality and Social Psychology Review, 17*(2), 124–141. https://doi.org/10.1177/1088868312467087

Crenshaw, K. (1989). Demarginalizing the intersection of race and sex: A Black feminist critique of antidiscrimination doctrine, feminist theory, and antiracist politics. *University of Chicago Legal Forum, 8,* 139–167. https://chicagounbound.uchicago.edu/uclf/vol1989/iss1/8/

Crenshaw, K. (1991). Mapping the margins: Intersectionality, identity politics, and violence against women of color. *Stanford Law Review, 43*(6), 1241–1299. https://doi.org/10.2307/1229039

Crenshaw, K. (2016). The urgency of intersectionality. *TED Women 2016.* Taken from www.ted.com/talks/kimberle_crenshaw_the_urgency_of_intersectionality

Curton, S. C., & Sutton, P. D. (2020). *Marriage rates in the United States, 1900-2018.* NCHS Health E-Stat. www.cdc.gov/nchs/data/hestat/marriage_rate_2018/marriage_rate_2018.htm

Doroshow, C. (2012). *Cooking in heels: A memoir cookbook.* Red Umbrella Project.

Drucker, Z. (2018). *Ceyenne Doroshow on going from homeless trans youth to holistic caregiver.* Vice. www.vice.com/en/article/mby4pq/ceyenne-doroshow-glits-transgender-center-non-profit-founder

Duggan, L. (2002). The new homonormativity: The sexual politics of neoliberalism. *Materializing democracy: Toward a revitalized cultural politics, 10,* 175–194.

Flint, C. (2004). *Spaces of hate: Geographies of discrimination and intolerance in the U.S.A.* Routledge.

Generations United. (2021). *Family matters: Multigenerational living is on the rise and here to stay.* www.gu.org/resources/multigenerational-families/

Giammattei, S. V., & Green, R. J. (2012). LGBTQ couple and family therapy: History and future directions. In Jerry J. Bigner and Joseph L. Wetchler (Eds.), *Handbook of LGBT-affirmative couple and family therapy* (pp. 21–42). Routledge.

Gokhale, D. (2005). The intersexion: A vision for a queer progressive agenda. In M. Adams et al. (Eds.), *Readings for diversity and social justice* (4th ed., pp. 391–393). Routledge.

Goldberg, A. E. (2022). *LGBTQ family building: A guide for prospective parents.* APA LifeTools.

Griffin, M. J. (2016). Intersecting intersectionalities and the failure of the law to protect transgender women of color in the United States. *Tulane Journal of Law & Sexuality*, *25*, 123.

Gude, O. (2004). Postmodern principles: In search of a 21st century art education. *Art Education*, *57*(1), 6–14.

Hardy, K. V., & Laszloffy, T. A. (1994). Deconstructing race in family therapy. *Journal of Feminist Family Therapy*, *5*(3–4), 5–33.

Hartwell, E. E., Heiden-Rootes, K. M., & Cooke. S. (2022). "There's a lot we don't understand about each other": Centering bisexual partners in couple therapy. In R. Harvey, M. Murphy, J. J. Bigner, & J. L. Wetchler (Eds.), *Handbook of LGBT-affirmative couple and family therapy* (2nd ed., pp. 89–104). Routledge.

Hartwell, E. E., Serovich, J. M., Grafsky, E. L., & Kerr, Z. Y. (2012). Coming out of the dark: Content analysis of articles pertaining to gay, lesbian, and bisexual issues in couple and family therapy journals. *Journal of Marital and Family Therapy*, *38*, 227–243.

Harvey, R., Murphy, M. J., & Laszloffy, T. A. (2022). Evolution of LGBTQ affirmative couple and family therapy. In R. Harvey, M. Murphy, J. Bigner, & J. Wetchler (Eds.), *Handbook of LGBTQ-affirmative couple and family therapy* (2nd ed., pp. 9–24). Routledge.

hooks, b. (1999). *Yearning: Race, gender, and cultural politics.* South End Press.

Hughes, D., Rodriguez, J., Smith, E. P., Johnson, D. J., Stevenson, H. C., & Spicer, P. (2006). Parents' ethnic-racial socialization practices: A review of research and directions for future study. *Developmental Psychology*, *42*(5), 747.

Kerr, M. E., & Bowen, M. (1988). *Family evaluation: An approach based on Bowen theory.* New York: Norton.

Long, J. K. (1996). Working with lesbians, gays, and bisexuals: Addressing heterosexism in supervision. *Family Process*, *35*, 377–388.

Long, J. K., Bonomo, J., Andrews, B. V., & Brown, J. M. (2006). Systemic therapeutic approaches with sexual minorities and their families. *Journal of GLBT Family Studies*, *2*(3–4), 7–37.

Long, J. K., & Serovich, J. M. (2003). Incorporating sexual orientation into MFT training programs: Infusion and inclusion. *Journal of Marital and Family Therapy, 29*(1), 59–67.

Makkreel, R. A. (2022). How the arts reorient experience and recontextualize the world. In *Philosophy of Culture as Theory, Method, and Way of Life* (pp. 342–362). Brill.

Matsuda, M. J. (1991). Beside my sister, facing the enemy: Legal theory out of coalition. *Stanford Law Review, 43*(6), 1183–1192. https://doi-org.dml.regis.edu/10.2307/1229035

McDowell, T. (2015). *Applying critical social theories to family therapy practice.* AFTA Springer Briefs in Family Therapy. Springer.

McGoldrick, M., Garcia Preto, N., & Carter, B. (2010). *The expanded family life cycle: Individual, family, and social perspectives* (4th ed.). Pearson.

McGoldrick, M., Garcia Preto, N., & Carter, B. (2016). *The expanding family life cycle: Individual, family, and social perspectives* (5th ed.). Pearson.

Menakem, R. (2017). *My grandmother's hands: Racialized trauma and the pathway to mending our hearts and bodies.* Central Recovery Press.

Mix, E. K. (2015). Appropriation and the art of the copy. *Choice, 52*(9), 1433–1445.

Morgensen, S. L. (2011). *Spaces between us: Queer settler colonialism and indigenous decolonization.* University of Minnesota Press.

Mukerjee, L. (2022, February). *Ceyenne Doroshow* [Interview]. Outwords. https://theoutwordsarchive.org/interview/ceyenne-doroshow/

Perel E. (2006). *Mating in captivity: Reconciling the erotic + the domestic.* HarperCollins.

Ritter, K., & Terndrup, A. I. (2002). *Handbook of affirmative psychotherapy with lesbians and gay men.* Guilford Press.

Sanders Thompson, V. L. (1994). Socialization to race and its relationship to racial identification among African Americans. *Journal of Black Psychology, 20*(2), 175–188. https://doi.org/10.1177/00957984940202006

Sanz, V. (2017). No way out of the binary: A critical history of the scientific production of sex. *Signs: Journal of Women in Culture and Society, 43*(1), 1–27

Sprenkle, D. H., & Blow, A. J. (2004). Common factors and our sacred models. *Journal of Marital and Family Therapy, 30*, 113–129.

Stone Fish, L., & Harvey, R. G. (2005). *Nurturing queer youth: Family therapy transformed.* WW Norton & Co.

Tilsen, J. (2013). *Therapeutic conversations with queer youth: Transcending homonormativity and constructing preferred realities.* Rowman & Littlefield.

Tilsen, J. (2021). *Queering your therapy practice: Queer theory, narrative therapy, and imagining new identities.* Routledge.

Umaña-Taylor, A. J., & Hill, N. E. (2020). Ethnic–racial socialization in the family: A decade's advance on precursors and outcomes. *Journal of Marriage and Family, 82*(1), 244–271.

Vaid-Menon, A. (2020). *Beyond the gender binary.* Penguin House.

Walters, M., Carter, B., Papp, P., & Silverstein, O. (1988). *The invisible web: Gender patterns in family relationships.* Guilford Press.

Warner, M. (1991). Introduction: Fear of a queer planet. *Social Text, 29,* 3–17.

Watzlawick, P., Hemlick Beavin, J., & Jackson, D. D. (1967). *Pragmatics of human communication: A study of interactional patterns, pathologies, and paradoxes.* New York: Norton.

Worthen, M. G. (2016). Hetero-cis–normativity and the gendering of transphobia. *International Journal of Transgenderism, 17*(1), 31–57.

Chapter 2

Queer-Contextualized Structural Family Therapy

Becky Diaz and Carla Vitola

An occasionally controversial figure within the family therapy field, Salvador Minuchin (October 13, 1921–October 30, 2017), began his work with families in the 1960s, subsequently developing and modifying structural family therapy (SFT) until he passed at the age of 96. Minuchin fundamentally believed that the way a family interacts and is organized shapes the individual. This was an outgrowth of both his personal experiences and his professional journey. Minuchin was the firstborn son of Russian Jewish parents who had immigrated to Argentina. As the oldest child, he acknowledged that his "responsible" nature was a product of his family context. When discussing the role of society in shaping his identity, he stated that as

> Part of a despised minority, I learned to despise my Jewishness, to try to pass, and to hate myself for it. I grew up divided, internalizing the prejudices of the Argentinean majority and fighting the unfairness of prejudices both inside and outside myself.
>
> (Minuchin & Nichols, 1993, p. 8)

While his family experiences may have inspired his interest in family dynamics, it wasn't until he worked at The Wiltwyck School for Boys that he moved away from his psychoanalytic training to a more systemic approach in clinical practice. Alongside his colleague, Braulio Montalvo, and influenced by Don Jackson and others, Minuchin began using a one-way mirror while working with entire families. After leaving Wiltwyck, Minuchin served as the director of the Philadelphia Child Guidance Institute, where he collaborated with Jay Haley, one of the creators of strategic family therapy (Gehart, 2016; Minuchin & Nichols, 1993).

DOI: 10.4324/9781003308188-2

Theoretical Assumptions of the Structural Family Therapy

Much has been written about SFT that is beyond the scope of this chapter (e.g., Minuchin, 1974; Minuchin, Colapinto, & Minuchin, 2007; Minuchin & Fishman, 1981; Minuchin & Nichols, 1993; Minuchin, Nichols, & Lee, 2007; Nichols, 2017). In our efforts to recontextualize SFT, we will focus on the assessment and restructuring of family organization. Minuchin (1974) posited that the individual must be approached and understood within their context. This is because individual concerns are not actually concerns of the individual, but rather the manifestations of relational qualities of a system that reflect the system's needs, challenges, and structure. For this reason, therapy from an SFT framework is not focused solely on the individual, but rather on the family, how it is organized, and its patterns of interactions (Minuchin & Fishman, 1981). Minuchin believed that a functional family is one whose structure is adaptable and flexible to deal with and move through life's changes and challenges. Minuchin was clear that no single structure was ideal for all families. Furthermore, he believed families should be viewed within their broader context, including their extended family, the community, hospitals, social service agencies, and society as a whole (Minuchin, Colapinto, & Minuchin, 2007). Minuchin described the difference between viewing families through systems theory and through individual psychology as the difference between a magnifying glass and a zoom lens. The individually oriented therapist can only see what is close-up—the intrapsychic world—while the family therapist has access to a broader view (Minuchin, 1974).

Family Structure and Assessment

A key assumption of SFT is that families have an organization—a structure—and that intervening at this level can help a family to reorganize their structure in a way that is more adaptive. Embedded in that assumption is that families sometimes structure themselves in ways that limit their ways of relating and as a result, limit the possibilities for the individuals in the family. **Family structure** involves the invisible set of functional demands that organize the ways in which family members interact. Through repetition across time, patterns are established for how, when, and to whom family members can relate (Minuchin, 1974). SFT focuses on helping families to create a structure that effectively meets their needs as they change throughout their lifespans (Colapinto, 2019). **Boundaries** are the invisible barriers in relationships that create the family structure. They are the rules that dictate who is involved and when and how someone participates (Minuchin, 1974). Boundaries can range from diffuse to disengaged. Diffuse boundaries are those that are open to the point of **enmeshment**. Enmeshment involves "excessive closeness" that can limit independence. On the other end is a disengaged boundary, which limits input and closeness and can result in distance and disconnection. A family system is made up of **subsystems**. These subsystems are organized by the nature of a relationship, such as parents or couple, siblings, or grandparents, or by other factors such as age or gender (Minuchin, Colapinto, & Minuchin, 2007). The subsystems also provide us with an understanding of how the family is organized.

Structural family therapists also assess for **triangulation** in the family structure. Triangulation occurs when at least one member of the family is drawn into the conflict of two other members to receive support, reduce anxiety, support a specific hierarchy, and overall, maintain the family structure (Minuchin, 1974). In SFT, the triangulated person can reduce the tension just by shifting the focus but other times they are caught in between and asked to take sides. Either way, SFT aims to reduce triangulation in the family and to support clear boundaries (Minuchin, 1974). One type of triangle is a **coalition**. Coalitions occur when family members join together against another member of the family (Minuchin, Colapinto, & Minuchin, 2007). Generally structural family therapists understand coalitions as problematic and seek to modify the structure to disengage the coalition (Nichols & Davis, 2017). This is different from **alliances** between family members, which involve a general closeness and may include two or more being involved in activities together (Nichols & Davis, 2017). Alliances can be as simple as siblings engaged together in a hobby, parents supporting each other in financial difficulties, or an older cousin coaching their younger cousin's baseball team.

Alliances and coalitions affect the family **hierarchy** because they materialize the relationships between subsystems. Minuchin assessed power in the form of influence as a way of determining the hierarchy in the family. He would consider who makes the decisions, who has a voice, how flexible or rigid the distribution of power is, and how clear the structure is to all the members in the system. In SFT, a healthy family structure should include parent(s) at the top of a hierarchy, in charge, while also providing developmentally appropriate care and nurturance in accordance with the family's life cycle stage. Correspondingly, parents would be less hierarchical with adolescents and adults than they would be with toddlers and young children (Colapinto, 2019).

A goal of SFT is to expand the presenting problem from an individually focused problem to a problem of the family. This means moving beyond a focus on the identified patient and instead to the family system

Box 2.1

Family structure
The invisible set of functional demands that organize the ways in which family members interact. With repetition, across time, patterns are established of how, when, and to whom to relate.

Boundaries
The invisible barriers in relationships. They form a part of creating the family structure. They are the rules that dictate who participates, and when, and how.

Enmeshment
Excessive closeness in a relationship that can limit independence.

Subsystems
Relationships, such as parents or couple, siblings, or grandparents, or by other factors such as age or gender.

Triangulation
When at least one member of the family is drawn into a conflict of two other members.

Coalitions
When family members join together against another member of the family.

Alliances
Family members involved in a general closeness and may include two or more being involved in activities together.

Hierarchy
How power is structured in the family and who has decision-making ability.

Identified patient
The "IP" is described as the symptom-bearer or official patient as identified by the family.

Complementarity
When a problem exists within an individual, then it can also be a creation of the family organization.

as a whole. The **identified patient** is described as "the symptom-bearer or official patient as identified by the family" (Nichols & Davis, 2017, p. 300). By inquiring about each member's view of the problem, the therapist provides the family with an opportunity to learn how their interactions shape and perpetuate the presenting problem. Another way to assess the structure of the family is through the concept of **complementarity**. Family systems embody complementarity when the dynamics of one subsystem are related to the dynamics of another subsystem such that this interdependence functions for the broader system. For instance, stress in the parental subsystem is related to stress in a parent/child dyad, which collectively functions to maintain existing coalitions and the hierarchical structure. A simple way to express complementarity back to the family is to reflect back to them how they relate to each other in predictable ways. For example, one partner pushes for connection and the other pulls away. The more partner one pushes for connection, the more partner two pulls away.

Goal Development and Intervention with Structural Family Therapy

Minuchin and Fishman (1981) wrote, "Any change in the family structure will change the family's worldview, and any change in the worldview will be followed by change in the family structure, including change in the use of the symptom to maintain the family organization" (p. 207). So how do structural family therapists do this? For starters, the therapist becomes part of the system through the process of **joining** (Minuchin & Fishman, 1981). Joining in SFT involves the development of a therapeutic relationship that allows the therapist to influence the family system. Joining requires "respect, empathy, curiosity, and a commitment to healing" (Minuchin et al., 2014, p. 4). It is far more than simply being a neutral observer. Joining is a way of being that continues throughout the therapy process which leaves the family feeling secure enough to be influenced, to move beyond what they have already attempted, try something else, and change (Minuchin & Fishman, 1981). Joining involves assuming a place of leadership and relating to each of the members of the family while maintaining fidelity to the system (Minuchin, 1974). In SFT, the therapist reflects strengths back to the family through **confirmation**. Therapists might compliment parents on their resilience and connect it to their willingness to fight for their family in therapy. This confirmation brings the family's strengths to the fore which they can then use to move toward change. Confirmation can also be seen as a form of **tracking**, a fundamental tool of a structural family therapist. Tracking involves differentiating between process and content and then making decisions based on what the therapist believes to be conducive to the therapeutic goals. Tracking can include attending to what is happening in the here-and-now or past events (Colapinto, 2019). When tracking, a therapist might follow the clients into the story, or rather the content of the concern. They might also help the clients explore what is occurring at the process level by asking about the interrelatedness of the relationships in the room. For instance, the therapist might ask a member of a couple relationship, "how have you decided to work together now that you have a newborn?" The therapist can also use a **reframe** to shift the view of the problem. A reframe involves the therapist presenting an expanded world-view of the problem that emphasizes bidirectionality and context. For example, if one person is unhappy that her partner is yelling during fights, and her partner is unhappy because she withdraws from their fights, the therapist can reframe this as both reciprocal and helpful: "so when your partner experiences you as pulling away, you really are trying to protect the relationship by turning the heat down."

SFT therapists use **structural mapping** to create a visual representation of the family. The therapist draws the boundaries and the structure of the family to determine how both are contributing to the clients' presenting concern. Structural mapping involves thinking systemically, gathering information, and then putting that into a concrete image that can be provided to the family and other care providers (Minuchin, Colapinto, & Minuchin, 2007). Completing a structural map with the family's participation facilitates client insight and brings the interrelatedness of family members to the fore. Minuchin and his colleagues provided useful options for how to draw various aspects of the family system. Therapists can use double lines for involvement and triple lines for over-involvement. Conflict can be shown with wavy lines or by a broken line. There are also symbols for clear, rigid, and diffuse boundaries (Minuchin, Colapinto, & Minuchin, 2007).

Joining, confirming, tracking, reframing, and mapping are all ways in which the therapist works to facilitate change. In addition to these strategies, SFT therapists also create **enactments**. Enactments vary to the degree in which a therapist shapes the in-session interactions of the clients, ranging from a gentle request that family members interact with each other to behavioral directives that are given to specific family members to reinforce structure. The intent of enactments is to create alternative ways of relating for family members. Therapists can use enactments to shape competence, whereby they highlight what families are doing that is helping them, and provide alternatives for moments when they are caught in their patterns. Therapists might also overlap boundary making with enactments to create

Box 2.2

Joining
An essential element that involves the development of a relationship with the family. Joining and accommodation are both used together to create the therapeutic system.

Confirmation
A consideration of what the family has to offer. Reflecting back strengths through confirmation, therapists can be effective in restructuring the family toward change.

Tracking
A fundamental tool of a structural family therapist. Tracking involves differentiating between process and content, making decisions based on what the therapist believes to be conducive to the therapeutic goals. Tracking can include attending to what is happening in the here-and-now, and also past events.

Reframe
An intervention where the therapist presents a more systemic, expanded, or bidirectional view of the problem.

Structural mapping
A tool where the therapist draws out the boundaries and the structure of the family. This involves thinking systemically, gathering information, and then putting that into a concrete image that can be provided to the family and other care providers.

Enactments
Therapists help the family to interact in new ways or actively shape interactions as they are happening in session.

an active space for change. Boundary making involves sculpting the interactions among family members. A common intervention that is used to shift boundaries is to have family members sit facing one another when speaking to each other. This sets the boundary that those seated in that arrangement will speak to one another. Rather than talking about what family should do differently, the therapist has them experience it in session

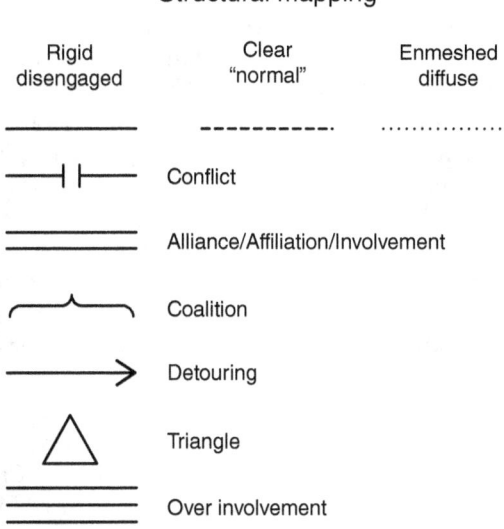

Figure 2.1 Key Symbols for Structural Mapping.

(Colapinto, 2019). Enactments also allow for increasing the intensity of an interaction, inviting other members of the family to participate, blocking members at times, and even extending the length of an interaction with statements as simple as, "keep going, stay in this." The therapist actively creates enactments, but as the sessions continue, like a director or conductor, they sit back to symbolize that the family is free to take over (Colapinto, 2019; Minuchin & Fishman, 1981).

Structural Family Therapy in Context

A key limitation that we will be addressing in this section is the lack of attention, consideration, and inclusion of queer families in SFT literature. We will use multiple iterations within the umbrella of LGBTQIA+ as we move throughout the chapter. We do so with the recognition that no matter our best intention, we will not be able to center all the identities within that broad and diverse spectrum, especially when attempting to think across intersections. In addition, we recognize that part of the diversity within the LGBTQIA+ community means that language can be limiting. There is no one clear undisputable name or title that will fit or encompass all, so we offer multiple options from a position of cultural humility.

When Salvador Minuchin and his colleagues developed SFT in the late 1960s, they did so partly in the interest of advocacy. This advocacy was primarily for poor families, single-parent families, and the teenagers they treated at the Wiltwyck School for Boys (Williams et al., 2016). Mental health professions, including marriage and family therapy, have historically not participated in advocacy or focused on changing oppressive systems. Minuchin and his colleagues stood apart from their contemporaries in this regard. At the same time Minuchin also failed to consider the impact of heteronormativity, white supremacy, and sexism in his own work. For example, in a recorded therapy session, Minuchin turns to the two young girls of an Italian-American family and asks them if they have boyfriends. When both of them replied no, he asked if it was because they were too young. There was no pause, no moment to consider the possibility of anything for these young women other than heterosexuality. This case was included in his book on working with psychosomatic families (Minuchin et al., 1978), and later, in his book *The Craft of Family Therapy: Challenging Certainties* (Minuchin et al., 2014). In the later discussions of the case, there is a missed opportunity to notice this assumption and address it. In the session, the intervention was intended to support the voices of the daughters, promote flexibility, and shift the boundaries in the family. What it also did was reinforce heteronormativity, cisnormativity, and patriarchy within the family. Similarly, Minuchin's repeated case example of an over-involved mother and peripheral father demonstrated how to unify and balance the hierarchy within the parental subsystem, but without any regard for how social systems influenced this common family structure (Dolan-Del Vecchio, 2019). SFT tends to focus on heterosexual nuclear families to the exclusion of families without children, extended or blended families, and multigenerational families. To use SFT inclusively with all families, we consider the context in which these families form, develop, and persist.

Queer-Contextualized Structural Family Therapy

Reimagining Structural Family Therapy

In the following section, we center queer and trans families so that we can transform the assessment and interventions of SFT. Minuchin was explicit throughout his career that therapy should be an operation performed with the family rather than an operation performed on them (Minuchin, Nichols, & Lee, 2007). By recontextualizing the process of joining and re-emphasizing collaboration, we modernize SFT so that it is inclusive, affirming, and centers queer families throughout the lifespan. Therapists have a key role to play in helping families see themselves as more than their presenting problem and more than the limited resources they believe themselves to have. A therapist can only do this if they take the time to do the self of the therapist work to queer-contextualize their own assumptions about health and family structure. Queer-contextualizing involves accountability when working with queer and trans families, who exist outside of our cultural norms and the norms in which SFT was created. A queer-contextualized SFT therapist considers their own values and assumptions in order to recognize how dominant beliefs can inhibit joining. Only by intentionally acknowledging those culturally held beliefs can a therapist build relationships and collaborate effectively with LGBTQ+ families. Doing this work is necessary for creating an affirming and safe space for all families.

Mapping the Family Structure

Minuchin considered the influence of social systems on the structure of poor families and included case workers and social services in his family assessments. He recognized that boundaries around these families were often diffuse due to the intense involvement and oversight of social welfare agencies. Similarly, queer families and their problems must be conceptualized within the context of patriarchy, heteronormativity, and cisnormativity. Further, this sociocultural context should include the family's structural map. SFT views presenting problems as the family's maladaptive attempts to adapt to changing circumstances. In queer families, the changing circumstances can include stigma and discrimination both within and outside the family. These oppressive forces organize families and influence their adaptability.

Heteronormativity and cisnormativity can organize families to dismiss or outright reject their queer and trans members. In response to this, queer individuals often form families of choice—a selected network of friends, family, ex-partners, and others who provide support and care (Blumer & Murphy, 2011; Sanders & Kroll, 2000; Wardecker & Matsick, 2020).

Families of choice are not defined by biology or legal marriage, although they might include people who are biologically or legally related. Families of choice require a broader view of who belongs in the structural map and what and who are represented. A queer-contextualized implementation of structural mapping would consider which adults occupy the parental, executive, or partner subsystems. It would also consider whether the roles and hierarchy are clear and functional. For families where children were adopted or conceived through surrogacy or other fertility methods, mapping might involve consideration for relationships between the subsystems

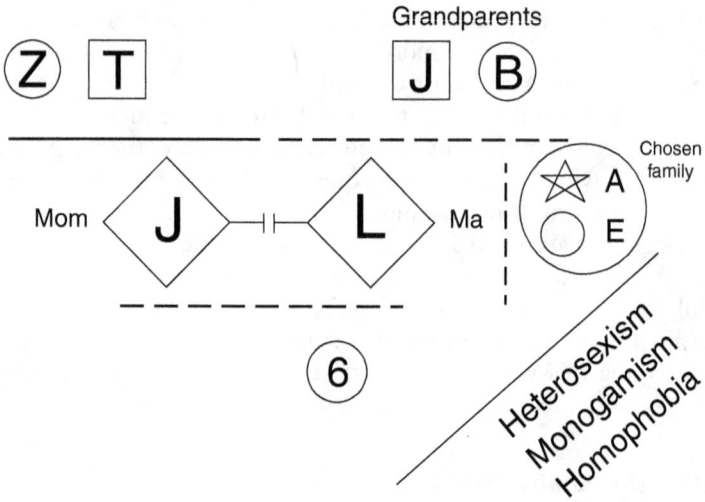

Figure 2.2 Sample Queer-Contextualized Family Map.

and the people whose bodies contributed to a child's life. Therapists often look to simplify, but simplifying structural maps loses context, richness, and complexity. Taking the time to get to know a family and do a true map is key to queer-contextualized SFT. Figure 2.2 presents a sample queer-contextualized family map for a two-parent family at the beginning of treatment. This map demonstrates clear boundaries between the adults and child, and includes the boundaries with families of origin and family of choice. Systems of oppression are also included. The boundaries with J's parents are disengaged, while L's parents are supportive, and those boundaries are clear.

In order to expand the definition of family, therapists must look at their own values and assumptions about family structure. Such self-of-the-therapist work is necessary to avoid imposing cultural norms onto families. In *Working with Families of the Poor*, Minuchin writes "our understanding of what children require for healthy development remains the same: security, nurturance, social contacts, and guidance" (Minuchin, Colapinto, & Minuchin, 2007, p. 133). Even these simple requirements represent cultural norms. Queerness has us ask, who defines and interprets these requirements? And whose access to these resources is limited by systems of oppression? Expanding structural maps to include a client-centered definition of family and their sociocultural context makes this intervention more inclusive for all families.

Contextualizing Family Structure

Hierarchy

When parents refuse to discuss queer or trans identities with their children, they are not only creating a rigid hierarchy but also perpetuating heterosexism and cissexism. This can lead to conflict or distancing between parents and children. A therapist steeped in Western values of individuality may normalize increasing distance between parents and children without recognizing the impact of homophobia on the family system. This misses how oppressive cultural forces actively restrict the family's flexibility and their ability to take care of each other. Such adaptability might include LGBTQ+ children teaching their family members about their own identity and experiences. Rather than seeing this as a hierarchical problem, we propose that families with LGBTQ+ adolescents and young adults might find their children possess a wealth of information about their needs, the needs of the family, and potential solutions. In fact, LGBTQ+ youth may embody the flexibility that is needed by the system. Parents who are open to learning from their children are not ceding hierarchy. Rather, they are demonstrating an ability to adapt in response to the needs of the least powerful members of their system. In doing so, SFT therapists can support families in benefitting from the positive outcomes that arise when LGBTQ+ youth are affirmed by their parents (Walker, 2013).

A queer-contextualized view of family structure also considers how power is held and used in family systems, as well as how the distribution of power in family systems reflects our broader cultural context. As marriage and family therapists (MFTs) we are in a unique position to support families, and parents in particular. With SFT, there is an assumption that we can and should support parents to take care of their children. This assumption is called into question, however, when considering conversion therapy. In queer-contextualized SFT, a parent's desire to change their child's sexual or gender identity is understood as organization by larger societal forces that create rigid boundaries and hierarchies within the family. Due to the overwhelming empirical data on the experiences of LGBTQ youth, a queer-contextualized SFT cannot support parents on this decision. Queer youths who experience identity rejection are more likely to experience depression, drug use, suicidal ideation, and participate in risky sexual behaviors (Heiden-Rootes et al., 2021; Przeworski et al., 2020; Ryan et al., 2009; Ryan et al., 2010; Ryan et al., 2018; Walker, 2013).

Boundaries

It is important to understand that all families are influenced by heteronormativity, but it is especially important to address and attend to the impact heteronormativity has on LGBTQ+ individuals and families. This is not just limited to identity management and the coming out process, but includes decisions about family growth, differences in "outness" among partners, the impact of internalized homophobia, and of course having to navigate a world that is pathologizing and limits autonomy (McGoldrick et al., 2016). Boundaries remain a clear and important part of assessing family structure from a queer-contextualized SFT framework. Assuming there are universally good and bad boundaries, however, may block a therapist from looking at a client's context with curiosity. A primary issue of the original assumptions of SFT is that the model assumes there is a "normal" that functions as a standard against which clients are judged as healthy or not. This "normal" was influenced by a cultural context that centers white middle-class cisheteronormative families and positions LGBTQ families, especially those who are of color or are financially poor, as outside the "norm." Queer-contextualization allows us to respect the authentic closeness and connection of many lesbian couples that have often been labeled as enmeshment or fusion (Ackbar & Senn, 2010). Rather than viewing closeness as enmeshment, a queer-contextualized SFT framework views increased closeness as a strengthening of bonds through clear boundaries and a resilient base against heterosexism.

Queer-Contextualized Interventions

A queer-contextualized structural therapist considers context when assessing for coalitions. Consider a family in which there are two parents and a trans child. If one parent is more accepting than the other of the child's gender identity, there might be a coalition between the child and the more accepting parent. In the original SFT, this would be conceptualized as a simple break or disengagement in the couple subsystem, and an emphasis would be placed on bringing the couple closer together. But placed in a queer context, we can see this disengagement as a symptom of the larger cissexist culture. Using the stroke and kick intervention (Minuchin, Nichols, & Lee, 2007), a therapist in this situation can acknowledge that both parents are fighting according to their values to give the best to their child, and they are even willing to sacrifice their marriage for their values (stroke). However, this forces their child to choose between fighting for themselves or their family (kick). In this example, the therapist would also present a reframe of the presenting problem. Rather than placing the locus of rejection on the family, a queer-contextualized reframe would extend beyond the family system. This is a family looking to survive oppression and, in doing so, has come up with different ideas for how to do that. The reframe allows for the family to see each other as resources to stand up against oppression rather than to break apart.

While the goal with the above family would be to create clear boundaries between both parents and child, the rejection from one parent must be taken into consideration. Family rejection is correlated with increased risk of substance abuse, self-harm, and suicidal ideation, whereas family acceptance has a positive impact on mental and physical health (Ryan et al., 2009). Before opening communication between the rejecting parent and their child, the therapist must first work to create a frame of support with that parent. This process might include exploring their past, their values, and what led them to become a parent in the first place, giving them an opportunity to process their fears and worries, and providing them with developmental information on the benefits of affirming their child. The leverage that structural family therapists have to promote change in a family is the love that the members have for each other. This leverage is the same for queer-contextualized SFT. Believing in and confirming that love, even at times reframing hurtful behavior to acknowledge the positive intent, can help a family to move toward third-order change.

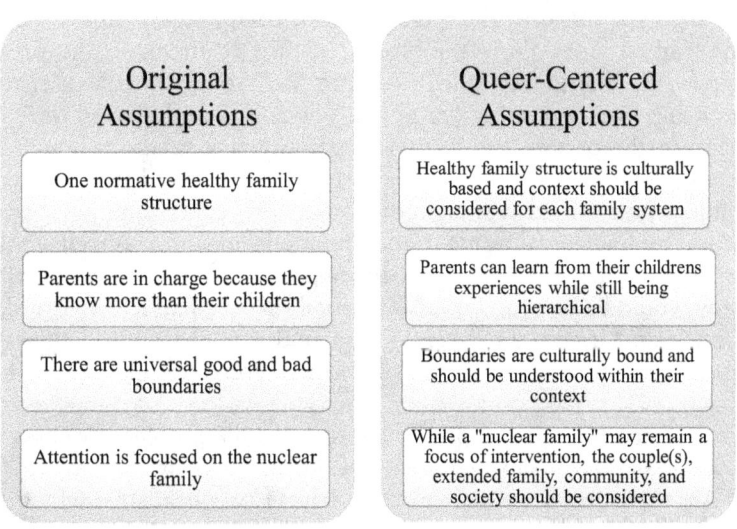

Figure 2.3 Comparison of Assumptions in the Original and Queer-Contextualized Structural Family Therapy Theory.

Case Study

This case study is based on the second author's (CV) work with a lesbian couple, whose identifying details have been altered for confidentiality, and who have given permission to share pieces of their story for learning purposes. Melissa and Alex, both in their early thirties, came to therapy due to a lack of physical and emotional intimacy in their relationship. They had been married for eight years, had a three-year-old son, and were expecting their second child. Melissa, a cisgender Latinx woman, carried and supplied the eggs for both children and was now a stay-at-home parent after years of working in health care. Her parents divorced when she was young, and she and her sister were primarily raised by their maternal grandmother, who had recently died. She reported a history of emotional, sexual, and physical trauma and mental health issues in her family. Alex also experienced trauma as a child, reporting emotional abuse and neglect. Alex currently identifies as female, although she is exploring her gender identity and sexuality in individual therapy. She is the only child of a Korean mother and a Black father and was raised outside the United States. The couple chose a sperm donor with a similar racial background as Alex. She works from home in the tech industry.

Initial Assessment

In the first few sessions, the therapist prioritized joining with the couple as she learned more about the history of their relationship and presenting problem. The therapist learned that Melissa has often felt that the relationship wasn't meeting her needs. The couple had opened their relationship in the past to support Melissa's intimacy needs, although they were monogamous at the time of therapy. Alex believed that her gender dysphoria, possible asexuality, and difficulty expressing emotions were all tied together and contributing to their relationship issues, as well as Alex's own persistent depression and anxiety. She was hopeful that her individual therapy would be helpful, but also worried that she had let Melissa down too much and it was too late. Melissa said that she wanted to stay in the marriage, but not at the cost of her need for emotional and physical intimacy.

When asked how they typically try to solve the problem, Melissa said that when she asks Alex for what she wants—a conversation, cuddles, sex—Alex will just stare at her "like I have two heads!" Melissa then becomes angry, and Alex will freeze or shut down until Melissa eventually storms off. Melissa says she puts up a wall, and won't talk to Alex about anything except the essentials for a few days. When the therapist asked Alex what her experience of these interactions was, Alex said, "I feel frozen. I know I should do something. I know I am letting her down. But I just can't seem to come up with anything worth saying." Alex said that when Melissa's wall is up, she just hides in her home office and works, coming out only to eat and sleep.

The therapist also asked about their support systems to get a sense for their sociocultural context and the boundaries around their family of creation. Melissa reported growing up with a strong value of "familismo." She was taught that families should be loyal and stick together no matter what—including abuse. Melissa felt it was important to stay loyal to her family, but struggled because her grandmother was the only adult who had accepted her sexuality and protected her from her mother's abuse. She maintained a distant relationship with everyone except her younger sister, who she was close to. Alex said her sexuality was also an issue for her parents, but that it was the last straw in a long history of "not being good enough." She had not talked to them in years and did not think they knew she had a child. On the other hand, the couple reported a strong and supportive chosen family who they felt they could rely on.

Family Structure

When conceptualizing the structure of this family, the therapist was careful to account for the couple's sociocultural context. The couple describe rigid disengaged boundaries between themselves and between them and their families-of-origin. Rather than view these as an indication of pathology in the family system, the therapist recognized that these boundaries were adaptive in the context of the abuse and oppression Melissa and Alex experienced in their childhoods. Further, the cultural context for these boundaries was different for each partner. In Melissa's family, the expectation was that everyone was highly involved in each other's lives, so she often felt conflicted about the distance she kept between herself and most of her family. On the other hand, Alex's family was more emotionally and geographically distant, as both of her parents had moved away from their countries of birth. While they had both created rigid and protective boundaries with their family of origin, those boundaries carried different cultural meaning for each of them.

Melissa and Alex's roles in their demand/withdraw pattern reflect the cultural norms their families-of-origin—Alex, who comes from a distant family, withdraws, and Melissa, who comes from an enmeshed family, demands. This pattern has become more polarized since the birth of their son, with Melissa's demands escalating to yelling and swearing, and Alex withdrawing for days at a time. The therapist noted that the last few years had been a time of significant change for the family with the birth of their son, and that they will face new challenges when the second child was born.

Despite feeling stuck, the couple has many strengths. They both survived abusive childhoods, and even with those wounds, had fostered many close friendships in adulthood, and formed a strong network of chosen family. They were both incredibly resourceful as individuals—putting themselves through college and building careers that provided financial stability and fulfillment—and as a couple—navigating a maze of fertility treatment, insurance providers, and legal documents to have their two children.

As the therapist gathered information about the family roles, rules, and structure, she drew a structural map and shared it with the clients throughout the conversation (see Figure 2.4). She pointed out the clear boundary and hierarchy between the parents (who choose their symbols: heart and "splat") and their children (a sun and an egg) as an element of their family that was currently working well. The therapist pointed out the conflictual relationships and rigid boundaries between each partner and their parents, as well as the close relationship Melissa had with her grandmother and the generally positive relationship with her younger sister. Because she was practicing from a QC SFT lens, the therapist thought of the structural map as encompassing their entire relational landscape—not just nuclear and extended family. She asked the couple who else should be included on this map of their most important relationships. Melissa and Alex described several people who they considered chosen family. They selected symbols for each, and the therapist added them on the side of the map with a clear boundary (not pictured). The QC SFT therapist then explained that all of these relationships exist in the context of heterosexism and racism, and that those contexts should be considered as they worked together in therapy. For example, the therapist

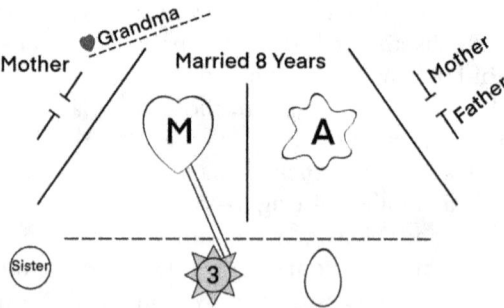

Figure 2.4 Queer-Contextualized Structural Map for Melissa and Alex.

suggested that the rigid boundaries between Melissa and Alex and the parents might be considered adaptive, given the rejection and abuse they each faced in their families. The therapist pointed to the rigid boundary between the partners and said,

> It makes sense that there is a rigid boundary between you, given how you both had to protect yourself growing up. But I suspect that this wall of protection is causing more damage to your relationship than it is doing to protect either of you. How would you feel about working together to create a boundary that works better for you and your family?

Rather than only focusing on the rigid boundary as the issue, the QC SFT therapist contextualized the structure of the couple's relationship within their family-of-origin history and larger sociocultural context.

Therapy Goals, Process, and Interventions

A common goal in SFT is to increase flexibility in a family system, so that it can adapt better to a changing environment, new stressors, or the growth and development of its members. The flexibility of the rules, roles, hierarchy, and boundaries of a system are changed through interventions like reframing and enactments. In the case of Melissa and Alex, their boundaries have become increasingly rigid and their pattern of interaction more entrenched as they have taken on the stressors of parenthood. In QC SFT, we recognize that these boundaries have been adaptive for the couple in oppressive contexts, and while they have the internal resources necessary to change their relationship, societal forces have prevented them from accessing those skills. Therefore, the primary therapeutic goal will be to increase the flexibility of the system by clarifying boundaries (i.e., increasing the flow of information) and interrupting complementary patterns (i.e., demand/withdraw)—by recognizing these structures as embedded within a larger sociocultural context. It is this last part that is unique to QC SFT.

In the first session, the therapist began to interrupt the couple's pattern by reframing their complementarity. The therapist listened as the couple described their fights, how worked up Melissa would get, and how scared and shut down Alex would get. Both partners agreed that Alex was the problem, and it was Alex who needed to change to meet Melissa's needs. The therapist wanted to offer the couple a view of the problem that was shared, which is part of original SFT, but also because their view of Alex as the problem created a power imbalance similar to the societal systems that oppressed them both, which is a perspective unique to QC SFT. Systems like racism and heterosexism rely on one group holding power over another—in this case, framing Alex as the problem gave Melissa power over Alex. To begin the process of interrupting this dynamic, the therapist offered a reframe.

Therapist: Melissa, you are fighting so hard to connect with Alex and I can see how much this disconnection hurts you. Alex, you desperately want to connect with Melissa, too, but you are afraid you will disappoint her, so you hide. You both want to connect with each other, and when your attempts fail, it has you both feeling defeated. Am I getting that right?

Melissa: Yes, I don't know what to do to get through to her. I'm desperate.

Therapist: What about you, Alex? Can you see how you are both stuck in a cycle of wanting to connect, but not knowing how?

Alex: Yes. I do want to connect with her. I just don't know how.

Therapist: Sounds like you two both want to feel connected to one another, but you are getting stuck in your attempts. I think there might be some really good reasons why you are getting stuck. Would you be willing to explore why you are getting stuck and also try some ways to get unstuck?

Here, the QC SFT therapist is setting the stage to explore the cultural and sociocultural context for their stuck patterns of interaction. She is also getting the clients' consent to explore this dynamic and to try to interrupt it.

When both partners agree that they are caught in a cycle and have similar goals, it starts to break down the polarizing positions of their complementary cycle. This work continues in subsequent sessions through additional reframing and the use of enactments. In the second session, the therapist uses the stroke and kick method to expand the reframe to include the couple's sociocultural context. Melissa was reporting on the previous week, where she tried to avoid making demands of Alex but was quietly upset that Alex did not seem to be making any changes. When prompted by the therapist, Alex shared that she really wanted to do something to connect with Melissa, but she was afraid that if she did the wrong thing, Melissa would get angry: "I didn't want to screw up a peaceful week." The therapist addressed both partners with a compliment (stroke), "It sounds like you spent quite a bit of energy this week trying not to rock the boat, out of your strong desire to keep this marriage together. You are both working incredibly hard for this relationship." Alex nodded and Melissa let out a long exhale, and the therapist continued with the kick, "However, not rocking the boat is costing you, isn't it? It's costing you communication, honesty, connection. It's costing you the relationship it sounds like you both truly desire." The couple sat quietly for a while. Finally, Alex said, "I can see that by trying not to rock the boat, we are making things worse. But it also feels like a really bad idea to rock the boat. Like, we don't know what will happen." From there, the therapist had a conversation with the partners about why rocking the boat felt so scary to them, in hopes of connecting this part of their pattern to their cultural context. Melissa and Alex talked about the cost of being their authentic selves in their families-of-origin. To place their pattern in their larger sociocultural context, the therapist also asked about the message they received as queer women of color from society.

"Don't rock the boat!" Alex said emphatically.

"No one cares about what I need. I cannot count on feeling safe or protected or cared for *out there*," Melissa said quietly. Seeing that Melissa had softened, the therapist used this as an opportunity to introduce a new interaction through the use of an enactment.

"Which makes it really hard when you don't feel cared for *in here*," the therapist pointed to the couple. Using QC SFT, the therapist could see how the rigid protective boundaries each partner had with the outside world were being replicated within their relationship, and how this type of boundary was not working for them. The therapist wanted to give the couple an opportunity to open that boundary a little.

Therapist:	Alex, we're not going to rock the boat just yet, but I'm going to ask you to make a little wave. Can you turn to Melissa and ask her what it is like for her when she does not feel cared for in your relationship?
Alex:	(turns to Melissa and takes a few breaths) What is it like for you when you don't feel cared for in our relationship?
Melissa:	(begins crying) I feel like I'm being abandoned and that I'm all alone in the world. I feel like I'm not worth being taken care of.
Therapist:	Alex, can you tell Melissa how it feels to hear that?
Alex:	(still facing Melissa) It breaks my heart to hear you say that. I know you feel that way in your family, but I didn't know you felt that way with me. I feel terrible that I've made you feel that way.
Melissa:	I don't want you to feel terrible. Because when you feel bad, you hide. I just want you to be here, to listen, like you're doing right now.
Alex:	Okay. I can do that.

The therapist, Melissa, and Alex spent the remainder of the session talking about what it would look like to practice these conversations at home.

They set clear guidelines for the conversations—that Alex was to initiate, ask Melissa to share her thoughts and feelings, Melissa was to respond without anger, and Alex was to actively listen. The couple agreed that either one of them could pass if it wasn't a good time for the conversation. These guidelines were important to keep the couple from repeating their stuck interactional pattern of Melissa demanding and Alex withdrawing. Instead, they created a small, concrete opportunity for Alex to approach Melissa. Alex was invested in trying this because she saw how their usual way of relating was rooted in their painful histories and the dominant culture. She wanted their relationship to be a safe space for Melissa. Rather than demand something of Alex, Melissa was given an opportunity to share her more vulnerable feelings and to be heard. This intervention was not much different from original SFT, except that the therapist intentionally assessed for the impact of sociocultural context and family history on the family structure, and incorporated those elements into the interventions. This empowers the clients to understand that their "problematic" ways of being have their roots in adapting and surviving in oppressive contexts.

This specific enactment was just a starting point in interrupting this couple's pattern. In subsequent sessions, the therapists continued to introduce different elements to their interactions, including opportunities for Alex to share her feelings and for both partners to make requests and to negotiate. The therapist continued to relate their pattern and stuck ways of interacting back to their families-of-origin and their sociocultural context, reminding the couple that their attempts to solve their relational issues made sense in those oppressive contexts, and offering them the choice to create a context of liberation in their own family.

Hopes for the Future of Marriage and Family Therapy

It is an honor to be an MFT. As MFTs we have an immense responsibility to support one of the most important—and at times delicate—systems of our society. Through this chapter, we hope to have provided resources for therapists who are looking to expand their lenses to better serve and affirm LGBTQ+ families. Recontextualizing SFT allows us to see the strengths of queer families, their resiliency, and to question what we consider normal and functional. We hope that MFTs can consider the importance of advocacy and acknowledging power inequalities across many systems. These inequalities affect the families we care for and affect us, and ignoring that upholds the power structures that limit our freedom. We can use our position of power to provide families with an affirming space that does not exist in our society. SFT has an excellent and well-developed framework

What do I believe about what makes a family functional?

What do I picture when I think of the word *family?*

What kind of boundaries do I find important in a family?

What caregivers do I generally work with? Why?

A good parent to me is…

A good child to me is…

My views on closeness and distance in families are…

How children should treat their parents/caregivers is….

What that looks like is…

What I learned from my own family that I carry into the therapy room is…

Blind spots that I know I have about queer families are…

Biases that I have implicitly or explicitly about queer people/families are…

What I am doing to learn about and understand LGBTQIA+ people and families is…

Figure 2.5 Questions for Reflection.

for assessing the organization of families. By queer-contextualizing SFT, we can reframe our biases around families, boundaries, and assessment of diverse family types. We understand that one of a therapist's many roles is getting clients from point A to point B; we can create the most meaningful change by boldly and proudly recognizing that this process looks different for everyone.

References

Ackbar, S., & Senn, C. Y. (2010). What's the confusion about fusion? Differentiating positive and negative closeness in lesbian relationships. *Journal of Marital and Family Therapy, 36*(4), 416–430.

Blumer, M. L. C., & Murphy, M. J. (2011). Alaskan Gay males' couple experiences of societal non-support: Coping through families of choice and therapeutic means. *Contemporary Family Therapy, 33*(3), 273–290. https://doi.org/10.1007/s10591-011-9147-5

Colapinto, J. (2019). Structural family therapy. In B. H. Fiese, M. Celano, K. D. Deater-Deckard, E. N. Jouriles, & M. A. Whisman (Eds.), *APA handbook of contemporary family psychology: Family therapy and training* (pp. 107–121). American Psychological Association.

Dolan-Del Vecchio, K. (2019). Dismantling white male privilege within family therapy. In M. McGoldrick & K. V. Hardy (Eds.), *Re-visioning family therapy: Addressing diversity in clinical practice* (pp. 226–235). Guilford Press.

Gehart, D. R. (2016). *Theory and treatment planning in family therapy: A competency-based approach.* Cengage Learning.

Heiden-Rootes, K., McGeorge, C. R., Salas, J., & Levine, S. (2021). The effects of gender identity change efforts on Black, Latinx, and White transgender and gender nonbinary adults: Implications for ethical clinical practice. *Journal of Marital and Family Therapy, 48*(3), 927–944. https://doi.org/10.1111/jmft.12575

McGoldrick, M., Carter, E. A., & Garcia-Preto, N. (2016). *The expanding family life cycle: Individual, family, and social perspectives* (5th ed.). Pearson.

Minuchin, P., Colapinto, J., & Minuchin, S. (2007). *Working with families of the poor* (2nd ed.). Guilford Press.

Minuchin, S. (1974). *Families and family therapy.* Harvard University Press.

Minuchin, S., & Fishman, H. C. (1981). *Family therapy techniques.* Harvard University Press.

Minuchin, S., & Nichols, M. P. (1993). *Family healing: Tales of hope and renewal from family therapy.* Toronto.

Minuchin, S., Nichols, M. P., & Lee, W.-Y. (2007). *Assessing families and couples: From symptom to system.* Pearson/Allyn and Bacon.

Minuchin, S., Reiter, M. D., Borda, C., Walker, S. A., Pascale, R., & Reynolds, H. T. M. (2014). *The craft of family therapy: Challenging certainties.* Routledge, Taylor & Francis Group.

Minuchin, S., Rosman, B. L., & Baker, L. (1978). *Psychosomatic families: Anorexia nervosa in context.* Harvard University Press.

Nichols, M. P. (2017). *The essentials of family therapy* (6th ed.). Pearson.

Nichols, M. P., & Davis, S. D. (2017). *Family therapy: Concepts and methods* (11th ed.). Pearson.

Przeworski, A., Peterson, E., & Piedra, A. (2020). A systematic review of the efficacy, harmful effects, and ethical issues related to sexual orientation change efforts. *Clinical Psychology: Science and Practice, 28*(1), 81–100. https://doi.org/10.1111/cpsp.12377

Ryan, C., Huebner, D., Diaz, R. M., & Sanchez, J. (2009). Family rejection as a predictor of negative health outcomes in White and Latino lesbian, gay, and bisexual young adults. *Pediatrics, 123*(1), 346–352. https://doi.org/10.1542/peds.2007-3524

Ryan, C., Russell, S. T., Huebner, D., Diaz, R., & Sanchez, J. (2010). Family acceptance in adolescence and the health of LGBT young adults. *Journal of Child and Adolescent Psychiatric Nursing, 23*(4), 205–213. https://doi.org/10.1111/j.1744-6171.2010.00246.x

Ryan, C., Toomey, R. B., Diaz, R. M., & Russell, S. T. (2018). Parent-initiated sexual orientation change efforts with LGBT adolescents: Implications for young adult mental health and adjustment. *Journal of Homosexuality, 67*(2), 1–15. https://doi.org/10.1080/00918369.2018.1538407

Sanders, G. L., & Kroll, I. T. (2000). Generating stories of resilience: Helping gay and lesbian youth and their families. *Journal of Marital and Family Therapy*, 26(4), 433–442. https://doi.org/10.1111/j.1752-0606.2000.tb00314.x

Walker, M. D. (2013). When clients want your help to "pray away the gay": Implications for couple and family therapists. *Journal of Feminist Family Therapy*, 25(2), 112–134. https://doi.org/10.1080/08952833.2013.777875

Wardecker, B. M., & Matsick, J. L. (2020). Families of choice and community connectedness: A brief guide to the social strengths of LGBTQ older adults. *Journal of Gerontological Nursing*, 46(2), 5–8. https://doi.org/10.3928/00989 134-20200113-01

Williams, N. D., Foye, A., & Lewis, F. (2016). Applying structural family therapy in the changing context of the modern African American single mother. *Journal of Feminist Family Therapy*, 28(1), 30–47. https://doi.org/10.1080/08952 833.2015.1130547

Chapter 3

Queer-Contextualized Strategic Family Therapy

Logan Parrott, Pia Alexander, Tomoyo Kawano, and Kristi Harrison

Strategic family therapy occupies an important place in the history of family therapy, having developed alongside many seminal family systems and general systems concepts. Strategic therapy is known for brevity and creative interventions, representing a radical departure from the psychoanalytic tradition prevailing at the time. Strategic therapy generally refers to several brief therapies, including the Mental Research Institute (MRI) (e.g., Watzlawick et al., 1967) and Milan models(e.g., Selvini Palazzoli et al., 1989), as well as the strategic approaches developed by Haley (1987) and Madanes (1981), which form the basis for the reimagined model presented in this chapter. The variants of strategic therapy all depart from insight-focused psychoanalytic therapy, viewing people and problems in terms of circular causality, rather than linear causality, staying problem-focused and working briefly, and attending to communication patterns and power dynamics within families (Stanton, 1981).

Strategic therapy, particularly as formulated by Haley and Madanes, does not prescribe particular structural goals; instead, the therapist attends to the unique problem presented by the client, tailoring interventions to specific circumstances (Haley, 1976). The therapist trusts that, although a family may be stuck in repeated attempts to solve the problem, they can generate more lasting and effective solutions with direction and creativity (Haley, 1987).

Theoretical Assumptions of Strategic Therapy

Structure and Hierarchy

Strategic family therapy draws its assumptions from several influences, including Minunchin's structural therapy, systems theory/cybernetics, Watzlawick's communication theory, and Ericksonian psychotherapy (Haley, 1987; Stanton, 1981). Strategic therapy, like structural therapy, considers a clear **hierarchy** essential to solving therapeutic problems,

DOI: 10.4324/9781003308188-3

which are seen as more likely around life cycle transitions where family members may be "stuck" (Haley, 1987; Haley & Richeport-Haley, 2005). According to the model, rules and roles should be flexible within a family while preserving clear hierarchy or organizational structure when resolving problems (Haley, 1987; Madanes, 1981). For strategic therapy, in contrast to structural therapy, changing the hierarchy is not the primary objective of therapy but rather a means to problem resolution (Haley, 1976; Madanes, 1981). Although Haley (1987) portrays strategic therapy as taking a non-normative stance with respect to family structure and processes, literature on strategic therapy is riddled with normative assumptions around gender, sexuality, and relationship structures, a concern addressed further in the critique section later.

Box 3.1

Hierarchy A ranking within the family system where some members have more power or influence than other family members.

First-order change Occurs when the family attempts to return things to normal (homeostasis) by changing their behaviors.

Second-order change Occurs when the family addresses the underlying rules of their relationships and creates a new homeostasis.

Problem A problem is a disruption to the homeostasis of the family. The family may view the problem as an external force, or a disruptive/misbehaving family member, while the therapist perceives the problem as a harmful or unproductive interaction *between* family members.

Cybernetics and Circularity of Interactions

Drawing from systems theory and cybernetics, strategic therapy conceptualizes the family as a homeostatic system that maintains its current state by attempting to solve **problems** through either **first-order** or **second-order** change (Watzlawick et al., 1974). With first-order change, attempts to solve the problem may *become* the problem because attempted solutions constitute "more of the same" at the process level and do not actually change the relational patterns. With second-order change, change occurs in the underlying "rules" or structures of relationships to create a new pattern of interaction (Watzlawick et al., 1974). Circular, repeating patterns of action are the primary focus of strategic therapy, and when sequences change, individuals can also change (Haley, 1987). In this model, pathology is defined by interactional patterns that are rigid and repetitive. Given the primary focus on circularity and sequences of interaction, identifying cycles of interaction is a primary aim during the strategic therapy assessment process. The focus on circular interactions conveys an essential assumption about the strategic view of health, namely that health goes hand in hand with flexibility and diversity of perspectives within a system. This is an important consideration when recontextualizing strategic therapy to center queer people and experiences.

Levels of Communication

Another defining assumption of strategic therapy is its focus on multiple levels or channels of communication within relational systems. Consistent with its roots in communications theory (e.g., Watzlawick et al., 1967), strategic therapy includes the idea that people in relationships communicate through both stated and unstated means, and that we are always communicating even when saying nothing (Haley, 1987). Strategic therapy incorporates a classic family systems concept called the double-bind, a situation that occurs when overt verbal communication conflicts with unstated messages about the nature of a relationship such that levels of channels of communication are conflicting and mutually exclusive (Foreman, 1990; Haley, 1976). Levels of communication are important in strategic therapy, particularly in terms of how family systems may demonstrate hesitation to change despite overtly stating a desire to change.

Metaphor

Related to communication is strategic therapy's use of metaphor. According to the model, clients' stated desire for change may conflict with unconscious or unstated motivations to *not* change, and the therapist overtly asking for a particular action may evoke a pattern of resistance (Haley, 1987). Strategic therapists utilize metaphor, an Ericksonian technique, as an indirect way of influencing clients' problems. Haley (1987) acknowledged ethical considerations around using metaphor to influence an aspect of a client's life that is not being specifically being named, noting that "the therapist is changing some aspects of a person's life outside the person's awareness, ostensibly, and without an explicit contract that this area is to be changed" (p. 76). Haley's (1987) recognition of the ethical dilemmas notwithstanding, the willingness of strategic therapists to work outside of clients' awareness is reflective of the strategic model's attention to, and willingness to, use therapist power to effect therapeutic change, an issue described in the next section and critiqued further below.

Power in Relationships and in Therapy

Power is a primary focus in the strategic model's view of relationships, including family relationships and the therapeutic relationship (Haley, 1987). Haley saw the organization of systems as inevitably involving hierarchy or power structure. This power structure may be clear and overt, or it may be covert and potentially involve conflict about who is in control. As part of its view of problem formation, strategic therapy includes the assumption that problems or symptoms are accompanied by some form of power struggle within a relational system (Haley, 1987). Given the perceived role of power struggles in problem formation, strategic therapy advocates that the therapist's beneficent use of power is an inescapable therapeutic responsibility (Haley, 1987; Madanes, 1981). Haley saw the therapist as a disruptor of existing relational patterns (Haley, 1987). The therapist is at once a part of the system and above the system: "[The] therapist should take charge of what is happening. If the family takes charge, it will go on as it has in the past, and there will be no change" (Haley, 1976, p. 3). Traditionally, strategic therapists utilize their own power to encourage clients to be flexible, use their imaginations, and change their communication patterns (Madanes, 1981). While there is merit in this approach, it also disregards the power that society holds in a family's life, a concern critiqued further below.

Strategic Therapy: Process and Interventions

The strategy in strategic therapy involves changing, specifically *interrupting*, problem-maintaining sequences to allow a relational system to develop new patterns of interaction free of the problem (Haley, 1987). Strategic therapists approach this change with the aim of solving problems in as brief a time as possible, moving quickly from joining to assessment to intervention, often all within the first session (Haley, 1987). From the moment of first contact with the client system, strategic therapists analyze patterns and power within relationships, carefully considering how they might **position** themselves relationally so as to have the most productive influence within the system (Haley, 1987; Stanton, 1981). Prioritizing problem resolution over insight, strategic therapists work with each person's stated motivations rather than confronting areas of resistance.

Box 3.2

Positioning/positionality The specific way that power differentials shape social identity and access.

Directive A hallmark of strategic family therapy. An indirect directive in which the therapist arranges the situation, so that whether or not the client follows their directive, change occurs. Paradox utilizes the therapeutic double-bind to create a win-win situation for the client.

Strategic therapists conduct assessment through direct questioning and observation of the client system as they interact with each other to talk about the problem in session (Haley, 1987). The aim of assessment is for the therapist to identify problem-maintaining sequences in order to plan a strategy for interrupting the pattern using **directives** (Haley, 1987). In traditional strategic therapy, directives typically involve working outside of the clients' awareness (Haley, 1987). Haley referred to misleading clients for change as "the beneficial lie," a stance critiqued for being manipulative or unethical (Foreman, 1990, p. 201; Kleckner et al., 1992). Ethical concerns with working outside of client awareness is one of several resounding critiques of this model.

Thinking Critically About Strategic Therapy: Power, Sociocultural Context, and Embodiment

Since its introduction, the strategic model has evolved through discourse among strategic therapists and through critiques from those outside of strategic therapy. Despite this evolution, the vast majority of scholarship on strategic therapy centers privileged social locations and carries cis-heteronormative biases that have pervaded and continue to pervade family therapy scholarship. Haley and Madanes were both presumably cisgender and straight and had the associated privilege of living in a cultural context where their being and bodies are "the norm." The strategic literature is riddled with biased examples of interactional patterns involving "the wife" and "the husband" and "the children." Consideration of gender, even in narrow binary terms, is largely missing from the strategic model (Luepnitz, 1988). While these biases in strategic literature are far more than superficial, cis-heteronormativity may not be essential to the model. There are, nonetheless, concerns hindering the model's applicability as a queer-affirming model, including its reliance on therapist power, neglect of oppression within sociocultural contexts, and discounting intraindividual, particularly embodied, experiences. These areas of concern are important to interrogate before reimagining the model.

Therapist (Ab)Use of Power

One resounding critique of strategic therapy concerns the power held by the therapist, specifically, that strategic therapists make therapeutic decisions unilaterally rather than collaboratively (Duncan, 1992; Luepnitz, 1988; McDowell et al., 2022). The therapist is the authority on systemic patterns, therapeutic conversation, and change in general; strategic assumptions give the therapist power over clients' lives without the responsibility of sharing their rationalizations. The mechanism for change in strategic therapy is the influence of the therapist, who directs the clients in achieving their goals. It is not the therapist's authority that is problematic per se, but rather the potential use of this authority to impose oppressive assumptions about family structure in pursuit of change. Existing power structures and hierarchies follow both therapists and families into their therapy sessions. A belief in therapist neutrality is insufficient for ensuring that the therapist does not replicate oppressive structures (Luepnitz, 1988; McDowell et al., 2022). While the strategic model clearly acknowledges the importance of power, and specifically the ethical considerations around therapists' use of power (Haley, 1987), strategic therapy is not concerned first and foremost with relational justice but rather with problem resolution (McDowell et al., 2022). This relates to a second major area of critique around strategic therapy's failure to address larger power structures.

Not Attending to Sociocultural Context

A second major critique of strategic therapy challenges the model in terms of addressing power structures and cultural context surrounding family systems. How can a model that sees power as organizing relationships not directly address the significant effects of oppression and marginalization, or the positionality of the therapist and clients? Haley (1987) acknowledged the effects of oppression and social context, but conveyed an arguably ineffectual either-or stance: that a therapist can *either* focus on larger systems change *or* focus pragmatically on solving the client's problem without regard for the social context. Haley (1987) asserted that therapists ought to focus on hierarchical structures *within* the family, rather than on sociocultural context, because family structure was what they could influence. Haley's (1987) stance suggests that the consideration of sociopolitical context is supplemental rather than primary, incorporated only to the extent that it aids symptom resolution.

By contrast, more recent socioculturally attuned strategic approaches consider family systems in the context of societal power structures, taking into account how societal power structures may influence problem-maintaining sequences and contribute to incongruence in hierarchies across levels of communication (McDowell et al., 2022). By placing family systems in the context of societal power structures, reimagined strategic therapy can center queerness by considering resistance to oppression as a primary lens for conceptualizing and changing sequences of interaction.

Neglect of Intraindividual Experiences, Particularly Embodied Experiences

Perhaps *the* defining assumption of strategic therapy is its prioritization of systemic context over intraindividual dimensions. As a result, the model not only deemphasizes client insight but also other intraindividual factors like emotion, individual histories, and embodied experiences. While the strategic literature does counter this critique, suggesting that the model *does* actually address emotion and individual histories (Haley, 1987; Kleckner et al., 1992), there are many instances where the strategic literature reflects a rigid discounting of intraindividual experiences, particularly emotion. For example, Stanton (1981) says of strategic therapists that "their approach is essentially a behaviorally-oriented 'black box' in which 'insight' or 'awareness' are not considered necessary or important for change to occur. Understanding one's motivation is of little value if one does not do something about one's problems" (p. 372). This description of strategic therapy indicates a paternalistic attitude wherein key dimensions of experience are delegitimized; in the context of experiences of hegemonic power structures, the claim that "understanding one's motivation [to resist oppression] is of little value" is alarming in its ability to maintain privilege and preserve oppressive structures. The collusion with oppression relates to the therapist's abuse of power addressed earlier; however, there is an additional, distinct critique of strategic therapy related to the discounting of individual "perceptions and subjective 'feelings,'" particularly the omission of embodied experiences in strategic therapy.

Abundant trauma research documents the embodied nature of trauma and healing (e.g., Dieterich-Hartwell & Melsom, 2022; Johnson, 2009; Lanius et al., 2011; Streater, 2022). Arguably, the neglect of the body in the strategic model promotes collusion with oppression. Dance/movement therapist Bennett Leighton (2018), who draws on the work of bell hooks and Judith Butler, described a crucial relationship between disconnection from our bodies and oppression, noting that "separation from the body is the crux of oppression" and that oppression works specifically through the exploitation and domination of bodies (p. 24).

Omission of the body in strategic therapy is of particular concern when considering the potential for therapist abuse of power. By discounting embodiment, classic strategic therapy obfuscates a dimension of experience where the most profound power dynamics are at play, particularly for people whose intersectional identities (and intersectional bodies) are oppressed and delegitimized. Put in terms of the model's own terminology, disembodied strategic therapy places people who experience oppression into a double-bind wherein they experience conflicting hierarchies and cannot name the (embodied, emotional) level where the most powerful oppression is operating. From this perspective, recontextualizing strategic therapy to incorporate the body is not just a creative reimagining of the model but an ethical necessity.

Strategic Therapy Reimagined: Embodied, Dance/Movement-Informed Queer-Contextualized Strategic Therapy

When recontextualizing strategic therapy, there are features of the original model worth retaining. For example, at its core, the model emphasizes circular causality and the interdependence of people in relationships and of systems and their contexts. Despite the pervasiveness of patriarchal and cis-heteronormative biases in strategic literature, the model's core assumptions endorse a non-pathologizing view of people, experiences, and problem-solving. Moreover, there is value in the model's focus on channels or levels of communication and the challenges that arise from conflicting messages, particularly with regard to who has power in relationships. At the same time, as presented in the critique of the model, there are also features of the model worth reimagining, including how therapists share power in therapeutic relationships, how the model attends to sociocultural context and power, and the extent to which the model actively accounts for the embodied experiences of people within systems. The creative integration of dance/movement therapy (DMT) allows for reinventing the strategic model in ways that complement the features of the model worth retaining, while specifically addressing concerns about power, social context, and embodiment.

Dance/Movement Therapy as a Complement to Strategic Therapy

Dance/movement therapy is a discipline that utilizes the body and dance as psychotherapeutic tools "to promote emotional, social, cognitive, and physical integration of the individual, for the purpose of improving health and well-being" (ADTA, 2017). It is a process-oriented approach that is client-led and collaborative and often facilitated in groups. Our queer-contexualized strategic therapy draws on areas of alignment and areas of complementarity between DMT and strategic therapy to address power, circularity, and communication in relational patterns by actively incorporating embodied information and change. Like strategic therapy, DMT is experiential in nature. DMT's emphasis on nonverbal communication addresses an important "level" of communication that traditional strategic therapy neglects, while at the same time the creativity and playfulness of DMT are a natural fit for the ethos of traditional strategic therapy.

Box 3.3

Dance/movement therapy "The psychotherapeutic use of movement to promote emotional, social, cognitive, and physical integration of the individual, for the purpose of improving health and well-being" (ADTA, 2017). The body and movement are utilized both as an in-context assessment tool and as an intervention.

Strategic Therapy Reimagined: Assumptions and Conceptualization

Our reimagined strategic therapy reaffirms a systemic, contextual, and circular view of people and the problems that bring them into therapy, with the important addition of attending to the embodied aspects of systemic interactions (see Figure 3.1). Sequences of interaction remain a primary focus for assessment, conceptualization, and intervention, as do patterns of hierarchy and power in relational sequences. However, drawing from DMT, the embodied dimension of interactional patterns becomes a primary area of focus in this reimagining of strategic therapy, which holds the assumption that oppression, trauma, and liberation all operate through bodies. Thus, queer-contextualized strategic therapy emphasizes embodiment as a powerful way of incorporating understandings of oppression and liberation into the circularity of relationships.

The importance of sociocultural and political context is a primary assumption in this revisioned strategic approach. Addressing power and hierarchy *within* systems requires addressing larger sociocultural power structures (McDowell et al., 2022), particularly with regard to dominant discourses around gender, sexuality, and other dimensions of diversity related to queerness. Countering hegemony and increasing equity are explicit aims in this reimagined strategic approach; this expands on Haley's

Original Assumptions	Queer-Contextualized Assumptions
Relationships contain circular causality, people are interdependent in both relationships and in the contexts of their family systems	Relationships contain circular causality, people are interdependent in both familial relationships and in the contexts of their broader systems
Therapist has authority; they join with the family to interrupt their problem-causing circular processes	Therapist is a co-creator; clients are experts of their own embodied lived experiences, and are empowered to change the circular processes they are in.
People communicate on multiple levels, and problems are associated with conflicting messages across levels. The therapist strategically targets problem-maintaining patterns of communication to resolve the problem.	People communicate on multiple levels, and problems are associated with conflicting messages across levels. The therapist collaborates with the family to understand and reshape communication.
Strategic therapy looks at power dynamics within the family system to promote therapeutic change.	Therapists expand their understanding of power both outward and downward

Figure 3.1 Comparison of Assumptions in the Original and the Queer-Contextualized Versions of Strategic Family Therapy.

(1987) original view of systemic health defined in terms of increasing flexibility and diversity within systems. Centering queerness entails explicitly creating space for the plurality of experiences in gender, sexuality, erotic, and romantic domains. Additionally, analysis of sociocultural and political context means that resistance to oppression becomes a primary lens for interpreting problem-maintaining cycles and changing sequences of interaction (McDowell et al., 2022); this is particularly important when centering queer people and experiences while acknowledging patriarchal, cis-heteronormative, and binary biases of current dominant discourses. Particularly by accounting for the embodied nature of power and oppression, this DMT-informed strategic approach considers systemic patterns, including the embodied interactions among people, in the context of larger sociopolitical power structures.

Box 3.4

Embodiment Highlighting our implicit use of the body in communication by making it explicit and intentional.

One of the most utilized DMT interventions, particularly with queer clients, is the use of **embodiment** to deepen the understanding of a client's experiences of privilege and marginalization (Kawano et al., 2018). The therapist's attention to their own bodily presentation can be incorporated to examine how similarities and differences in bodies impact relational power dynamics. While traditional strategic conceptualizations look at the relationships in hierarchical terms of who has power, this reimagined strategic approach explores the roles that members take on, investigating the emergent, interconnected, embodied experiences of each person. Sequences of interaction, as well as communication and metacommunication, are addressed through observation that takes into account embodiment. Integrating DMT and systems thinking allows therapists to "move easily between verbal and nonverbal streams of communication" (Dulicai, 2015, p. 145). For example, paying attention to nonverbal, embodied aspects of communication can offer the strategic therapist further insight into the rules and organizations of the system. Attuning to clients' physical positioning can facilitate joining and alliances, something as simple as positioning parents together can reconfirm their alliance, while having a child reach for their parents, even as part of a role-playing exercise, could be seen as a metaphor for their supportive needs.

Strategic Therapy Reimagined: The Stance of the Therapist

In DMT, the body is a site of self- and other-knowledge, a site for agency, inquiry, and potential for change. In traditional strategic therapy, therapists rely on exercising power over clients, expecting that clients follow the therapist's directives both during sessions and outside of therapy. In our reimagined strategic approach, sessions are client-led, reflecting instead a sense of mutuality and power-with rather than power-over. Whereas conventional strategic therapy may value the authority of the therapist as an "expert" to facilitate change, queer-contextualized strategic therapy views the clients as experts on their own lives. Drawing on DMT, the role of the therapist is to develop a relationship through listening and attuning to others with our bodies.

Conventional strategic therapists promote change by raising intensity and interrupting patterns, often by working outside of client awareness.

In contrast to the classic strategic stance where the therapist tries to outpace clients in order to circumvent resistance, DMTs work collaboratively, countering classic strategic therapy's cis-heteropatriarchal roots, positioning the therapist not as an authoritative, paternalistic disruptor of patterns but, instead, as an amplifier of what clients bring to session. The clients' worldview is repeatedly and viscerally centered through honoring their bodies and movements. Moving at their client's pace, the therapist's job is to improvise and co-create with what is emerging in the moment, using interventions such as metaphor, reframing, and meta-narratives. To join in the metaphorical dance and meet the client where they are, the following practices integrate bodies and movement into reimagined strategic interventions.

Strategic Therapy Reimagined: Interventions and Tools for Change

In conventional strategic therapy, change is therapist-choreographed and accomplished through directive interventions that interrupt problem-maintaining sequences and resolve conflicting messages about the power structure or hierarchy within relationships. Classic strategic therapists use a combination of behavioral directives and meaning-focused interventions such as metaphors and reframing. In our reimagined strategic model, the integration of embodied concepts allows therapists to collaboratively address multiple levels of communication (the spoken versus unspoken) in ways that honor clients' felt experiences and identities. As in the classic strategic therapy, the selection of interventions is highly individualized and is based on a conceptualization of how the presenting problem is situated within sequences of interaction. In reimagined strategic therapy, the aims are to interrupt rigid, repetitive sequences, to clarify power structures both within family systems and in broader sociopolitical contexts, and to free systems to reorganize in ways that allow individuals and systems greater flexibility and diversity. Guided by these aims, we reimagine two classic strategic interventions that incorporate DMT's emphasis on embodiment and empowerment: metaphor and reframing.

Metaphor

Metaphor can be used to help clients both with understanding of and indirectly communicating about problems (Haley & Richeport-Haley, 2005; Napoli, 2021; Samaritter, 2013). When clients are reluctant to talk about a topic, for example a child's emerging gender identity, instead a therapist might, for example, ask each family member about their taste in music (or art or movies) as a way of indirectly addressing individuality and self-expression. Discussing individual tastes in music or movies, as a metaphor, serves the dual benefit of reinforcing the idea of multiple perspectives (increasing flexibility and diversity) while also providing fruitful sources of discussion about the human themes or social discourses addressed within media. Eventually, the therapist might help the clients connect the two topics (self-expression in music and gender identity) or may allow the parallel to remain implicit (Kopp, 2013).

In addition to using discussion of creative arts as a strategic metaphor, movement can itself serve as a strategic metaphor. In our reimagined strategic therapy, movement can serve to symbolize interactional patterns; movement can become a metaphor through which new sequences of interaction are symbolically explored. For example, a therapist can invite the client to explore their reluctance through movement and tuning into their body. Where do they feel their "reluctance?" What does it look like? Feel like? Smell like? Taste like? They might respond and say it tastes like "sour lemons." The therapist might ask what the client can do with sour lemons, and they might add honey to make it less sour and more palatable. What was the honey in real life? Is it a person? A thought? And so on, until arriving at new understandings about the problem. In traditional strategic therapy, there is no collaboration on the metaphor; clients may not even understand or recognize that they are working with metaphor. In this reimagined strategic approach, clients are asked to involve their own metaphors, suffused with their own meanings. For queer clients, this relieves the burden of explaining their existence to a well-meaning but unknowledgeable therapist. Discussing the specifics of a client's gender and sexuality are not important; rather, the therapist trusts their expression and choice of metaphor and lets go of the need to correct, edit, or lead. They not only collaborate with the client but also allow them to exercise agency and lead the session where they need it to go.

Box 3.5

Metaphor Applying symbolism to the client family's life in order to express an idea or feeling, using another topic to represent and discuss parallel dynamics.

Reframing Requires the therapist to first reconceptualize the problem/presenting challenge in a more positive/solvable way, and then helps the clients to envision this reinterpretation by directly inviting them to view their communication and interactions in a more positive way.

Reframing

Reframing refers to changing the meaning of the problem (Haley, 1976). Reframing is not simply positivity in the face of adversity; rather, reframing refers to changing the client's understanding of a problem when the original framing maintains the problem. For example, a client who is depressed and cut off from their family may, indirectly, see themselves as the problem using the following logic: *My family cut me off, and I am sad about this. But I shouldn't be sad because I am upset at my family. I have no control over my feelings, and having no control over my feelings is a bad thing.* While it is difficult to define depression out of existence, shifting the context around the problem changes the frame the problem is in. In reimagined strategic therapy, societal contexts of oppression and liberation are often the foundation for reframes (McDowell et al., 2022). For example, depression may instead be framed as an act of resistance, the body's intuition to invite in rest, healing, and connection. Reframing also happens through movement. Clients can be asked to act out their beliefs and, through directives, try out different scenarios.

Ethics of Embodied Practice

One important ethical consideration concerns the way that biases may operate through attitudes about how bodies look, work, and move. Socially constructed narratives about dance and bodily attitude have historically centered cisgender, heterosexual, able-bodied, white European ways of being (Amighi & Loman, 2018; Kawano & Chang, 2019). Without critically examining the socially constructed norms about bodies, embodied therapy can replicate marginalization by relying on oppressive scripts regarding a standard body on which all people's ways of being are judged. It is the job of the therapist to critically examine societal narratives about bodies. Furthermore, while bodies can be a source of agency and a site to reclaim power, bodies are often also where traumatic experiences reside. Embodied work has been a part of the family therapy's theory and practice since the field's inception (e.g., see the work of Virginia Satir), and we maintain that embodied approaches fall within the scope of practice of couple and family therapists; however, ethical responsibilities regarding scope of competence mean that therapists doing embodied work should seek out relevant knowledge and skills related to the embodied nature of trauma and embodied or somatic interventions. This chapter serves as a starting point for development of such competency.

Case Example: The Perry-Hallett Family

The following case example, a composite of multiple clients with whom the authors have worked, illustrates the application of our reimagined, embodied strategic therapy model. The family in this case, the Perry-Hallett family, identifies as a multiethnic French-American and African-American Polish family, whose members are spiritual and nonreligious.

Initial Contact and Case Background

Dee (60, she/her) contacted the family therapy practice during the early months of the COVID-19 pandemic; her eldest child, Emily (24, she/her), had moved home as a result of the pandemic. Since then, Emily and her younger sibling Morgan (19, she/them) have been locked in "continuous verbal conflicts" that Dee described as escalating and disrupting an otherwise "very peaceful home environment." Dee and her husband Reginald (61, he/him) have been married for over 30 years, are both college-educated and work in well-paying professional fields, with Dee working especially long hours. Both parents identify as cisgender, heterosexual, and monogamous.

Emily identifies as a cisgender lesbian woman. She is career-oriented and, following the completion of college and a graduate degree, has worked in increasingly advanced positions within her chosen field. She left the family home post college and has moved back due to the financial uncertainty of the pandemic. During the intake call, Dee reported having a "fine" relationship with Emily but stated that Emily and Morgan have historically been quite distant and are now locked in conflict.

Morgan identifies as a genderqueer person. Morgan has not attended college and has worked in retail settings during and after high school, continuing in-person employment during the pandemic quarantine. Dee reported that Morgan's willingness to risk exposure to illness has been one of the many topics of conflict among the siblings.

The Initial Interview: Assessment and Conceptualization

Both Dee and Reginald are highly motivated during the first session. Emily is more engaged than Morgan, responding to therapist's questions freely. During the early part of the session, Reginald shares that Morgan is only attending at his request. Reginald describes that he and Morgan have a "close and trusting" relationship, particularly because they have spent a lot of time together since the pandemic started.

Reginald explains being "visibly shaken" by an argument he overheard where Emily and Morgan were yelling at each other about Morgan's gender identity disclosure. Since that incident, Morgan has remained with-drawn and prefers to stay in their bedroom, including during meals, avoid-ing interaction with the rest of the family. Morgan describes "feeling cut off" from their typical routine within the home. When Morgan and Emily encounter each other in the home, there is typically little verbal communi-cation. Emily and Morgan both disagree with their parents' assertion that the verbal conflict is ongoing and; in contrast, both siblings describe their present relationship as "reserved" or "detached." Morgan shares with the family therapist that their family prefers "silence to conflict."

The family members convey mixed messages about the focus of their conflict, including about how gender and sexual identities figure into the siblings' conflict. Emily describes feeling "blindsided and intention-ally left-out" of Morgan's disclosure to their parents that they are queer, a disclosure that occurred while Emily was living away from the family home. Emily also expresses frustration with Morgan's decisions around work, describing Morgan's choice to continue to work and socialize in person as "irresponsible," especially given that they are doing "menial work that is not worth the risk." Morgan describes being content with their own "coming out" process and did not see this process as relevant to the conflict with Emily or as warranting coming to therapy. Reginald and Dee both convey their acceptance of Emily and Morgan, including their children's educational and career decisions and their sexuality and gender. All four members of the family agree that reducing arguing and restoring peace is their primary goal and that they hope just a few sessions can help them achieve this.

In the initial interview, the therapist asks what troubles the family, initially seeking a verbal response and then using an embodied strategic approach that incorporates movement to help the family share other layers of its relational processes.

Therapist: I'm curious to hear from each of you about how you would describe the problem.

Morgan: Between the pandemic and Emily moving home, I can't do what I usually do, and I'm isolated from everyone that knows me well. I just want Emily to back off and give me space!

Emily: Morgan comes and goes without regard for anyone else's feelings. I feel shut out. Everyone's withholding stuff from me, no one tells me anything!

Reginald: Everyone is tense all the time. I don't understand what they're fighting about. It stresses me out.

Dee: I just want things to return to normal and no matter what I do they just keep yelling and disrupting the peace.

These brief responses illustrate one layer of the family's cycle of inter-action, in which Emily is seeking out and focusing on Morgan, while Morgan withdraws, and Reginald and Dee minimize conflict in order to "keep the peace." A therapist following the classic strategic model might view the presenting problem as one of *hierarchy versus equality*, perhaps complicated by developmental transitions and life stressors, including the pandemic. The clients are in an ambiguous position hier-archically as they face the stressors of the pandemic and developmental transitions around emerging adulthood. In a classic strategic approach, the therapist might view the aim of therapy as helping the parents clarify the hierarchy and establish expectations for "acceptable" communica-tion within the household, given its developmental stage, a stance that may inadvertently uphold societal norms about family communication or reinforce a cis-heteronormative status quo about each member's role in the family.

In this session, the queer-contextualized strategic therapist first validates the verbal accounts each person offers about the problem and their experi-ence of it and then uses movement to invite the family into intentional and congruent metacommunication (communication about their communica-tion). This is a collaborative, transparent way to address underlying power struggles or conflicting communication that occurs when verbal signals are inconsistent with nonverbal ones. The therapist seeks to understand how each member of the family system interprets each other's behaviors using an embodied strategic approach:

Therapist: It sounds like each of you is experiencing the problem in different ways from each other and in ways that may feel confusing to you. To shed further light on your interactions, would you each be willing to actually show me, through actions rather than words, how you are presently experien-cing your relationships?

The family members agree to this exercise, acting out their views of their communication. During this process, the therapist observes Dee's dem-onstration of waving her arms above her head in multiple busy circles. Reginald pushes his arms out in front of him as though he is repeatedly pushing away negative energy or heavy objects. Morgan and Emily stand silently facing away from each other and turn occasionally to pantomime talking signs at each other with their hands. As the clients carry out this exercise, the therapist verbally reflects to the client family what they are observing for confirmation:

Therapist:	I'm curious, what did you take from each other's actions?
Morgan:	I'm not angry with her, I'd just like space and for her to respect my decisions.
Emily:	It's tough to connect with Morgan, it feels like our backs are to each other.
Reginald:	I'm not sure that I have a good read on their conflict. It feels heavy to me but I don't really know what it's about.
Dee:	My movements were about confusion, exhaustion and chaos.
Therapist:	Observing all of you here, I get the impression that you may each be feeling a little helpless. Or maybe even a lot helpless. Like you don't know what to do to resolve this. Does that fit with your experience? [*All four nod in agreement. The therapist allows a long pause, providing space for the four clients to absorb the commonality in their experience. After the pause…*] I'm curious…if we had other people here who could serve as actors to portray the other forces affecting your family right now, who or what would also be part of this scene.
Emily and Morgan, in unison:	The pandemic! [*they laugh*]
Emily:	The stress of the pandemic is a huge part of this. It's like we're all in a pressure cooker. That should definitely be part of this scene. [*Another pause occurs.*]
Morgan:	This might sound strange, but I also feel like the world's expectations of me should also be a character in this scene. It's like everyone has a right to tell me how to be.
Therapist:	Can you say more about this? If we actually saw this in the room right now, what would it look like?
Morgan:	Like a huge figure lording over me and pointing its finger at me, telling me what to do.

Using the opportunity to communicate *about* their relationships through movement, new dimensions of the systemic interactions begin to emerge, allowing this queer-contextualized strategic therapy to account for sequences of interaction affected by sociocultural context. We get a sense for life cycle areas where family members may be "stuck" (Haley & Richeport-Haley, 2005), but also a glimpse into how the symptoms (conflict) involve resistance to cis-heteronormative assumptions about individuals and relationships (McDowell et al., 2022). This expands the view of the presenting problem and uses embodiment to consensually engage the family system such that the therapy holds the literal "problem" sequence presented by the family—"constant verbal conflict" of the siblings—and its the metaphorical presentation of the tension in their relationship, which is eventually revealed as a negotiation between the desire to give support (Emily) and the need to assert a personal boundary (Morgan), stances which may be viewed in the context of the broader sociocultural power dynamics around gender and sexuality identities.

*During this initial session, the therapist lays the foundation for **reframing** the problem, emphasizing areas of commonality despite the sibling arguing and laying the groundwork for incorporating resistance to oppression as part of the problem-maintaining cycle. The conceptualization in terms of hierarchy and conflictual communication patterns (disempowered/confused parents, avoidant/arguing adult children) is expanded by inviting new views of the conflict, brought forward through embodiment. Building on the imagery Emily and Morgan offered regarding the effects of the pandemic and the imposing figure lording over them, the therapist concludes the initial session by asking the family members to remember this scene, and, before the next session, to work together to identify an empowering piece of music that supports their resistance to the effects of the pandemic and the towering figure.*

Intervention: Music as Metaphor

Therapist: I'm wondering if you would be willing to discuss a piece of music that you collectively enjoy, something with lyrics that you wouldn't mind moving to?

Emily: We used to go to Martinique Carnival and visit some of our French family members there. I can think of a few carnival songs that we might all know the lyrics to or songs from our school assemblies when we were younger. Other than that, our tastes differ quite a bit!

Morgan: I would definitely agree.

The therapist amplifies this moment of agreement between siblings using humor and slows down the pacing of the moment by inviting each member of the family to demonstrate with a movement how it feels to hear agreement. Dee and Reginald each demonstrate movements indicating peace or ease. Morgan decidedly shrugs (communicating humor), and Emily places both hands over her heart.

Therapist: Morgan, do you mind sharing the experience that inspired your movement?
Emily: Relief. I feel included.

The therapist reflects to the family their understanding of the way that music and movement can be tools for exploring differences in communication in the family, and emphasizes Morgan and Emily's agreement as a moment of family union as well as unity and empowerment in their identities. The family is not protected from the pressures of the outside world, as these pressures inform the urgency or pacing of movement for each member of the family. The family feels more able to discuss agreements regarding pacing that feels generous and respectful and begin to generate solutions to the presenting problem. One solution that emerges from the family is an agreement that the siblings will intentionally connect more by phone or in person outside of the family home, so that the physical space is no longer the only place where information is shared or where family members "catch up" with each other. Family members reached agreement on how to consciously manage anxiousness around the ever-changing sociopolitical environment, particularly as it relates to queer persons and their families, so that there is less expectation for each member of the family to respond in the same way to new information.

Concluding Thoughts

The queer community is as varied as any community; in a random sample of queer people, the only thing they have in common may be sexual or gender identity that differs from the supposed cis-heterosexual norm. Strategic therapy, as originally imagined, is a thoughtful modality that strives to promote family flexibility and rapid change; however, by failing to account for the inherent power imbalance queer people experience in a cis-heteronormative society, traditional strategic therapy can easily become an exhausting repetition of the status quo hierarchy. Instead of introducing another authority figure to a system, it is our hope that a reimagined strategic therapy helps families fully realize what power they do have over their lives.

What do you understand about your own power as a therapist?

What are your assumptions about the ways that sequences of interaction play a role in the situations that bring people to therapy?

What "more of the same" solutions has the Perry-Hallett family tried, and how do power differences in the family hierarchy influence these attempted solutions?

Thinking about therapy as an embodied experience, consider what you tend to notice about a person when they first enter a room? What do you think people notice about you and your embodied self?

What aspects of your identity remain invisible to clients?

What is your relationship with your body? How does it feel for you to be embodied?

What would you need in order to incorporate embodiment into your clinical practice?

Figure 3.2 Questions for Reflection.

References

ADTA. (2017). *What is dance/movement therapy?* American Dance Therapy Association. Retrieved from https://adta.memberclicks.net/what-is-dancemovement-therapy

Amighi, J. K., & Loman, S. (2018). Reviewing the body attitude and interpreting movement patterns through KMP diagrams. In J. K. Amighi, S. Loman, & K. M. Sossin (Eds.), *The meaning of movement* (2nd ed., pp. 319–345). Routledge.

Bennett Leighton, L. (2018). The trauma of oppression: A somatic perspective. In C. Caldwell & L. Bennett Leighton (Eds.), *Oppression and the body: Roots, resistance, and resolutions* (pp. 17–30). North Atlantic Books.

Dieterich-Hartwell, R., & Melsom, A. M. (Eds.). (2022). *Dance/movement therapy for trauma survivors: Theoretical, clinical, and cultural perspectives.* Routledge.

Dulicai, D. (2015). Family dance/movement therapy: A systems model. In S. Chaiklin & H. Wengrower (Eds.), *The art and science of dance/movement therapy* (pp. 125–137). Routledge.

Duncan, B. L. (1992). Strategic therapy, eclecticism, and the therapeutic relationship. *Journal of Marital and Family Therapy, 18*(1), 17–24. doi: 10.1111/j.1752-0606.1992.tb01733.x

Foreman, D. M. (1990). The ethical use of paradoxical interventions in psychotherapy. *Journal of Medical Ethics, 16*(4), 200–205. doi:10.1136/jme.16.4.200

Haley, J. (1976). Problem-solving therapy: New strategies for effective family therapy. *Social Work, 22*(3), 241. https://doi.org/10.1093/sw/22.3.241

Haley, J. (1987). *Problem-solving therapy* (2nd ed.). Jossey-Bass.

Haley, J., & Richeport-Haley, M. (2005). *The art of strategic therapy.* Brunner-Routledge.

Johnson, R. (2009). Oppression embodied: The intersecting dimensions of trauma, oppression, and somatic psychology. *The USA Body Psychotherapy Journal, 8*(1), 19-31.

Kawano, T., & Chang, M. (2019). Applying Critical Consciousness to Dance/Movement Therapy Pedagogy and the Politics of the Body. American Journal of Dance Therapy, 41(2), 234–255. https://doi.org/10.1007/s10465-019-09315-5

Kawano, T., Cruz, R. F., & Tan, X. (2018). Dance/movement therapists' attitudes and actions regarding LGBTQI and gender nonconforming communities. *American Journal of Dance Therapy, 40,* 202–223.

Kleckner, T., Bland, C., Frank, L., Amendt, J. H., & Bryant, R. D. (1992). The myth of the unfeeling strategic therapist. *Journal of Marital and Family Therapy, 18*(1), 41–51. doi: 10.1111/j.1752-0606.1992.tb01737.x. PMID: 26274006

Kopp, R. R. (2013). *Metaphor therapy: Using client generated metaphors in psychotherapy.* Routledge.

Lanius, R. A., Bluhm, R. L., & Frewen, P. A. (2011). How understanding the neurobiology of complex post-traumatic stress disorder can inform clinical practice: A social cognitive and affective neuroscience approach. *Acta Psychiatrica Scandinavica, 124*(5), 331–348. https://doi.org/10.1111/j.1600-0447.2011.01755.x

Luepnitz, D. A. (1988). *The family interpreted: Psychoanalysis, feminism, and family therapy.* Basic Books.

Madanes, C. (1981). *Strategic family therapy.* Jossey-Bass.

McDowell, T., Knudson-Martin, C., & Bermudez, J. M. (2022). *Socioculturally attuned family therapy: Guidelines for equitable theory and practice* (2nd ed.). Routledge. doi: 10.4324/9781003216520

Napoli, M. (2021). *In and through the body: The benefits of dance/movement therapy on the mental health of LGBTQIA+ adults: A literature review.* Expressive Therapies Capstone Theses, 436.

Samaritter, R. (2013). The use of metaphors in dance movement therapy. *Body, Movement and Dance in Psychotherapy, 4,* 33–43. doi: 10.1080/17432970802682274

Selvini Palazzoli, M., Cirillo, S., Selvini, M., & Sorrentino, A. M. (1989). *Family games: General models of psychotic processes in the family.* W.W. Norton.

Stanton, M. D. (1981). Strategic approaches to family therapy. In A. S. Gurman & D. P. Kniskern (Eds.), *Handbook of family therapy* (pp. 361–402). Brunner/Mazel.

Streater, O. K. N. (2022). Truth, justice and bodily accountability: Dance movement therapy as an innovative trauma treatment modality. *Body, Movement and Dance in Psychotherapy*, *17*(1), 34–53.

Watzlawick, P., Beavin, J. H., & Jackson, D. D. A. (1967). *Pragmatics of human communication*. W. W. Norton.

Watzlawick, P., Weakland, J. H., & Fisch, R. (1974). *Change: Principles of problem formation and problem resolution*. W. W. Norton.

Chapter 4

Queer-Contextualized Satir Family Therapy

Lindsay L. Edwards

As a founding member of the Mental Research Institute at Palo Alto, Virginia Satir (1916–1988) offered an important diverging perspective during the early days of systemic therapy. Although based in the ideas of circular causality, nonsummativity, and communication theory (Haber, 2002), Satir was known to have found problematized views of families and their presenting concerns to be limited (Brothers, 2019). Offering a counterpoint to problem-focused systemic therapy, Satir created a clinical framework centered on the humanistic assumption that people and their systems are naturally inclined toward growth and wholeness (Woods & Martin, 1984).

The developmental story of Satir Family Therapy is the story of Virginia Satir herself. As a lifelong learner, Satir's ideas about the origins of distress and clinical intervention evolved as she followed her life's pursuit to understand people (Haber, 2002). Satir's own account of her model development focuses primarily on the impact her experiences – within her family of origin, as a teacher, working with clients, and encountering other scholars – had on her thinking about families (Satir, 1982). In Satir (1982), she relays the significance of reading *"Toward a Theory of Schizophrenia"* by Bateson, Jackson, Haley, and Weakland (1956) since it confirmed what she was already noticing in her work with families. Satir also recounts how meeting humanists and somatics at the Esalen Institute shifted her focus to **growth** and the "affective domain" of experience (1982, p. 21). The evolution of Satir's ideas can be seen throughout the 12 books she authored during her career (see Satir, 1967; Satir, 1972; Satir, 1976; Satir & Baldwin, 1983; Satir, 1988 for her flagship books), with the most comprehensive description of the model being published posthumously (Satir et al., 1991). Embodying the growth she encouraged in others, Satir's thoughts on family systems and intervention evolved as she worked with clients, conducted workshops internationally, and relentlessly pursued her own development. As a result, Satir Family Therapy is

DOI: 10.4324/9781003308188-4

a masterful integration of systems theory, communication theory, humanistic psychology, and experiential intervention.

Box 4.1

Growth The energy of life, which is the persistent unfolding of potential and the evolution of individuals and systems from the smallest of origins to an expanded wholeness.

Theoretical Assumptions

Healthy Systems

Informed by humanistic psychology, Satir Family Therapy assumes people are naturally inclined toward growth, want to feel good about themselves, and need to be valued. These foundational assumptions offer a framework for understanding how problems develop within systems and how therapists can use clients' own momentum toward growth to inspire change. From a Satir framework, the identified patient's "problematic" behavior is evidence of stymied growth for an entire system and is viewed as an attempt to reclaim self-worth. In healthy systems, there is balance between what family members contribute to a system and receive from a system (Satir et al., 1991). Furthermore, healthy systems allow family members to experience *intra*personal and *inter*personal congruence so that they can express their needs and wants to others in the system (Brothers, 2019). Family members and their relationships grow unencumbered and authentically, so people feel cared for, respected, connected but autonomous, and balanced. Additionally, discomfort and pain are viewed as signals for change or as indications of a normal growth process, rather than as signs of dysfunction or abnormality (Satir et al., 1991).

Box 4.2

*Intra*personal Congruence A state of sentience where we are conscious of genuine emotions and somatic experiences that allow us to access our essential self.

*Inter*personal Congruence Communicating so that there is harmony between what we are genuinely experiencing and what we show others through our body language, vocal pitch, and vocal rhythm.

Systems in Distress

Family members in distressed systems contribute more than what they receive, making the system "unfair and unjust, yet stable" (Satir et al., 1991, p. 100). Simultaneously, family members are not considered equally valuable, and family roles reinforce a hierarchical structure of superiority and submissiveness. In this case, pain and discomfort are considered undesirable obstacles and as indications of flaws within people and/or relationships (Satir et al., 1991). Unhealthy systems remain rigidly imbalanced because family members are forced to cope with the demands of the system by "conforming to something that works against them" in order to survive (Satir, 1982, p. 18). This coping results in a "stress ballet" of *in*congruent communication where family members move in and out of survival stances like placating, blaming, super-reasonable, and irrelevant in order to hide their genuine experiences (Satir et al., 1991, p. 31). Such survival stances occur when family members are *intra*personally *in*congruent, meaning they are unaware of or do not acknowledge their **essential self**, their authentic emotions, and their somatic experiences.

Box 4.3

*In*congruent Communication Communication where there are conflicting messages between the report component (the words used by a person) and the command component (metacommunication about interpreting the words).

Essential Self Unique essence that is core to each person and inherently valuable because of its singularity.

Systemic Elements of Satir Family Therapy

In alignment with systems theory, these incongruent survival stances are complementary and self-propagating. By their very nature, each survival stance is related to and contingent on the other survival stances. It is impossible to take a blamer stance if there is no one to blame, and one cannot placate without fearing the loss of another person. Satir viewed survival stances as interconnected, since each style of incongruence requires a partner for implementation, and she held that these interpersonal dynamics functioned for the homeostasis of a system. Satir also understood that developmental learning occurs predominantly in our bodies. We "learn from our caretakers by their breath, their touch, and their movement more than their words" (Satir et al., 1991, p. 20). Our early experiences with family shape how we engage in relationships by teaching us what we can expect from others, what others expect from us, and what we should expect from ourselves (Satir, 1982). When these **family rules** demand *inter*personal *in*congruence, they tell us we cannot share our essential selves with others, and we cannot have our own experience in a family. Thus, the level of congruence in our family shapes who we become by granting or denying us access to our authentic selves (Brothers, 2019). As Satir et al. (1991) put so eloquently, "... the infant whose survival depended on others becomes the child whose identity depends on others" (p. 22). As awareness of the value of our uniqueness atrophies, we disconnect from our experiences to avoid the painful feelings of inadequacy in our most essential relationships. We no longer experience our emotions or physical sensations. Our identity and feelings of worth become dependent on external sources, and we suffer from low **self-esteem** (Satir & Baldwin, 1983). Then, given the nature of interpersonal process, children raised in incongruent systems become partners and parents with low self-esteem who are disconnected from their experiences and communicate incongruently – recreating and perpetuating the family incongruence.

Box 4.4

Family Rules Perceptions, behaviors, and beliefs that we learn in our families of origin that are often inhuman and leave us living inhuman lives.

Self-Esteem Conscious valuing of one's essential self.

Threat/Reward Model Relating to others through hierarchy so that the value of each person varies, people live according to others' expectations, events are explained in a linear way, difference indicates pathology, and change is undesirable.

Growth Model Relating to others through equality so that people embrace and value their own uniqueness, events are explained systemically, difference is an opportunity for connection and evolution, and change is essential and inevitable.

Problem Conceptualization

Problems emerge in families when the **threat/reward model** of relationship is predominant rather than the **growth model**. In a threat/reward system, family rules are rigid and inhumane, people are incongruent, and relationships are hierarchical. Each person's value is determined by how well they conform to and obey the expectations of others, which diminishes differences and uniqueness among family members. Problems are attributed to individuals, which allow members of the system to remain disconnected from their experiences and authentic selves. This disconnection maintains the homeostasis of a system by preventing family members from being consciously aware of their emotions and somatic experiences. Satir (1982) recounts how it is possible to wash your hands without experiencing the sensation of touch, or to eat food without experiencing its smell or taste – and so it is with emotions; we can speak about pain, shame, pleasure, and joy without experiencing any of them. Romantic partners who are disconnected from their own pain, cannot tolerate expressions of pain in each other. Instead, couples argue over who caused the other more injury, without ever feeling the very pain they argue over. Parents, who are disconnected from their essential selves, cannot embrace and value the uniqueness of their children. Instead, they reinforce similarity and require conformity without acknowledging the various ways that they themselves are unique (Satir et al., 1991). Thus, conflict and distress function systemically to keep family members out of touch with their painful feelings of shame, sadness, and loneliness.

Assessment

Satir Family Therapists assess the level of **congruent communication** in a family and how much the members focus on an individual person or a specific relationship as the "problem." Assessing these aspects of process provides the therapist with information on how the symptom functions for the system and to what extent the family relates through threat/reward dynamics. Satir Family Therapists use this information to decipher why the growth of a particular system remains stunted and what is needed in order for a system to grow. This is in contrast to a problematized view of systems which diagnose issues for individuals and relationships. Individual diagnoses, and even static hypotheses about systemic dynamics, are considered "freeze frame(s) of an interaction," according to Satir (Brothers, 2019, p. 91). These interactions occur between the individuals of a family and between families and larger cultural systems. As such, a person's depressive symptoms are not features of the individual but, instead, are features of homeostasis in the family and cultural systems. Correspondingly, Satir Family Therapists prioritize relational explanations for presenting concerns over individual diagnosis.

Box 4.5

Congruent Communication Communication where there is harmony between the report component (the words used by a person) and the command component (metacommunication about interpreting the words).

Goal Development

From a Satir framework, the goal for any client system is to help members move from a threat/reward model to a growth model of relating (Brothers, 2019). A growth-oriented system includes people who are both *intrap*ersonally and *inter*personally congruent. When family members are congruent, they nurture and value their own uniqueness, prioritize parity over hierarchy, are connected to their emotional and somatic experiences, and embrace change as a natural process even when it is uncomfortable (Satir et al., 1991). Although it is reasonable for therapists to conceptualize clients' goals in terms of the model language, Satir was clear that goals should be stated using words that are relatable to clients and reflect their experience (Satir, 1988). Without a resonant clinical goal, clients' homeostasis will overtake any progress toward their desired change.

Intervention

Satir Family Therapy is considered an experiential model because its interventions emphasize change through in-the-moment connection to experience. Although insight is sometimes used to consolidate experience, the primary tools for change are interventions that connect clients to their essential selves through emotional and somatic experiences in the here and now. More specifically, change is thought to occur when clients experience their feelings and body sensations, which together increase their consciousness of their essential self (Satir, 1982). Well-known techniques of the model include *family reconstruction, family sculpting, making contact, metaphor*, and *self-mandala* (Satir et al., 1991). Each of these techniques is meant to facilitate clients' increasingly authentic encounters with each other and the therapist.

To successfully use these techniques, therapists must first cultivate their own congruence since this is what gives the techniques their traction (Satir et al., 1991). Not surprisingly, Satir's workshops were largely focused on helping therapists grow their congruence, rather than on providing instruction for specific techniques (Brothers, 2019). Therapists who are connected to their own experiences, as well as the value of their own uniqueness, can generate relational experiences where clients' essential selves emerge, their self-esteem grows, and interpersonal conflict dissolves. As a result, family systems undergo second-order change and the family's growth-orientation becomes autogenic.

Critical Considerations

Critical evaluations of Satir Family Therapy are few and far between, but some feminist authors have argued that Satir did not sufficiently address power and the effects of oppression on family systems (Freeman, 1999; Luepnitz, 1988; Maxey, 2021). Luepnitz (1988) contends that Satir's humanistic assumptions do not account for the way power impacts our ability to change in systems, nor can low self-esteem account for complex social problems like genocide, slavery, and poverty. Luepnitz also notes that Satir did not see the expansion of feminism as a part of her work, citing the following quote from Satir "*I am for personhood. I want to help women find their self-worth and take their place in society. But not at the expense of men*" (Luepnitz, 1988, p. 81). Despite this, Luepnitz maintains that elements of the model fit with a feminist framework – namely that Satir prioritized nurturance in her change model. Nurturance, as a therapeutic strategy, is in alignment with feminist ideals and "a matter so taboo under patriarchy that it must always be disguised as 'unconditional positive regard' or 'positive countertransference' or 'multidirectional partiality'" (Luepnitz, 1988, p. 78). Luepnitz also speculates that the accessibility and relational aspects of Satir's work, which are associated with femininity in the United States, likely explain the devaluing of Satir's contributions to the field and the oversimplification of her highly sophisticated work. Given her context as the only woman founder of family therapy, it makes sense that Satir would have strategically worked at the process level in place of engaging in content level advocacy for gender equality. Interestingly, Freeman (1999) observed from her analysis of Satir's original writing, recordings, notes, and interviews that Satir addressed power and gender at the process level. Although not an explicit goal of Satir, gender equality is certainly an outcome of the model interventions.

A Queer Evaluation

In a more recent critique, Maxey (2021) contends that the model does not consider the impact of systemic oppression on families. As a result, Satir can be practiced in a way that overlooks how racism, transphobia, homophobia, gender essentialism, and monogamism shape the theoretical assumptions of the model. One can easily find evidence of dominant and oppressive cultural beliefs about gender, sexuality, and relationship structures in the foundational texts written by Satir. The most obvious cishetmononormative assumption of the model is with the concept of the *primary survival triad*. According to Satir, the primary survival triad comprises a mother, a father, and a child (Satir, 1967, 1991; Satir & Baldwin, 1983). Satir described it as the first system in a series of systems someone will come into contact with, and correspondingly, it is the "essential source of identity of the 'self'" (Satir & Baldwin, 1983). Implicit in this concept is the assumption that there are exactly two primary caregivers for a child, that these caregivers are genetically related to the child, and that they are an opposite gender pair who are romantically involved, monogamous, and legally married. Such implicit bias surrounding the structure and formation of families does not account for the expansive, adaptive, and creative ways that lesbian, gay, bisexual, transgender, and queer (LGBTQ+) family systems form.

Additionally, essentialist and binary assumptions of gender, sexuality, and relationship structure are found throughout Satir's written work. For instance, as Satir discusses family rules, she refers to males, females, wives, and husbands (Satir, 1972). Also, her case examples in Satir et al. (1991) included cishetmononormative couples with biological children. Of course, Satir's use of cishetmononormative language and case examples can be understood as an artifact of the times, and yet it is important to ask how cishetmononormativity shaped Satir's thinking about health, dysfunction, family structure, and the process of change.

Effects of Oppression on Process

According to Maxey (2021), Satir did not explicitly address how sociopolitical contexts shape personhood and influence congruence and self-esteem. Without considering the effects of oppression on personhood, self-esteem, and congruence, the model would ignore the connection between internalized oppression and self-esteem, as well as the substantial risk associated with visibility (i.e., interpersonal congruence) for LGBTQ+ people. The risk of visibility for LGBTQ+ people can be seen in the overwhelming amount of research that shows that LGBTQ+ people face discrimination in all aspects of life, including in families, and are frequently the targets of hate crimes in the form of harassment, violence, and murder (Kutateladze, 2022; McKay, Lindquist, & Misra, 2019). In essence, LGBTQ+ people are forced to remain incongruent under threats of isolation, violence, and death. Additionally, the pervasiveness of transphobia, homophobia, and monogamism directly impact LGBTQ+ people's self-perceptions, resulting in internalized oppression. This internalized oppression can leave LGBTQ+ people second-guessing their experiences, doubting themselves, and experiencing shame and low self-worth to a much greater extent than those who are not targeted by transphobia, homophobia, and monogamism (Rood et al., 2017).

Maxey's (2021) point that oppression shapes congruence and self-esteem is critical. With this, Maxey's claim that Satir does not account for oppression overlooks that it is a process-oriented model that addresses oppression through process. The work of Moane (1999) is useful for explaining how this is the case, since it describes how process is shaped by hierarchy and how process-level dynamics perpetuate inequality. Integrating the ideas of numerous feminist and anti-colonialism theorists, such as Lee Maracle, Frantz Fanon, Jean Baker Miller, bell hooks, and Paulo Freire, Moane describes the intrapsychic and interpersonal patterns experienced by those living under oppression at the bottom of a hierarchy, as well as by those living as oppressors at the top. These process-level patterns are strikingly similar for all people involved in a hierarchy and occur in four domains – self and identity, emotions, interpersonal relationships, and mental health. Each of these domains are not only shaped by oppression but operate in concert to maintain hierarchy.

In her discussion of self and identity, Moane (1999) explains "there is a general emphasis firstly on loss and restriction of identity related to the erasure of history and culture" in hierarchical systems (p. 85). Self-knowledge is restricted, and experiential truths are distorted through the colonization of self for people at both the top and bottom of a hierarchy. For people living under oppression, colonization of self manifests as assimilation, self-doubt/hatred, feelings of inferiority, and a loss of culture and history (Moane, 1999). Consider how the history of LGBTQ+ liberation movements, and even the existence of LGBTQ+ people, has been sidelined and erased from U.S. history (Bronski, 2011). For those living at the top of a hierarchy as oppressors, colonization of self similarly manifests as the mystification of historical and cultural background, in addition to an inaccurate self-concept that contributes to an unsubstantiated and inflated self-confidence, feelings of entitlement, and expected exaltation. One example of mystified historical and cultural background for those living as oppressors is the tendency for people socialized white in the U.S. to describe their cultural heritage as American – having entirely forgotten their own family's migration story.

Moane (1999) also describes how, in a hierarchy, the full range of emotional experience is restricted so that painful emotions are not expressed. This restriction of genuine emotions occurs at all levels of a hierarchy and functions to maintain the hierarchical structure. It is important to note that the cost of expressing genuine emotions in a hierarchy is not the same for those living under oppression as it is for those living as oppressors. Moane describes how authentic expressions of anger from minoritized people, born from the grief and pain of living under oppression, are met with retaliation from oppressors. For those with the least amount of power in a hierarchy, this retaliation can be lethal. At the top of a hierarchy, however, authenticity is predominantly met with isolation and a loss of power and influence. People living as oppressors restrict vulnerable emotions in order to retain positional power in a system – sometimes carrying out retaliation. Those living under oppression, however, restrict genuine emotions for the sake of survival since the cost of authenticity is markedly more extreme. In each case, what occurs is dissimulation – the concealment of the authentic self and genuine emotions.

Countering Oppressive Systems with Satir Family Therapy

Moane's (1999) ideas about self and identity, as well as dissimulation, have a great deal of conceptual overlap with Satir Family Therapy. Much like Moane, Satir saw that relational patterns are both shaped by and perpetuate hierarchy. What Moane called dissimulation, Satir understood as interpersonal incongruence. Satir's thinking about low self-esteem as disconnection from one's essential self and experiences is akin to Moane's description of constricted self-knowledge and restricted emotional experiences. Furthermore, Satir's thinking that hierarchy is maintained in family systems through incongruence is remarkably similar to Moane's determination that hierarchy is upheld when the individuals at both the top and bottom of a hierarchy are disconnected from their history and culture, their genuine experiences, and an accurate self-concept. Interestingly, the language Satir used to reference unhealthy systemic dynamics evolved from the *threat/reward model* in Satir and Baldwin (1983) to the *dominant/submissive model* in Satir (1988), and finally, to the *hierarchical model* in Satir et al., (1991). This evolution suggests that, as Satir wrote, she came ever closer to articulating the role of power in family dynamics and labeling the source of systemic distress for what it is – hierarchy.

Given these parallels, Satir's articulation of the relationship between self-esteem and the hierarchical model of relating (i.e., threat/reward) provides a framework for understanding how hierarchy shapes process and how process maintains hierarchy both inside and outside of family systems. By working at the process level, Satir created a model for change that was content neutral and, correspondingly, could be used to address power and hierarchy through the discussion of any content at any systemic level. Thus, Satir Family Therapy not only accounts for the influence of oppression on relational dynamics and individual process but also offers a framework for dismantling hierarchy at the micro- and macro level. Said more directly, Satir Family Therapy offers an antidote to oppression through experiential connections to one's essential self.

In fact, Brothers (2019) notes this potential for the model in a chapter she titled *Gun Power and Seed Power*. In this chapter, Brothers describes Satir's vision for addressing injustices within the broader system of humankind. Brothers notes how only people who are in contact with and value their essential selves (i.e., intrapersonal congruence) can value the uniqueness of others. Furthermore, when we value ourselves *because* we are unique, not *despite* our uniqueness, the need to compare ourselves to others becomes obsolete, and we no longer need to dominate or submit (Brothers, 2019). Intrapersonal congruence also dissolves hierarchy since it is a sentient state that facilitates our emotional attunement with others. Simply put, we feel what others feel when they feel it. In a state of emotional attunement, we cannot enact transphobia, racism, cissexism, homophobia, or other forms of oppression without feeling the pain we are causing to another person through our actions. In essence, hierarchy can no longer be sustained when the members of a system are interpersonally congruent. See Figures 4.1 and 4.2 for visual representations of the connection between hierarchy and congruence under the growth model and the hierarchical model.

Considering Satir's work alongside Moane (1999), it is evident that incongruence in families is a sociological phenomenon and not strictly a feature of families. Whether intentional or not, Satir accounted for the impact of oppression on personhood, congruence, and self-esteem by articulating the relationship between hierarchy and incongruence. As a result, fostering intrapersonal and interpersonal congruence within families

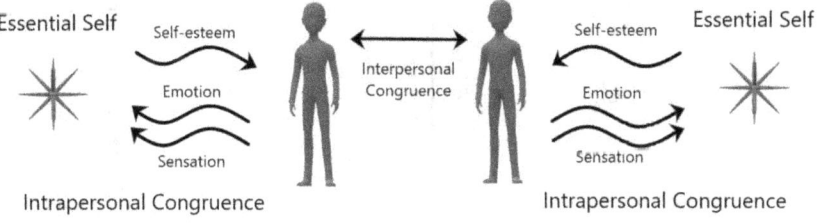

Figure 4.1 Growth Model of Relating.

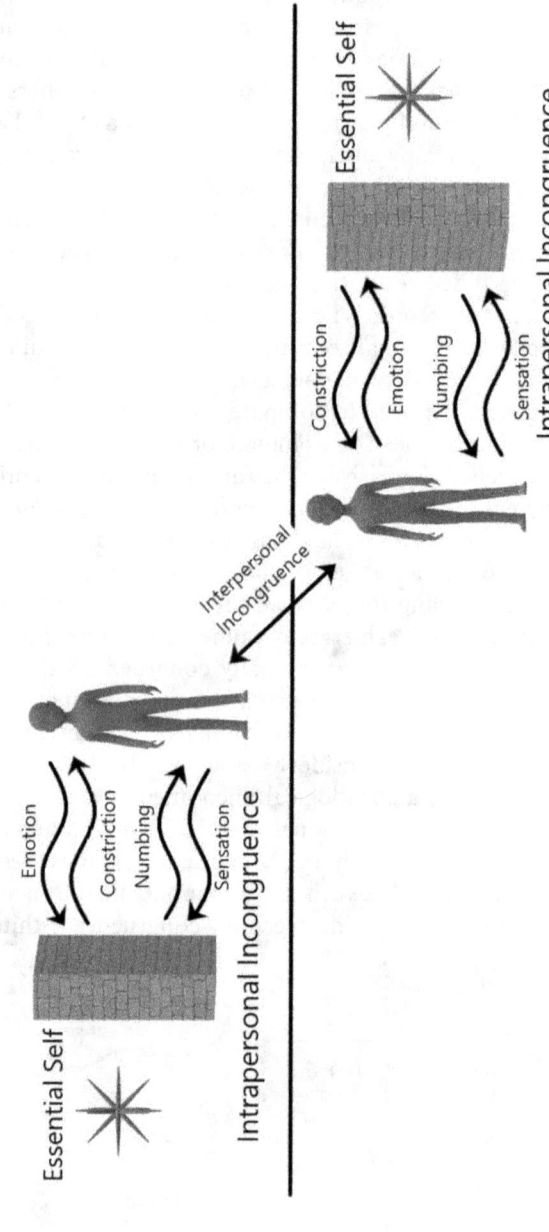

Figure 4.2 Hierarchical Model of Relating.

has the potential to create second-order change at the society level. Satir said it best, "By knowing how to heal the family, I know how to heal the world" (Laign, 1988, p. 20).

Necessary Adjustments

With the extraordinary potential that Satir Family Therapy holds for countering oppression, it is reasonable to wonder what, if any, limitations exist for the model. Limitations do exist, and they stem from the societal, political, and historical context within which the model was developed, a context shaped by white supremacy, heteronormativity, cisnormativity, patriarchy, and monogamism. As a result of this context, the model was developed largely around white, cisgender, straight, and mononormative people. To interrogate the core assumptions of Satir for cishetmononormativity and white supremacy, we must ask how the model's assumptions about health and dysfunction, family structure, and change might have been different if created around the lives and relationships of LGBTQ+ people – especially LGBTQ+ people of color.

As previously mentioned, a Satir framework assumes that families are healthiest when they are growth-oriented, the communication is congruent, and the members experience high levels of self-esteem. In such a system, people experience harmony and intimacy through congruent encounters which are "life giving" (Brothers, 2019, p. 168). Although the necessity of harmony and intimacy for individual and systemic health is undeniable, this perspective is predicated on the assumption that living incongruently in hierarchical systems has a greater cost than living congruently. The costs of living incongruently, according to the model, are dysfunctional relationship dynamics, poor psychological health, and even physical illness (Brothers, 2019). In fact, Satir spoke later in her career about her belief that chronic incongruence would take a toll on a person's body by "training the glands not to perform their normal function simply by continually restraining their output" (Brothers, 2019, p. 153). Satir came to believe that the cost of incongruence could be physical illness and even death from diseases like cancer (Brothers, 2019). Satir's thinking about the mind/body/relationship connection was pioneering, but the assumption that incongruence costs more than congruence overlooks the pervasive amount of violence faced by people targeted by oppressive systems like racism, transphobia, homophobia, and patriarchy (Lenning, Brightman, & Buist, 2021). For people facing oppression, living incongruently is often necessary for surviving in a hostile environment. This brings into question the assumption that congruence is the embodiment of health and should be the goal of all therapeutic encounters.

For some, the long-term health outcomes of interpersonal incongruence might involve less risk than having to face abusive and violent retaliation from sharing authentic expressions of anger toward white supremacy, disclosing one's queerness, and/or living one's true gender identity. This does not mean that people targeted in systems of dominance do not also suffer terrible, and sometimes immediate, mental and physical health outcomes, while protecting true aspects of themselves through incongruence. Consider the overwhelming amount of empirical research that shows how internalized stigma contributes to adverse health outcomes for LGBTQ+ people (Hatzenbuehler & Pachankis, 2016; Hatzenbuehler, Phelan, & Link, 2013). The point here is that if Satir had created her model around LGBTQ+ people and relationships, it would not automatically balance in favor of congruence for all members of a system. Instead, the model would include a cost analysis during assessment that considers each clients' sociocultural background, determines potential implications for congruence both inside and outside of the family system, and examines the impact of sociocultural background on communication stances and the distribution of power within the system. Such an assessment would give particular attention to experiences of rejection within families to determine how this rejection reflects broader systems of dominance and, correspondingly, intensifies struggles with self-esteem and interpersonal incongruence for family members. Such efforts would be in the interest of helping clients decide *for themselves* how to move forward with therapy.

In addition to this change, the model would not include the concept of a primary survival triad but, instead, would make general reference to family systems without defining a specific structure. Intergenerational transmission of process and the importance of caregiver involvement in therapy would, however, remain essential assumptions of the model since they are related to the distribution of power in a family. Assumptions about the mechanism of change itself would also remain intact. In particular, the experiential nature of the model, as well as the value and power placed with uniqueness, would remain core to the model given the significance of these ideas for dismantling hierarchy. See Figure 4.3 for a comparison of the theoretical assumptions of Satir Family Therapy with those that underpin queer-contextualized Satir Family Therapy.

Queer-Contextualized Satir Family Therapy

One foundational assumption underpins queer-contextualized Satir Family Therapy (QCSFT) – namely that humans are healthiest when they can live connected to and value their own uniqueness and the uniqueness of others. Such a state is born from and facilitates genuine intimate connection with others, where difference is not an indication of pathology but a moment

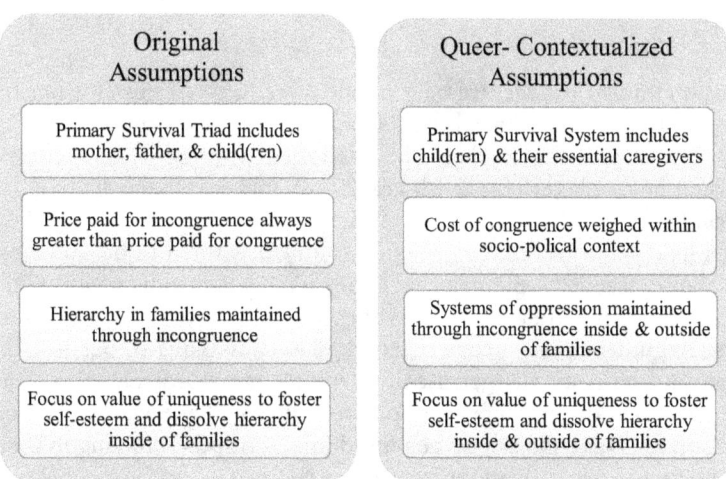

Original Assumptions	Queer-Contextualized Assumptions
Primary Survival Triad includes mother, father, & child(ren)	Primary Survival System includes child(ren) & their essential caregivers
Price paid for incongruence always greater than price paid for congruence	Cost of congruence weighed within socio-polical context
Hierarchy in families maintained through incongruence	Systems of oppression maintained through incongruence inside & outside of families
Focus on value of uniqueness to foster self-esteem and dissolve hierarchy inside of families	Focus on value of uniqueness to foster self-esteem and dissolve hierarchy inside & outside of families

Figure 4.3 Comparison of Theoretical Assumptions.

of naturally occurring growth. Furthermore, uniqueness is viewed as both beautiful and powerful. This is in stark contrast with the perception of difference under the hierarchical model, where "our existing differences usually serve as an unspoken rationale for accepting the dominant/submissive power differential in our relationships" (Satir et al., 1991, p. 8). With a queer heart, QCSFT makes the inherent value of each person and their unique lived experiences central aspects of clinical work with *all* clients.

Case Illustration

Important implications for each phase of therapy stem from this core assumption of QCSFT. Additionally, there are distinct self-of-the-therapist considerations when working from this framework. The following is a case illustration that shows the unique aspects of QCSFT in action and notes important reflections for therapists to consider as they work.

Client Information

Rachel (45), James (43), Blake (15), and Sarah (8) are a family of four who live in a suburb of a large midwestern city. Rachel and James self-identify as white, cisgender, and heterosexual and have been legally married for 19 years. Blake identifies as a white, transgender, and pansexual. He also asked the therapist to use he/him pronouns. Sarah identified as white on her intake paperwork but did not indicate a gender identity or sexuality.

Initial Contact

Rachel contacted the therapist by phone to request services for her transgender son Blake, who "needs help from someone who knows about these things." According to Rachel, Blake stopped wanting to do things with her when he reached the seventh grade and, instead, spent the bulk of his time on the computer in his room. It was around this time that Blake told Rachel he did not feel like a girl and no longer wanted to be called by his given name. Rachel explained that "they have been trying to use Blake to refer to him," but they sometimes forget, and this often results in arguments. Arguments also occur when Rachel asks Blake about his day at school, and he responds generically or with one-word sentences. Rachel also mentioned during her initial phone call that Blake was being bullied in school, and that she hoped he would talk about the bullying in therapy since he would not talk about it with her.

Assessment/Case Conceptualization

Similar to the original version of the model, QCSFT assessment is focused on incongruence in the system and whether an individual person or a specific relationship is identified as the "problem." QCSFT therapists use this information to determine if the system operates under a hierarchical model and, correspondingly, how power is distributed within the system. The framing of a presenting concern can be especially helpful for determining the balance of power among family members. This is because family members with the least amount of power are often framed as the problem and are the ones who come or are sent to therapy. In contrast, those with the most amount of power in a system are not viewed as connected to the problem and, as a result, often attend sessions as collateral or do not attend therapy at all.

Rachel, having good intentions, called to request individual therapy for Blake, hoping that the therapist would provide him with support. Such a request stems from important assumptions about the problem – namely that the problem exists with Blake alone, that the problem is related to him being transgender, and that she and James are incapable of providing Blake with support since they "don't know about these things." What remains outside the frame of this problem (and unseen) is how Rachel and James are struggling to parent across difference. Their struggle to parent Blake, who they perceived as different from them, stems from their own incongruence and use of a hierarchical model of relating that leaves them out of touch with their own uniqueness and the uniqueness of their other child Sarah – who they perceive to be similar to them. This view of the "problem" also overlooks that Rachel and James are struggling with a placator/blamer dynamic that has left them feeling isolated and lonely in their marriage. As a result, Blake's withdrawal from the family has uniquely impacted Rachel since she copes with her isolation through her parenting relationship with Blake. These overlooked aspects of the problem prevent Rachel and James from being a resource for Blake, but because of their power in the system, they are not viewed as connected to the "problem."

In addition to obscuring the parents' involvement in the presenting concern, Rachel's frame of the problem establishes an unseen agenda for therapy. This frame enlists the therapist as an agent of the parents who want the therapist to inquire about the bullying and provide support to Blake in order to eliminate the *family's* conflict. If left unaddressed, this frame of the problem will undercut the therapy by positioning Blake as the person who is responsible for carrying out the *family's* needed change. Said differently, the least powerful family member would have responsibility for systemic change despite having little to no influence over it, and the most powerful family members would have influence over the change with little to no responsibility for it. Seeing Blake individually would collude with the system and absolve the parents of their responsibility for the change that they alone have the power to influence – effectively binding the therapy. To address this, the therapist would need to expand the therapeutic system by contextualizing the problem within the family members' relationships. During the initial phone call with Rachel, the therapist insisted that the entire family attend therapy sessions together, noting that Blake's struggles had likely impacted, and been impacted by, his relationships with other family members. When the request was met with hesitation, the therapist assured Rachel that therapy would provide support for Blake *and* address the impact on their various relationships.

Although Satir viewed presenting concerns in terms of hierarchy and considered parental involvement important, her decision to involve parents was not linked to power in the same way it is for QCSFT. A QCSFT framework explicitly connects power to the framing of a problem and views the involvement of more powerful family members as critical. In place of the stagnant concept of the primary survival triad, QCSFT conceptualizes the treatment unit in terms of power over and responsibility for systemic change. Involving powerful family members is necessary for second-order change, but most importantly, it avoids reifying societal injustices that occur within families. If the therapist had agreed to see Blake alone, the emphasis on gender identity, rather than the family's hierarchical model of relating, would have reinforced a cisnormative assumption that Blake's transgender identity was the "problem."

Using a QCSFT framework also requires a therapist to back further away from the initial frame of the problem and consider how the family members' incongruence is not strictly a feature of the family dynamics but of cultural oppression manifested through family dynamics. Thus, a QCSFT case conceptualization articulates how incongruence within family systems stems from societal-based hierarchies like gender socialization and white supremacy. Having been socialized white, cisgender, and straight, both Rachel and James embody the incongruence that occurs for people living as oppressors, which leaves them unable to experience painful emotions and embrace their own and other's differences. For Rachel, who has also been socialized as a woman and suffered the effects of patriarchy, the pain of knowing she might have caused injury in another is uniquely unbearable. As a result, both parents operate from a hierarchical model where they remain detached from their experiences. From this perspective, their focus on Blake functions for them as powerful members of the system and reinforces culturally rooted oppression.

Goal Development

A QCSFT therapist initiates a collaborative goal development process following the formulation of a case conceptualization that describes the functioning of incongruence and the distribution of power in a system. From a QCSFT framework, goal development prioritizes client autonomy by discussing the risks and rewards of increased congruence for each family member, beginning with the most powerful. QCSFT therapists start with powerful family members in order to increase their involvement in and responsibility for the family change – bringing these into greater alignment with their power in the system. With the current frame of the problem, there is a wide gap between Rachel and James' power over the change and their involvement in family change. There is also less risk associated with increased congruence for them as cishetmonogamous white parents. As a result, the therapist focused on helping Rachel and James explore their experience of having been parented and parenting themselves, noting what their hopes were for their children and how these hopes came to be. Building upon the parents' values instead of family rules, the therapist facilitated a family discussion where members spoke of wanting to know each other better and be connected. Following the establishment of this goal, the therapist asked the clients to consider what it would require of each of them to know each other better and what was at risk if they were genuinely connected. These efforts were in the interest of acknowledging the systemic functioning of their current relational dynamics before helping the family decide for themselves if they would pursue second-order change.

Intervention

In total alignment with Satir Family Therapy, QCSFT therapists use experiential interventions to elicit clients' emotional and somatic experiences in the here-and-now. Doing so connects family members to their essential selves and the complexities of human experience. Through these interventions, clients come to find that, at the experience level nothing is only one thing, and we are all contemporaneously the same and different. In sessions with Rachel, James, Blake, and Sarah, the therapist focused on exploring their lived relational experiences. Beginning with James, who typically embodies a placator stance and easily disappears during discussion of the problem, the therapist asked what it is like for him to witness the conflict between Rachel and Blake. In a state of intrapersonal incongruence, James responded to the therapist by explaining that the conflict between Rachel and Blake has been difficult for the two of them. Intent on eliciting James' lived experience, the therapist acknowledged his response, while also asking him to distinguish between his experience and the experiences of other family members. The therapist asked "James, I am beginning to grasp how the arguments between Rachel and Blake are impacting them, but I have yet to hear how they impact you. Can you describe what it is like for *you* to witness these arguments?" In response to this and subsequent questions from the therapist, James described feelings of shame, rooted in a deep fear of incompetence, that emerge for him when the arguments occur. Following a similar strategy with Rachel, the therapist worked to progressively evoke her lived experience as a parent, asking her questions like

> Rachel, when you realize that Blake is struggling and needs support, what feelings emerge for you? Where do you feel this fear in your body? How would you like Blake to feel when you are parenting him? What does this tell you about yourself and your own experiences having been parented?

To emphasize the distinctiveness of Sarah, whose identity had been overtaken by Rachel's descriptions of Sarah, the therapist asked

> Sarah, I imagine that you see a lot, but are often rendered invisible during this conflict. What does it feel like for you to see your mother and Blake argue? What feelings are you left to deal with on your own?

To Blake, the most intrapersonally congruent member of the family, given his position as an outsider, the therapist asked "Blake, what does it feel like for you to show others your true self? When others acknowledge your true self, what does this feel like for you?" In response, Blake spoke of feeling both fearful and happy. Noting the complexity of his experience, the therapist encouraged Blake to share the details of those moments when his genuineness had resulted in both pain and joy for him.

Concluding Thoughts

Unlike any other family therapy model, QCSFT holds the potential for radical change, both inside and outside of family systems. With its emphasis on the inherent value of uniqueness and growth through difference, QCSFT is uniquely suited for work with clients suffering the effects of heteronormativity, cisnormativity, white supremacy, and gender essentialism. To do this work, however, therapists must explore their own moments of incongruence, noting when they hide true aspects of themselves and considering how gender and racial socialization contribute to their incongruence. Such personal growth, while often painful, is necessary for practicing QCSFT, since therapists must be able to experience their own joy and pain in order to help others do the same. Although a monumental task, given our individualistic and pathologizing culture context, a therapist's diligent investment in their own growth serves them, their loved ones, and their community.

When you feel hurt by or frustrated with someone you care about, is it difficult for you to mention this to them?

How do you personalize behavior in conflict? Do you leave disagreements thinking that the other person in the argument is (selfish/hateful/disrespectful/nosey/harsh/judgmental)?

After an argument, do you focus on what the other person did that upset you?

When you are around others who are expressing raw pain, do you begin to feel pain, or do you notice a numbing occurring for you in the moment?

Do you notice moments in your own life where your lived experience falls outside of what is culturally defined as "normal"? Do these moments leave you feeling ashamed?

Do you avoid situations you know will leave you feeling sad or ashamed? In what way does this reflect your gender and racial socialization?

When people share how they are feeling, does it distract from the task at hand? How does this reflect your gender and racial socialization?

How does your gender and racial socialization contribute to your level of congruence and the style of your communication?

What do you focus on when listening to clients describe presenting concerns? What aspects do you miss? How does power define what you miss?

Figure 4.4 Questions for Reflection.

References

Bateson, G., Jackson, D. D., Haley, J., & Weakland, J. (1956). Toward a theory of schizophrenia. *Behavioral Science*, *1*(4), 251–264.

Bronski, M. (2011). *A queer history of the United States*. Beacon Press.

Brothers, B. J. (2019). *Well-being write large: The essential work of Virgina Satir*. Beyond Words Publishing.

Freeman, M. L. (1999). Gender matters in the Satir growth model. *American Journal of Family Therapy*, *27*(4), 345–363. https://doi.org/10.1080/01926189 9261907

Haber, R. (2002). Virginia Satir: An integrated, humanistic approach. *Contemporary Family Therapy*, *24*(1), 23–34.

Hatzenbuehler, M. L., & Pachankis, J. E. (2016). Stigma and minority stress as social determinants of health among lesbian, gay, bisexual, and transgender youth: Research evidence and clinical implications. *The Pediatric Clinics of North America*, *63*(6), 985–997. https://doi.org/10.1016/j.pcl.2016.07.003

Hatzenbuehler, M. L., Phelan, J. C., & Link, B. G. (2013). Stigma as a fundamental cause of population health inequalities. *American journal of public health*, *103*(5), 813–821. https://doi.org/10.2105/AJPH.2012.301069

Kutateladze, B. L. (2022). Acting "straight": Socio-behavioral consequences of anti-queer hate crime victimization, *Justice Quarterly*, *39*, 1036–1058. https://doi.org/10.1080/07418825.2021.1906931

Laign, J. (1988). Healing human spirits: Creating joy in living. Interview with Virginia Satir. *Focus on Chemically Dependent Families*, *11 (Oct/Nov)*, 20–32.

Lenning, E., Brightman, S., & Buist, C. L. (2021). The trifecta of violence: A sociohistorical comparison of lynching and violence against transgender women. *Critical criminology*, *29*, 151–172. https://doi.org/10.1007/s10612-020-09539-9

Luepnitz, D. A. (1988). *The family interpreted: Psychoanalysis, feminism, and family therapy*. BasicBooks.

Maxey, V. A. (2021). The intersectional growth model: The Satir growth model informed by intersectional feminism. *Contemporary Family Therapy: An International Journal*, *43*(1), 54–68. https://doi.org/10.1007/s10 591-020-09553-7

McKay, T., Lindquist, C. H., & Misra, S. (2019). Understanding (and acting on) 20 years of research on violence and LGBTQ + communities. *Trauma, Violence, & Abuse*, *20*(5), 665–678. DOI: 10.1177/1524838017728708

Moane, G. (1999). *Gender and colonialism: A psychological analysis of oppression and liberation*. Palgrave MacMillan.

Rood, B. A., Reisner, S. L., Puckett, J. A., Surace, F. I., Berman, A. K., & Pantalone, D. W. (2017). Internalized transphobia: Exploring perceptions of social messages in transgender and gender-nonconforming adults, *International Journal of Transgenderism*, *18*(4), 411–426. https://doi.org/10.1080/15532 739.2017.1329048

Satir, V. (1967). *Conjoint family therapy, revised edition*. Science & Behavior Books.

Satir, V. (1972). *Peoplemaking*. Science and Behavior Books.

Satir, V. (1976). *Making contact*. Celestial Arts.

Satir, V. (1982). The therapist and family therapy: Process model. In A. M. Horne & M. M. Ohlsen (Eds.), *Family counseling and therapy* (pp. 12–42). F. E. Peacock Publishers.

Satir, V. (1988). *The new peoplemaking*. Science & Behavior Books.

Satir, V., & Baldwin, M. (1983). *Satir step by step: A guide to creating change in families*. Science & Behavior Books.

Satir, V., Banmen, J., Gerber, J., & Gomori, M. (1991). *The Satir model: Family therapy and beyond*. Science and Behavioral Books.

Woods, M. D., & Martin, D. (1984). The work of Virginia Satir: Understanding her theory and technique. *American Journal of Family Therapy*, 12(4), 3–11. https://doi.org/10.1080/01926188408250192

Chapter 5

Queer-Contextualized Emotionally Focused Family Therapy

Caitlin Edwards, Robert Allan, and Andrea K. Wittenborn

Emotionally focused therapy (EFT; Johnson & Greenberg, 1985; Johnson, 2019) is an empirically supported treatment for couples in distress. Distress is conceptualized as repetitive, harmful interaction patterns that reinforce relational disconnection (Johnson, 2019). EFT attempts to change these patterns through increased intrapersonal and interpersonal emotional coherence and connection (Johnson, 2019). Grounded in **attachment theory** (Ainsworth et al., 1978; Bowlby, 1988) and emotion theory (Arnold, 1960), EFT integrates person-centered, systemic, structural, and experiential models of therapy. EFT has been shown to be efficacious (Spengler et al., 2022), specifically with partners coping with addiction (Fletcher & Macintosh, 2018), raising a child with autism (Lee et al., 2017), PTSD (Ganz et al., 2022), cancer (McLean et al., 2013), and depression (Wittenborn et al., 2019).

Box 5.1

Attachment theory is a developmental theory of personality, initially outlined by John Bowlby (1969, 1988) for early childhood development. Since the late 1980s (Hazan & Shaver, 1987; Fraley & Shaver, 2021), research has evolved to address adult attachment theory.

The EFT Tango is a macro-intervention used across all stages of EFT. There are five moves of the tango that facilitate therapist's understanding of where they are in any moment in a session. The five moves are mirroring present process, emotion assembly and deepening, choreographing engaged encounters or enactments, processing the encounter or enactment, and summarizing, integrating, and validating.

DOI: 10.4324/9781003308188-5

Interventions and Change Events

EFT uses experiential interventions (e.g., validation, empathic reflection, heightening, and others) to help clients deepen, distill, and disclose their emotions with the purpose of co-constructing a more responsive and emotionally attuned (i.e., securely attached) relationship (Johnson, 2019). These interventions are used throughout therapy within the context of the meta-process of the EFT Tango. The **EFT Tango** involves five moves that the therapist uses iteratively with the aim of creating more vulnerable interactions. Initially, here-and-now emotional experiences are accessed, which are followed by **emotion assembly**. Once an emotion has been assembled, that partner shares their new emotional experience via an enactment—a therapist-guided interaction. This enactment is then processed between partners before the therapist validates the client and helps each partner to integrate the experience as a new way of interacting (Johnson, 2019).

Box 5.2

The **EFT Tango** is a macro-intervention used across all stages of EFT. There are five moves of the tango that facilitate therapist's understanding of where they are in any moment in a session. The five moves are mirroring present process, emotion assembly and deepening, choreographing engaged encounters or enactment, processing the encounter or enactment, and summarizing, integrating, and validating.

Emotion assembly is when the therapist works with client(s) to piece together elements of emotion and places them in an interpersonal context that contributes to coherence of experience. The five elements of emotion are based on Magda Arnold's work (1960).

In addition to the Tango, there are three key change events: negative cycle de-escalation and stabilization, withdrawer re-engagement, and pursuer softening. De-escalation and stabilization, which occur in stage one, result in clients being able to take a meta-perspective

Figure 5.1 The EFT Tango.

on the cycle as the problem. In stage two, withdrawer re-engagement and pursuer softening deepen awareness of attachment fears and longings, which increases attunement and responsiveness between partners (Johnson, 2019).

Theoretical Foundations of EFT: Attachment Theory

EFT processes and change events occur through the lens of attachment theory (Bowlby, 1969; 1988), which describes the innate survival mechanism of establishing affectional bonds with significant others and the behavioral patterns that develop to meet relational needs. **Attachment "strategies"** (i.e., meeting one's relational needs through a process that is influenced by a "working model" of self and other) develop as caregivers respond to infants, especially during times of distress (Ainsworth et al., 1978). For example, a child who feels safe, seen, and soothed by their caregivers will likely utilize a secure attachment strategy to meet their relational needs because they learn they can reasonably expect these needs to be met (Siegel, 2012). Conversely, a child who is abused or neglected will learn that they cannot expect their needs to be met and may develop an insecure attachment strategy (Ainsworth et al., 1978). Attachment strategies, initially developed with one's first caregivers, can be used to understand how each family member interacts within the family and

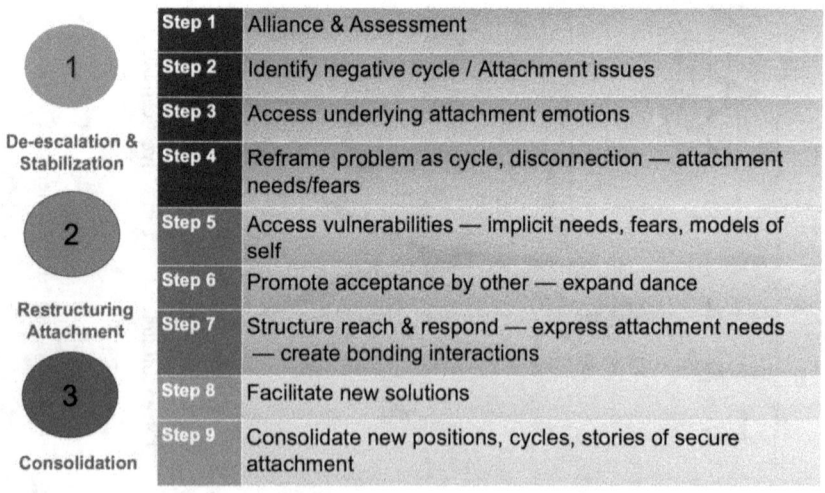

Figure 5.2 The Steps and Stages of EFT.

within larger systems based on their working models of self and other (Bowlby, 1988).

Box 5.3

Attachment strategies are ways of engaging with an attachment figure that serves to increase or decrease proximity. The term evolved from attachment style and lends itself to understanding these strategies occur in context and are interpersonal.

Secure attachment is one of four adult attachment strategies. A history with available and responsive attachment figures increases one's confidence that proximity-seeking is an effective emotion regulation strategy. Secure people maintain positive expectations about the availability and effectiveness of social support (Mikulincer & Shaver, 2008).

Conceptualization of Health

According to attachment theory, **secure attachment** is typically the result of a history of emotionally available, attuned, and responsive attachment figures (Feeney, 2004). Individuals using a secure attachment strategy can flexibly access a variety of emotional expression strategies depending on the context (Wang et al., 2022) and see others and themselves as resources for contact, care, and comfort during times of distress. In relationships, securely attached partners can identify their own internal experience of relational distress and confidently ask for their attachment needs to be met from a variety of attachment figures (Doherty & Feeney, 2004). Conversations between partners are characterized by coherence, vulnerability, and mutual empathy (Johnson, 2019).

Assumptions About Problems

EFT characterizes a lack of relational health as rigidly repetitive patterns of emotions and behaviors informed by insecure attachment strategies (i.e., **the negative cycle**) (Johnson, 2019). Partners who demonstrate a negative view of self and a positive view of other (i.e., **anxious attachment**) seek soothing from others, resulting in a "hyperactive" attachment strategy, which results in proximity-seeking that appears as rumination on perceived rejection and/or abandonment and demands for care (Mikulincer & Shaver, 2007, 2008). Partners who demonstrate a positive view of self and negative view of other (i.e., **avoidant attachment**) suppress their attachment needs and emotions and, when relationally distressed, manifest their attachment behaviors through defensiveness and distancing (Mikulincer & Shaver, 2007, 2008). The repetitive use of these strategies results in a negative interaction cycle, which blocks partners from safe, attuned connection. The negative cycle functions as homeostasis, resisting change and supporting previously established ways of attempting to connect (Johnson & Brubacher, 2016).

Box 5.4

The negative cycle is an emotional-behavioral interactional cycle that contributes to distress in relationships (Johnson & Brubacher, 2016). The self-reinforcing repetitive patterns lead to relationship(s) being experienced as distressed (Gottman, 1994).

Anxious attachment is one of the three insecure attachment strategies. People who use an anxious attachment strategy have learned through difficult and painful experiences that key attachment figures were unavailable and unresponsive. Thus, the primary attachment strategy—proximity-seeking—has often failed to accomplish its emotion-regulating goal. An anxious strategy includes expressing fears, exaggerating distress, or presenting oneself as vulnerable to pain and injury (Mikulincer & Shaver, 2008).

Avoidant attachment is another insecure attachment strategy. Here a person would deactivate their attachment needs (e.g., shutdown/withdraw) and focus more on self-reliance (Mikulincer & Shaver, 2008).

Recontextualizing EFT

Conceptualization of Attachment

Despite Bowlby's recognition of the sociocultural context of attachment (e.g., 1988), traditional dyadic conceptualizations of attachment focus more on the function of attachment security within and between persons without considering the influence of sociocultural systems. This keeps the focus on the micro-context of the relationship and overlooks the utility of secure attachment for protecting against the negative effects of a hostile sociocultural environment (e.g., Dunbar et al., 2021; Wang et al., 2022).

While attachment relationships exist between people, they also exist within oppressive systems, and secure attachment can act as a buffer to the negative impact of marginalization.

Box 5.5

An attachment figure is often a parent/caregiver, close friend, sibling, other relative, or higher power. They are a target for proximity-seeking and function as a "safe haven" in times of need. They are special and are resources to whom a person turns to when protection and support are needed (Mikulincer & Shaver, 2007).

A secure base is one of the functions of a secure attachment figure or resource. It is a felt sense of being able to depend on loved one(s) and pursue nonattachment goals or explore autonomously (Mikulincer & Shaver, 2007).

A common interpretation of attachment theory is that *one* person (i.e., the **attachment figure**) functions as a **secure base** and meets all attachment and relational needs of the other person. This interpretation leads to several mononormative assumptions about relationships—most importantly, that deep emotional engagement and other qualities of a secure base can only exist within monogamous dyadic relationships, and that people are too limited to engage in multiple, simultaneous emotionally attuned relationships. Research disputes these assumptions (e.g., Doherty & Feeney, 2004; Moors et al., 2019; Overall et al., 2003), demonstrating that the qualities of secure attachment (i.e., being able to ask and receive contact, care, and comfort) are not contingent upon sexual and emotional exclusivity. The assumption that only monogamous dyads can be healthy attachment figures is, therefore, a misinterpretation of adult attachment theory. It is, in fact, normal and natural for people to establish multiple, simultaneous attachment relationships that can include family, friends, and partners (e.g., Doherty & Feeney, 2004; Overall et al., 2003). Indeed, non-monogamous (NM) relationships are congruent with attachment theory—they are characterized by security (Ka et al., 2020; Moors et al., 2019), respect for autonomy, deep intimacy and closeness, and willingness to empathically communicate (Witherspoon, 2018). An NM interpretation of attachment theory allows for multiple romantic attachment relationships because secure attachment is seen as abundant, rather than scarce, and multiple partners do not threaten attachment security.

Case Conceptualization

Case conceptualization in EFT includes the presenting problem, client background, including attachment history, and delineation of the negative interaction cycle. Clients are typically identified as more pursuing or more withdrawing, which is informed by how they navigate emotional closeness and distance and respond to relational distress. Rigid interactional positions (e.g., frequent or severe pursuing or withdrawing) can lead to relational problems. EFT focuses on re-engaging withdrawers and softening pursuers; increased intrapersonal and interpersonal awareness gradually allows for more flexibility in responding to relational distress.

The most discussed negative interaction cycle in EFT is pursue-withdraw, which is characterized by cisgender heterosexual men engaging in withdraw behaviors and cisgender heterosexual women engaging in pursuit behaviors (Huerta et al., 2023). While this characterization does describe some relationships, its presumed universality is based on heterocentrism and the gender binary. It does not account for the impact of racial or gender socialization on attachment strategies, nor does it explain symmetrical patterns such as withdraw/withdraw or pursue/pursue. By centering this characterization, non-white, genderqueer, and non-binary people, as well as same-gender relationships and cisgender individuals whose attachment strategies differ from prescribed social norms, are marginalized. However, more recent work (i.e., Allan & Johnson, 2017; Guillory, 2021; Nightingale et al., 2019) is beginning to illustrate how these concepts can be addressed within the context of EFT.

Identity Integration

Move two of the EFT Tango outlines a process to first assemble emotional experience and then deepens it, thereby increasing emotional coherence. Historically, EFT therapists help clients develop reflective functioning and emotional coherence to own their position in the negative cycle and allow for corrective emotional experiencing, thereby increasing attachment security. What is missing from these descriptions of move two in the EFT Tango, and germane to a queer-contextualized understanding of EFT, is the importance of contextualizing the development of emotional coherence. Of particular importance is recognizing how bias, discrimination, and/or threats impact the management of emotional responses related to views of self and other. Consider how identity-related minority stressors function as forms of chronic and traumatic invalidation, essentially disrupting queer and trans individuals' ability to identify, understand, and effectively utilize their emotions (Cardona et al., 2022). In this light, the development of emotional coherence can be seen as a resource for managing identity-related stigma and contributing to identity development. For example, the development that comes with queer pride may be accompanied by righteous anger, motivating one to resist oppression and distancing oneself from heterosexual/cisgender individuals in favor of the safety of LGBTQ+ relationships (Cass, 1979). Healing identity-related trauma via EFT provides a method to repair **attachment injuries** related to oppression-based messages about a client's identity from both attachment figures, such as the client's family of origin, and the client's larger sociocultural context.

Box 5.6

An attachment injury is a form of significant abandonment or betrayal in a relationship. It leads to the relationship being experienced as insecure and partner(s) as untrustworthy or unreliable (Johnson, 2019).

Attachment theory provides a theoretical base for understanding *personality* development through habitual emotion regulation strategies (Fraley & Shaver, 2021). However, neither attachment theory nor EFT, as originally conceptualized, integrate *identity* development models or the impact of sociocultural context on identity. Identity is an individual's continuous sense of self defined by their individual characteristics and social roles, such as race, ability status, or gender. The parts of self that are acceptable and worthy of love and care are dictated by sociocultural contexts. Hierarchical systems prescribe that individuals with less power disown parts of themselves, such as their queerness. This can occur passively by means of social norms or overtly through experiences of isolation, prejudice, and violence. For example, queer-identifying children often internalize implicit or explicit sociocultural and familial messages that their identity is unacceptable, resulting in experiences of shame, judgment, and rejection (Grafsky, 2017). EFT has been developed, researched, and normed with couples holding dominant identities, resulting in little attention being paid to the effects of oppression and socialization processes on relational dynamics. Clients with marginalized identities may not feel sufficiently safe to bypass their defenses and protective strategies they use to navigate systems of power and oppression, which has direct implications for the effectiveness of EFT with clients targeted by oppressive systems.

Queer-Contextualized EFT: Centering Queerness

EFT, as originally developed, focuses on experiences of emotion and models of self and other within the context of caregiver and romantic relationships, with little attention to sociocultural context. Queer-contextualized EFT (QEFT) centers queer, trans, and NM relationships, and views models of self and other, emotional experiences, and attachment strategies as sociocultural phenomena that manifest within multiple attachment relationships. QEFT therapists resist the universality of the pursue/withdraw dynamic, instead focus on the extent to which one believes themselves to be worthy of love and care, and in what relationships love and care can be received. QEFT therapists also view some attachment injuries as manifestations of larger sociocultural wounds (i.e., white fathers socializing their white sons to be "real men").

QEFT therapists also maintain an open and welcoming stance to clients in a variety of relationship structures, honor all mechanisms used to navigate hostile environments, including insecure attachment strategies, engage with clients purposefully to identify and integrate their cultural experiences, allow clients to define health, actively consolidate positive relational cycles, and embrace the knowledge that identity impacts relational cycles. Furthermore, QEFT therapists would routinely and actively explore the sociocultural messages clients receive about when and how it is acceptable to feel and express emotion, as well as how these messages manifest in their working models of self and other and impact their attachment dynamics. QEFT therapists view securely attached relationships as a healthy way to navigate oppression.

The Queer-Contextualized EFT Therapist

QEFT therapists working with any client, but especially those from marginalized backgrounds, should begin therapy by inviting identity into the room as important context for understanding client experience. When working with queer and trans clients, this requires the therapist to have knowledge of the unique struggles faced by NM, queer, and trans individuals, including coming out processes, harassment and discrimination, the impact of religious trauma, and the importance of exploring identity-based language. One empirically supported method of inviting all aspects of a client's identity into therapy is therapist broaching (i.e., the discussion of therapist identities and the impact their identities may have on the therapeutic process [Day-Vines et al., 2018]). Broaching, while not specified in the original EFT model, encourages an open discussion of how sociocultural identities interact with experiences of power, privilege, and oppression to influence how people relate to each other—a central area of exploration in EFT.

An essential aspect of broaching is therapist's awareness of their own values, attitudes, and beliefs, and how these affect their sociocultural interactions with clients (Chu-Lien Chao, 2012; Sue & Sue, 2013). QEFT therapists should also know that they are trapped within dominant discourses. This necessitates self-of-the-therapist work in both QEFT training and supervision on internalized biases and prejudices such as those related to racism, heteronormativity, cisnormativity, mononormativity, classism, and ableism. This also warrants an exploration of how these systems of oppression impact the therapist's own attachment strategies and, subsequently, the therapist's tolerance for vulnerability. To work successfully with all relationships, but especially queer relationships, therapists must also explore their beliefs about fidelity, how trust is created and maintained, and how thriving relationships are structured.

Queer-Contextualized EFT: A Closer Look at Stages and Steps

Stage One: Cycle De-Escalation and Stabilization

Step One: Alliance Building and Assessment

Alliance in EFT is built through collaboration on tasks, matching client language, relentless empathy, validation of client experiences, and a focus on creating safety (Johnson, 2019). EFT is rooted in humanist and experiential models, which are welcoming to marginalized communities as they center clients' voices and trust clients' lived experiences. QEFT therapists can build on this foundation by acknowledging each client's abilities, strengths, and resilience as responses to cultural systems of oppression.

Assessment in EFT can involve asking the nine assessment questions outlined by Johnson (2019) in addition to taking an attachment history. A QEFT therapist broadens these questions to include a sociocultural history and an attachment history based on sexual, gender, and racial identities (Allan & Johnson, 2017; Guillory, 2021). This includes processing each person's experience of their own race, gender, sexual identity, ability status, relationship structures, and the messages received from society, family, and friends about these identities to determine how these experiences shape the client's working models of self and other. It includes a more involved assessment for safety, including support systems, communities of care, and chosen family. Assessment incorporates identity by exploring each person's sexual, gender, and racial identity in the context of identity development models, including coming out stories and any places where the person feels welcomed, accepted, and supported.

Another essential component of assessment in EFT is attachment strategy classification based on attachment behaviors. This classification is used to understand how each partner's attachment strategies create and maintain the negative cycle—which is essential to understanding how to soothe and work with each partner given their life history and sociocultural context. QEFT therapists conceptualize how gender and racial socialization interact with pursue-withdraw classifications, focusing on the *function* of the attachment behaviors in a sociocultural context. QEFT therapists should be knowledgeable of and ask about how gender and racial socialization influence attachment behaviors. For example, a transwoman might continue to engage in suppressing emotions other than anger if she was socialized according to masculine norms while growing up.

When asking attachment history questions, the EFT therapist should ask how clients learned to avoid and/or suppress emotion in relation to their identities. For example, "when was the first time you remember needing to hide feelings for someone because of your sexual orientation?" QEFT therapists also assess for sociocultural attachment injuries. Individuals who possess a marginalized identity may experience distinctive attachment injuries compared to white, cisgender, heterosexual, and/or monogamous individuals. Therefore, it is not sufficient to assess only for dyadic attachment injuries, but essential to contextualize these injuries within a client's sociocultural and sociopolitical context. For example, a trans client may need and not receive their partner's support for moving to a more trans-affirming area, engendering an attachment injury. The QEFT therapist, aware of current sociopolitical dynamics, understands this injury in the client's sociocultural context.

Step Two: Mapping the Cycle

Cycle mapping involves tracking the iterative negative interaction patterns between partners (Johnson, 2019). This is a strength of EFT, as it is non-judgmental and conceives of the cycle as something that has been co-created and can be co-deconstructed. Nightingale et al. (2019) discusses the importance of storytelling in socioculturally attuned EFT. For QEFT therapists, this will appear as spending more time discussing the *content* of a client's experience as opposed to the *process* of that experience. Spending time on discussing the content of a client's experience allows for the deconstruction of dominant discourses, which impact how a client has emotionally encoded social and relational experiences relating to their identities. This deconstruction empowers clients to center their own lived experiences in relation to dominant social discourses and helps clients to deconstruct sociocultural stigma, including how racism and homophobia have impacted relational dynamics.

Thus, when cycle mapping, the QEFT therapist integrates how differing experiences within LGBTQ + communities impact the cycle, how different stages of identity development impact relational processes, and how experiences of oppression impact asking for contact, care, and comfort. For example, two Black gay men may be at different stages in their racial and sexual identity development, leading one partner to internalize the dominant white culture more deeply. Therefore, when experiencing racial discrimination, this partner may not defend themselves or their partner, thereby threatening the safety and security of the relationship—processes that should be explored and mapped onto the relationship's negative cycle.

QEFT therapists reframe attachment strategies as protective responses to a hostile world and validate the challenges of creating a queer relationship in an unsupportive sociocultural context. When working with queer relationships, negative interaction cycles go beyond what happens between partners—for many marginalized individuals, these cycles are also a product of experiences of power, privilege, and oppression (Nightingale et al., 2019). By integrating experiences of oppression into negative interaction cycles, therapists affirm that what occurs on a societal level impacts their clients personally and empowers clients to understand how these experiences are enacted in their relationships. For example, when tracking a cycle between NM partners, the QEFT therapist should explore how compulsory monogamy impacts how and when each partner asks for contact, care, and comfort.

Step Three: Accessing Attachment Emotions

Step three involves introspectively accessing primary emotion (Johnson, 2019). EFT creates safety in this exploration by moving slowly and de-pathologizing client defenses (Johnson, 2019). A key aspect of step three is helping each partner share their more vulnerable emotions. Due to experiences of living in an unsafe, racist, heterocentric, and mononormative sociocultural context, these **enactments** should be done slowly and within the client's **window of tolerance**. Therapists should ensure partners can stay within their own window of tolerance by continuously checking in about the impact of emotional disclosure and validating the risks each partner takes. Several options exist for increasing safety during enactments, including processing an enactment directly with the therapist first, asking a client to share what is challenging about directly saying what is being uncovered, for example, "I am afraid of what you will say or do with what I say—this is the place where I have been told so many times in my life that there is something wrong with how I feel as a queer person," or go to Tango move 5 and summarize and validate the risk they are taking in exploring this aspect of their experience and noting that this is an important area to slowly explore.

> **Box 5.7**
>
> **An enactment** is also referred to as an engaged encounter. This is a therapist-facilitated process where one partner is asked to turn and speak to another partner (Johnson, 2019).
>
> **The window of tolerance** is the optimal zone of arousal for a person to function in everyday life. When in this zone, a person can effectively manage and communicate their emotions (Siegel, 2012).

Step Four: Reframing the Problem

At the end of stage one, clients are less likely to engage in escalated negative cycles and are more successful at repairing if negative cycles occur (Johnson, 2019). For the therapist, this step involves helping the client actively see the ways in which they and their partner(s) contribute to the cycle, and how connection is blocked by secondary emotions and action tendencies. QEFT therapists intentionally link experiences of discrimination, view of self and other, and client identities to attachment experiences and the negative cycle. Therapists help clients co-create a narrative that explains why it has been challenging to name and experience deeper attachment emotions, as well as celebrate vulnerability.

Stage Two: Reconstruction

Step Five: Promoting Identification of Disowned Needs and Aspects of Self

Stage two deepens awareness of attachment fears and longings, as well as increases active attunement and responsiveness between partners (Johnson, 2019). Specifically in step five, the therapist helps the client fully access deeper attachment emotions and parts of self that have been hidden and share these with their partner(s). QEFT therapists spend more time working slowly with shame, fear, and trauma related to identity and relationship behaviors. Therapists should be curious and compassionate about how each partner was taught to disown (i.e., cut off, deny, view as unworthy of love and care) their own attachment needs and suppress parts of their identity due to sociocultural influences and help them share this with their partner(s). It is vital to help clients connect larger sociocultural experiences to their view of self and other, as internalized homophobia, transphobia, and monogamism will likely need to be addressed and cared for in this step.

Step Six: Promoting Acceptance of Partners' Experiences

Step six involves helping each partner accept and support each other's new emotional experiences and integration of self. This may be challenging for individuals in queer relationships because of oppression, rejection by family of origin, and each partner's own level of identity development. It is important for the QEFT therapist to validate that interacting in this more vulnerable way may feel unsafe in certain contexts, and the QEFT therapist should help the client decide in what circumstances it feels safe to be vulnerable. Emotional coherence is an effective way of managing the stigma, discrimination, and physical threats associated with a queer identity (Wang et al, 2022). Therefore, as clients move through stage two, increasing their emotional coherence, they may become more effective at navigating systems of oppression. The QEFT therapist should praise each partner for their courage in sharing their disowned parts of self (e.g., desire and need for NM and/or gender identity transition) and attachment needs and fears, as well as affirm that these interactions may feel different from previous relationships.

Step Seven: Facilitating the Expression of Needs and Wants

Step seven involves all partners expressing newly accepted and owned needs and aspects of identity in the relationship. It is important that the QEFT therapist helps each partner understand that their needs and wants are legitimate and can be expressed without fear or shame in the context of safe and secure relationships. Therapists should also continue to move slowly and connect the challenges clients experience in asking for their needs and wants to larger experiences of sociocultural rejection. By the end of stage two, all partners should feel safe, sufficiently capable of self-regulation to seek closeness, and can ask for their relational needs to be met when facing discrimination, microaggressions, and/or prejudice. More specifically, attachment security developed in QEFT can help counter the effects of stigma and oppression. Positive views of self and other in relation to fluid identity conceptualizations are then celebrated, affirmed, and supported by partners and the therapist.

Stage Three: Integration and Consolidation

Step Eight: Finding New Solutions to Old Problems

Stage three, consolidation, involves the celebration of intrapersonal and interpersonal changes and the shift in focus in dealing with pragmatic problems (Johnson, 2019). Queer relationships will most likely not follow cisnormative, heteronormative, or mononormative scripts, and these ways of relating should be explored, supported, and concretized with the therapist. For example, queer relationships are often more egalitarian compared to heterosexual relationships—roles are shared and negotiated rather than assumed based on gender—therefore, it is important for QEFT therapists to explore the roles each partner holds in the relationship, especially in the context of increased attachment security. Marginalized clients routinely struggle to navigate prejudicial systems. In response, the QEFT therapist should spend more time working through pragmatic concerns, actively and personally connecting clients to community resources, and providing clients with "tools" to enhance the positive aspects of their relationships. This involves helping clients enact new interactional patterns based on their evolving identities and navigating how to reach for contact, care, and comfort when those identities come under attack.

Step Nine: Consolidation of New Positions

Step nine involves concretizing new relational patterns (Johnson, 2019). For queer and NM relationships, this involves building safety and relational confidence by anchoring each partner's more resourced self to the new interactions within the relationship. QEFT therapists affirm that NM and queer relationships are important sources of support and healing in a heterocentric, sexist, cisnormative, mononormative, and racist culture. Finally, QEFT therapists should honor the obstacles that the individuals and relationships have overcome, celebrating their relationship as a profound act of social resistance.

Case Example

Finn is a certified QEFT therapist and identifies as non-binary, white, and able-bodied. Gabriella and Jamie contact Finn for relationship therapy. They explain Jamie has recently come out as trans, and their ability to communicate safely and clearly has been negatively impacted by the rejection from both Jamie and Gabriella's families. Gabriella explains they are in a V: they have maintained a friends-with-benefits relationship with Monique for two months, while Jamie is their nesting partner of six years. Finn asks

Gabriella and Jamie who should attend therapy. Gabriella explains their relationship with Monique is new and not what they and Jamie need to focus on in therapy. Therefore, Gabriella and Jamie agree to attend couple therapy for now and invite Monique if needed.

During the intake session, Finn broaches their identities and invites Jamie and Gabriella to share any and all identities that feel salient to them. Gabriella identifies as a queer Chicana and uses they/she pronouns. Jamie shares that they use they/them pronouns and have identified as trans for six months. Jamie reported they identified as non-binary for two years and were assigned male at birth (AMAB). Jamie reported also identifying as multiracial, able-bodied, with a history of depression, anxiety, and non-suicidal self-injury. Gabriella and Jamie met on an NM dating app and were drawn to each other's queer activism. Finn continued by exploring how each aspect of these identities has informed Gabriella and Jamie's relationship, as well as the presenting problem.

Gabriella and Jamie explain they started to struggle significantly when Jamie came out as trans to their respective families. Both Gabriella and Jamie report their families have struggled with various aspects of their identities throughout their lives. Gabriella states "being queer and Chicana is challenging—my parents are more traditional, and they expected I would settle down and have kids, with a straight, cis man—but that's not me." Jamie stated,

> I've struggled with my gender my entire life—I just never felt like a "boy" or a "man." My dad and stepmom have not been accepting of me. Fortunately, my mom has been tolerant. I stayed with her until I was 17 and then left on my own to move to San Francisco.

Jamie explained their family had become somewhat more accepting over time. However, when Jamie decided that being trans more fully fit their identity, both Gabriella and Jamie's families became more overtly rejecting. These experiences were amplified by a recent move to a more conservative part of the United States for Gabriella's job. Gabriella and Jamie reported experiencing both overt and covert discrimination.

Finn conducts a conjoint intake session and two subsequent individual sessions to conduct an assessment and learn about Gabriella and Jamie's attachment and sexual histories. At the fourth session, Gabriella and Jamie arrive emotionally activated and report that Gabriella had received an emotionally abrasive text from Jamie's stepmother that morning and that Jamie had been called a "tranny fag" the previous evening. As a QEFT therapist, Finn validates the anger and pain Gabriella and Jamie are experiencing, while also allowing them to tell their story to fully explain the content of what occurred. As Finn does this, Gabriella clenches their fists and sighs. Finn sees this as an opportunity to begin the Tango. Finn asks, "What happened just now, Gabriella? You clenched your fists...you sighed.... What's going on as we talk about this?"

Gabriella angrily says, "I'm just so tired of this! I'm tired of being attacked for who we are! It's not fair to us!" Although step two of the Tango involves emotion assembly, during which Finn would focus on the embodied experience and meaning of "tired," in alignment with QEFT, Finn chooses to spend more time discussing the content and sociocultural discourses prior to emotion assembly. Finn asks Gabriella to tell them more about what is "unfair." Gabriella responds, "it's unfair—it makes me angry—that we are not 'acceptable.' Just because we do things differently, experience things differently, people put us in a place—a box—like we're bad or wrong." Finn follows with

> Gabriella, of course you're angry. Of course you would be angry about being put in a box that does not match your life and your experiences. It sounds like people are telling you that you are something you are not? And that you and Jamie, just by being yourselves, by engaging in a relationship, are refusing to be put in that box? And that's exhausting?

Gabriella nods, tears in their eyes, and Finn chooses to move to emotion assembly, focusing on Gabriella's anger. Finn adds a trauma-informed approach (SAMHSA, 2014) to QEFT, saying to Gabriella, "I'm going to ask about how you experience this in your body, is that okay?" Gabriella nods. Finn then asks Gabriella what the embodied experience of anger is like for them, when they experience that they are being put in a box by familial and sociocultural messages. Gabriella responds, "My anger is hot! And it's like I need to run." Finn validates these responses, as these embodied experiences tell Finn that Gabriella is attempting to respond to a potentially traumatic event with fight, flight, or freeze. Finn, mindful of Gabriella's trauma response, does not stay in their embodied experience and instead moves to meaning-making. Finn asks, "So, when you're feeling this anger, what does it say about how you see yourself?"

Tears well up in Gabriella's eyes before they state, "That some part of me is broken.... That some part of me is just wrong.... But another part of me says that can't be true...because how could I be so happy with Jamie if there was something wrong with us?"

Finn validates this response, knowing internalized homophobia is a part of living in oppressive systems. Finn reflects,

> Gabriella, it sounds like you're really struggling with this misalignment between what society tells you to be and who you truly are. And

when you experience this tension, you get angry and some part of you says that you're broken, but another says that it's impossible...that it's society that's broken, not you?"

Gabriella nods in agreement and Finn continues, "...so how do you talk about this anger and this feeling of brokenness with Jaime?"

Gabriella turns to Jamie, who takes Gabriella's hand. Gabriella grins ruefully stating, "I don't think I actually do a good job of that, huh?" Jamie shakes their head. Gabriella sighs, still looking at Jaime. "I think I just get irritated about other things. Like, I know we're going through this together, but it's just hard to talk about feeling broken with you. So, I end up yelling about your stepmom." Finn interrupts, "Instead of telling Jamie how much you need their support when you feel all the stress society puts on you?" Gabriella nods, "Yes...instead of that." Finn responds, "It makes so much sense that you do that, Gabriella. It's so hard when who we don't align with what society says is okay to be...it makes sense that these messages from society make you feel broken."

Finn then asks, "What was it like to share that with Jamie now?" Gabriella pauses, "It was good...there's less tension now that you know... but it's scary to share that with you." Finn nods, affirming Gabriella's experience, "I really hear that Gabriella, that it can be scary to share how society impacts us personally. Is it okay that I ask about what was happening for Jamie when you shared?" Gabriella nods, squeezing Jamie's hand. Jamie responds: "I just felt like I totally get it. Like my stepmom and the society we live in are just messed up. And I don't think it's wrong of you to feel messed up when we're living in a messed up society." Finn moves in with step five of the Tango, stating,

This is so important you two—look at what you just did here! As we begin to unpack that discriminatory message from Jamie's stepmother and the hostile incident at the store, Gabriella, your fists tense up and we explore how unfair it is to be put in a box, for others to try to force you to be who you are not, and these tears come that speak to how unfair that is for you and your relationship. You do this beautiful job of telling Jamie about how your anger shows up, but what is really happening is the sense of injustice and sadness about how those messages impact you. When you hear that Jamie, you reach for Gabriella, note that there is less tension, and it feels good to hear more about what is happening for Gabriella in those moments. You talked about how these messages society sends us can be so damaging—personally and in your relationship. And you did it in a completely new way! A new way that helped Jamie understand more about what's going on with you, Gabriella. That's really great work.

In this session, Finn moved from the sociocultural impacts on Gabriella's view of self to their intrapersonal and interpersonal experiences. Rather than only tracking how Gabriella's anger shows up between them, Finn helps Gabriella deconstruct how the narratives of transphobia impact their view of self and experience in the relationship. By asking just a little more information about content, Finn helped Gabriella unpack that it is Gabriella's sociopolitical context in which they find themselves that is damaging—not their relationship with Jamie. By externalizing these messages and helping Gabriella to share them, they begin to create a safe haven from discriminatory, damaging discourses.

Conclusion

Just as Finn helps Gabriella increase her coherence around her emotional experiences and turn to Jamie as a source of comfort when experiencing overt acts of prejudice and discrimination, a QEFT integrates client sociocultural context and relational dynamics to aid clients to utilize a secure attachment strategy as a source of protection. The creation of a secure attachment relationship provides opportunities for safety and bias management that cannot be found when using insecure strategies. Therefore, EFT, when queer-contextualized, offers a way to relationally subvert heterosexism, racism, and transphobia. Moreover, there are numerous strengths inherent for individuals with marginalized identities and in relationships

---

How have you been impacted by racism, homophobia, sexism, transphobia, and other forms of discrimination? Who do you talk to about this? How have those people responded? How have these experiences impacted your view of self and view of other as resources for contact, care, and comfort?

How have your cultural contexts (e.g., race, gender, sexual identity) shaped how you suppress and avoid emotion?

Who has been curious about your identities? Who has been able to comfort you when you experienced challenges related to your cultural contexts?

How do your identities impact your own negative relational cycles? How do you navigate your vulnerable emotions in these cycles?

How comfortable are you depending on others? Where did you learn this? How did your sociocultural contexts inform you about dependence?

How comfortable do you feel working with deep, vulnerable, and sometimes overwhelming emotion? How did you learn this? How did your sociocultural contexts inform how you engage with intense emotional experiences?

Figure 5.3 Questions for Reflection.

that evolve in challenging sociocultural contexts, such as queer, trans, and NM relationships—resiliency, self-awareness, creativity, courage, originality, adaptability, emotional expressiveness, deep intimacy, and strong attachments, among others. Furthering this work involves integrating both the resilience derived from living and loving in a hostile sociocultural context and drawing on the relational strengths inherent in queer, trans, and NM relationships.

References

Ainsworth, M. D. S., Blehar, M. C., Waters, E., & Wall, S. (1978). *Patterns of attachment: A psychological study of the strange situation.* Lawrence Erlbaum.

Allan, R., & Johnson, S. M. (2017). Conceptual and application issues: Emotionally focused therapy with gay male couples. *Innovations in Clinical and Educational Interventions, 16*(4), 286–305. https://doi.org/10.1080/15332 691.2016.1238800

Arnold, M. B. (1960). *Emotion and personality. Vol. 1. Psychological aspects.* Columbia University Press.

Bowlby, J. (1969). *Separation: Anxiety and anger.* Basic Books.

Bowlby, J. (1988). *Attachment. Attachment and loss: Vol. 1.* Basic Books.

Cardona, N. D., Madigan, R. J., & Sauer-Zavala, S. (2022). How minority stress becomes traumatic invalidation: An emotion-focused conceptualization of minority stress in sexual and gender minority people. *Clinical Psychology: Science and Practice, 29*(2), 185–195. https://doi.org/10.1037/cps0000054

Cass, V. C. (1979). Homosexuality identity formation: A theoretical model. *Journal of homosexuality, 4*(3), 219–235. https://doi.org/10.1300/J082v04n03_01

Chu-Lien Chao, C. (2012). Racial/ethnic identity, gender role attitudes, and multicultural counseling competence: The role of multicultural counseling training. *Journal of Counseling and Development, 90*(1), 35–44. https://doi.org/ 10.1111/j.1556-6676.2012.00006.x https://doi.org/10.1080/08964289.2016.1165173

Day-Vines, N. L., Booker Ammah, B., Steen, S., & Arnold, K. M. (2018). Getting comfortable with discomfort: Preparing counselor trainees to broach racial, ethnic, and culturalfactors with clients during counseling. *International Journal for the Advancement of Counselling, 40*, 89–104. https://doi.org/10.1007/s10 447-017-9308-9

Doherty, N. A., & Feency J. A. (2004). The composition of attachment networks throughout the adult years. *Personal Relationships, 11*(4), 469–488. https://doi. org/10.1111/j.1475-6811.2004.00093.x

Dunbar, A. S., Lozada, F. T., HaRim Ahn, L., & Leerkes, E. M. (2021). Mothers' preparation for bias and responses to children's distress predict positive adjustment among Black children: An attachment perspective. *Attachment and Human Development, 24*(3), 287–303. https://doi.org/10.1080/14616 734.2021.1976922

Feeney, J. A. (2004). Adult attachment and relationship functioning under stressful conditions: Understanding partners' responses to conflict and challenge. In W. S.

Rholes & J. A. Simpson (Eds.), *Adult attachment: Theory, research, and clinical implications* (pp. 339–364). Guilford Publications.

Fletcher, K., & MacIntosh, H. (2018). Emotionally focused therapy in the context of addictions: A case study. *The Family Journal, 26*(3), 330–340. https://doi.org/10.1177/1066480718795125

Fraley, R. C., & Shaver, P. R. (2021). Attachment theory and its place in contemporary personality theory and research. In O. P. John & R. W. Robins (Eds.), *Handbook of personality: Theory and research* (pp. 642–666). The Guilford Press.

Ganz, M. B., Rasmussen, H. F., McDougall, T. V., Corner, G. W., Black, T. T., & De Los Santos, H. F. (2022). Emotionally focused couple therapy within VA healthcare: Reductions in relationship distress, PTSD, and depressive symptoms as a function of attachment-based couple treatment. *Couple and Family Psychology: Research and Practice, 11*(1), 15–32. https://doi.org/10.1037/cfp 0000210

Gottman, J. M. (1994). *What predicts divorce? The relationship between marital processes and marital outcomes.* (1st ed., pp. 37–65). Routledge.

Grafsky, E. L. (2017). Deciding to come out to parents: Toward a model of sexual orientation disclosure decisions. *Family Process.* https://doi.org/10.1111/famp.12313

Guillory, P. T. (2021). *Emotionally focused therapy with African American couples: Love heals.* Routledge.

Hazan, C., & Shaver, P. (1987). Romantic love conceptualized as an attachment process. *Journal of Personality and Social Psychology, 52*(3), 511–524. https://doi.org/10.1037/0022-3514.52.3.511

Huerta, P., Edwards, C., Asiimwe, R., PettyJohn, M., White, J., Morgan, P., & Wittenborn, A. K. (2023). Exploratory analysis of pursue-withdraw patterns, attachment, and gender among couples in Emotionally Focused Therapy. *The American Journal of Family Therapy, 51*(1), 57–75.

Johnson, S. M. (2019). *Attachment theory in practice: Emotionally focused therapy (EFT) with individuals, couples, and families.* Guilford Publications.

Johnson, S. M. & Brubacher, L. (2016). Clarifying the negative cycle in emotionally focused couple therapy (EFT). In G. E. Weeks, S. T. Fife, & C. M. Peterson (Eds.), *Techniques for the couple therapist: Essential interventions from the experts* (pp. 443–448). Routledge.

Johnson, S. M., & Greenberg, L. S. (1985). Differential effects of experiential and problem solving interventions in resolving marital conflict. *Journal of Consulting and Clinical Psychology, 53*, 175–184. https://doi.org/10.1037/0022-006X.53.2.175

Ka, W. L., Bottcher, S., & Walker, B. R. (2020). Attitudes toward consensual nonmonogamy predicted by sociosexual behavior and avoidant attachment. *Current Psychology, 41*, 4312–4320. https://doi.org/10.1007/s12144-020-00941-8

Lee, N. A., Furrow, J. L., & Bradley, B. A. (2017). Emotionally focused couple therapy for parents raising a child with an Autism Spectrum Disorder: A pilot study. *The Journal of Marital and Family Therapy, 43*(2), 213–226. https://doi.org/10.1111/jmft.12225

McLean, L. M., Walton, T., Rodin, G., Esplen, M. J., Jones, J. J. (2013). A couple-based intervention for patients and caregivers facing end-stage cancer: Outcomes of a randomized controlled trial. *Psychooncology*, 22(1), 28–38. https://doi. org/10.1002/pon.2046

Mikulincer, M., & Shaver, P. R. (2007). *Attachment in adulthood: Structure, dynamics, and Change.* Guilford Press.

Mikulincer, M., & Shaver, P. R. (2008). Adult attachment and affect regulation. In Cassidy, J., Shaver, P. R. (Eds.), *Handbook of attachment: Theory, research, and clinical Applications* (pp. 503–531). Guilford Press.

Moors, A. C., Ryan, W., & Chopik, W. J. (2019). Multiple loves: The effects of attachment with multiple concurrent romantic partners on relational functioning. *Personality and Individual Differences*, 147, 102–110. https://doi.org/10.1016/j.paid.2019.04.023

Nightingale, M., Awosan, C. I., & Stavrianoplous, K. (2019). Emotionally focused therapy: A culturally sensitive approach for African American heterosexual couples. *Journal of Family Psychotherapy*, 30(3), 221–244. https://doi.org/10.1080/08975353.2019.1666497

Overall, N. C., Fletcher, G. J. O., & Friesen, M. D. (2003). Mapping the intimate relationship mind: Comparisons between three models of attachment representations. *Personality and Social Psychology Bulletin*, 29(12), 1479–1493. https://doi.org/10.1177/0146167203251519

SAMHSA (2014). SAMHSA's concept of trauma and guidance for a trauma-informed approach. Retrieved on January 10, 2023, from: www.health.ny.gov/health_care/medicaid/program/medicaid_health_homes/docs/samhsa_trauma_concept_paper.pdf

Siegel, D. J. (2012). *The developing mind: How relationships and the brain interact to shape who we are* (2nd ed.). Guilford Press.

Spengler, P. M., Lee, N. A., Wiebe, S. A., & Wittenborn, A. K. (2022). A comprehensive meta analysis on the efficacy of emotionally focused couple therapy. *Couple and family psychology: Research and practice.* Advance online publication. https://doi.org/10.1037/cfp0000233

Sue, D.W,. & Sue, D. (2013). *Counseling the culturally diverse.* John Wiley & Sons.

Wang, K., Maiolatesi, A. J., Burton, C. L., Scheer, J. R., & Pachankis, J. E. (2022). Emotion regulation in context: Expressive flexibility as a stigma coping resource for sexual minority men. *Psychology of Sexual Orientation and Gender Diversity*, 9(2), 214–221. https://doi.org/10.1037/sgd0000503

Witherspoon, R. G. (2018). Exploring polyamorous resilience and strength factors: A structural equation modeling approach. (80141959). [Doctoral Dissertation, Alliant University]. Proquest.

Wittenborn, A. K., Liu, T., Ridenour, T. A., Lachmar, E. M., Rouleau, E., & Seedall, R. B. (2019). Randomized controlled trial of emotionally focused couple therapy compared to treatment as usual for depression: Outcomes and mechanisms of change. *Journal of Marital and Family Therapy*, 45, 395–409. https://doi.org/10.1111/jmft.12350

Chapter 6

Queer-Contextualized Bowen Family Therapy

Erica E. Hartwell

Bowen Family Systems Theory

Murray Bowen (January 31, 1913–October 9, 1990) developed and refined Family Systems Theory, known as Bowen Family Systems Theory (BFST) or the Bowen Theory, over several decades of observing and coaching families in clinical and community settings (Bowen, 1978; Kerr & Bowen, 1988). He defined two complementary life forces at work in human relationships: one that promotes togetherness and one that promotes individuality (Bowen, 1978). These two forces motivate all systems (e.g., individuals, couples, families, clans, institutions, societies, etc.) to maintain viability, that is, the ability to survive or continue to exist (Buckley, 1967). Threats to viability provoke **anxiety** in the system. Bowen believed that constant, low-level anxiety was a natural part of life, because it keeps organisms alert to threats and focused on survival needs. Some threats are real, like violence. But most threats are only perceived to be dangerous when really, they are survivable, like criticism from your boss or coldness from your partner. Whether the threats are real or perceived, they trigger anxiety. Enough threats, or stress, over a long period of time can lead to chronic anxiety, which can lead to symptoms like depression, substance use, or physical illness. While symptoms can manage the anxiety in a system, they do not release or relieve the anxiety. To do that, the anxiety must be faced and resolved. Facing anxiety means consciously recognizing it and choosing how to respond, rather than reacting automatically in stressful situations. How well one responds to anxiety can depend on one's level of differentiation of self.

Bowen explained our different reactions to anxiety through the concept of differentiation. **Differentiation** is the ability to know the difference between our thoughts and emotions and to recognize that our thoughts and emotions are separate from other people's (Kerr, 1984; Kerr & Bowen, 1988; Smith, 2019). People with lower differentiation are more likely to be **emotionally reactive** in close relationships by reacting automatically to anxiety-provoking situations, rather than responding thoughtfully

DOI: 10.4324/9781003308188-6

(Bowen, 1978). Our level of differentiation is shaped in large part by the **nuclear family emotional system** in which we grew up. However, children in the same family can range in their level of differentiation due to the **family projection process.** Anxiety is off-loaded in different ways and to different degrees onto different members of the family. For example, one child might take on the role of being the sick one, the problem, or the scapegoat. Another child might be in the role of the golden child, the good one, or the invisible one. Regardless of how we label it, these different roles shape each child's emotional reactivity and maturity. So, children growing up in the same family will end up with slightly different levels of differentiation, some lower or higher but all within range of their parents. In this way, anxiety and differentiation travel through the generations of a family and create branches with progressively higher or lower functioning. This is called the **multigenerational transmission process.**

Bowen believed that anxiety moved around an emotional system in predictable ways and that our reactions could be categorized in one of four **relational patterns:** distance, conflict, over/underfunctioning, and triangles (Kerr & Bowen, 1988). Triangles occur when anxiety is high between two people, and a third person is used as a mediator, messenger, or confidante. The triangle temporarily reduces anxiety and stabilizes the dyadic relationship. In addition to these four relational patterns, Bowen also defined **emotional cutoff** as an extreme form of reactivity that only occurred when anxiety was very high, or differentiation was very low in a system. It is important to note that these patterns are natural and normal and occur in all relationships to some degree. They are only a problem when systems can get stuck in them and members find themselves unable to deal with anxiety in thoughtful and effective ways. In order to get unstuck, Bowen believed we needed to observe our reactions to others and interrupt the emotional process.

The Bowen Approach to Therapy

BFST aims to increase differentiation in three ways: (1) defining and clarifying emotional process, (2) demonstrating differentiation, and (3) coaching the client to observe process (Bowen, 1978; Kerr & Bowen, 1988; Papero, 1990).

Defining the Emotional Process

BFST begins with a "survey of the emotional field or system" (Papero, 1990, p. 68). The therapist gets a sense of how the family has functioned over time and across generations, so that they can place the presenting problem

---

Box 6.1

Anxiety A natural part of life that keeps organisms alert to threats and focused on survival needs.

Differentiation The ability to know the difference between our thoughts and emotions and to recognize that our thoughts and emotions are separate from other people's.

Emotional reactivity The tendency to respond automatically and intensely to anxiety-provoking situations, rather than responding thoughtfully. It is characterized by quick, often impulsive emotional responses such as anger, fear, or frustration, which can lead to reactive behaviors like yelling, withdrawing, or shutting down.

Nuclear family emotional system Any group of individuals who spend a significant amount of time together and start to pass anxiety around the system.

Family projection process The process by which anxiety is off-loaded in different ways and to different degrees onto different members of the family.

Multigenerational transmission process The process by which anxiety and differentiation travel through the generations of a family and create branches with progressively higher or lower functioning.

Relational patterns Predictable ways in which anxiety moves around an emotional system, categorized into distance, conflict, over/under-functioning, and triangles.

Emotional cutoff An extreme form of reactivity that occurs when anxiety is very high, or differentiation is very low in a system.

---

in a larger context and assess levels of anxiety, differentiation, and relational patterns. This is typically done through a **genogram** (McGoldrick et al., 2020), which is a diagram that maps the "facts" of the family members (e.g., name, age, gender, physical or emotional health concerns, etc.), how members are related (e.g., married, divorced, living together, adopted, etc.), the emotional nature of relationships between members (e.g., close, distant, cutoff, etc.), and cultural and contextual factors (e.g., immigration, religious affiliations, ethnicity, etc.). There are many ways to collect and map the information for a genogram. I typically start sketching a genogram while I am asking basic assessment questions: what the problem is, what have you tried to solve the problem, how does each person understand the problem. From there, I ask about extended family and any significant events in the family's history. The symbols I use and the questions I ask are not as important as my ability to use systems thinking while I construct the genogram. Systems thinking requires a broad perspective over a narrow one—trying to understand the operation of the whole system and how each piece fits together, rather than looking at each piece individually (Papero, 1990). I am looking for patterns as I ask questions to get at the family's emotional process. As the client and I continue to add relationship lines to the genogram, a pattern of interlocking triangles emerges, and we have a visual of the emotional process in the family.

Box 6.2

Genogram A diagram that maps the facts of the family members, how members are related, the emotional nature of relationships between members, and cultural and contextual factors.

Process question Insight-oriented questions asked by the therapist to uncover the pattern of behavior and reactivity in an emotional system.

Although many consider the genogram to be the hallmark intervention of BFST, the foundational clinical technique is the **process question**. By asking questions of each family member, the therapist uncovers information to define and clarify the emotional process within the family. These questions are not meant to be confrontational, although they may be difficult for family members to answer if they are unaccustomed to examining their own reactions. The therapist may ask family members to describe particular behaviors and feelings that accompany them. Although the therapist might ask about emotions, process questions are insight-oriented, meaning they aim to elicit thought or reflection. For example, if one partner begins to get angry in a couple therapy session, the therapist might ask the other partner, "Did you notice the change in your partner's tone of voice? What were your thoughts when you heard that?" The goal is to get the clients noticing and talking *about* their emotional reactions, rather than being *in* them. This is distinct from an experiential approach, which aims to elicit feelings and experiences to enact change. Talking about process helps the client take a step back and look at their relational systems from a broader perspective, which is the first step in helping the client to think systemically and a key component of increasing differentiation.

Demonstrating Differentiation

While process questions and genograms are essential tools to define the emotional process, a differentiated therapist is necessary to effect any change through BFST. Bowen believed that calm is contagious. He was not interested in raising intensity or anxiety in the therapy room; he always wanted to lower it so that people could be more thoughtful about their own process. To do this, the Bowen therapist asks direct process questions to one person at a time. If there is more than one person in the room, the others simply listen unless asked a question by the therapist. Bowen would not ask family members to speak to each other in session until they had progressed enough to manage their reactivity in those interactions. If clients are directed to speak to each other too early in therapy, they are likely to fall into their well-worn relational pattern, which is helpful in models that utilize enactments, but not so in BFST.

Despite their best efforts, it is natural that therapists will have their own anxiety and emotional reactions in the room. When this happens, it is important to carefully observe those reactions and work to respond to client systems from a calm and neutral position. Of this, Bowen (1978) said, "When I feel myself inwardly cheering the hero, or hating the villain in the family drama, or pulling for the family victim to assert himself, I consider it time to work on my own functioning" (p. 83). The therapist's own differentiation work is essential to be a calm and connected presence in the face of an emotional system.

One way to demonstrate differentiation is to take the I-position, which is stating what one thinks or believes without needing anyone to agree, or what one will or will not do, and then following through (Bowen, 1978). In a way, it is about taking responsibility for oneself and one's boundaries. Typically, the therapist will take the I-position frequently in the beginning of therapy, when anxiety is high and the togetherness force is strong. The therapist may take this position in response to a client pushing for the therapist to agree with them, asking for advice or direction, seeking approval, or becoming critical or angry (Titelman, 1998). For example, if a client asks, "don't you agree?" and I do not agree, I might say "I am listening to what you are saying, and I understand your point, though I don't agree with your interpretation." Saying this is not an attempt to get the client to listen to my interpretation, and it is not necessarily an attempt to get the client to change. I am simply defining my opinions and, therefore, myself. At the same time, this is still an intervention, because I am defining myself while remaining connected to the system, which is demonstrating differentiation. Over time, as anxiety lowers, the therapist will coach the client to take the I-position and to observe their own process.

Coaching Clients to Observe Process

At the beginning of therapy and any other time anxiety is high, the therapist leads by example and projects calm onto the client system. Bowen believed that learning was not possible when anxiety was high. However, once the anxiety in the client system is low enough, the therapist begins explaining the thinking behind their approach, including the theoretical concepts, and teaching clients to observe their own process.

Therapeutic Goals and Progress

The goal of BFST is to reduce anxiety in the system and to increase differentiation, which will improve adaptiveness (Kerr & Bowen, 1988). Reducing anxiety happens largely in the therapy room, whereas increasing differentiation most often occurs in the family of origin (FOO). Bowen would often assign his clients to "go home" to their immediate family members to work on taking nonreactive I-positions, to detriangulate themselves from conflict, and to build authentic person-to-person relationships with individual family members (Guerin et al., 1987; Kerr, 1981; McGoldrick, 1995). He believed that if a person could differentiate a self in their FOO, they could more easily do so in other relational systems.

Queer-Contextualized Bowen Family Systems Theory

If asked to name models of family therapy that center queer and trans lives and relationships, BFST would probably not be at the top of your list. In fact, it might not be on your list at all. And for good reason. For starters, Murray Bowen, himself, was—from what we know—a cisgender, heterosexual, white psychiatrist who developed the bulk of his theory in the United States during the 1950s and 1960s. Although the emergence of family therapy was a radical departure from the field of psychiatry at the time, neither psychiatry nor family therapy integrated any ideals from the countercultural movements that defined the 1960s. In fact, both fields staunchly supported the status quo (Hardy, 1989; Hare-Mustin, 1987; Stryker, 2017). BFST, like the rest of the mental health zeitgeist, is rooted in capitalism, white supremacy, and patriarchy. As a result, it often fails to account for the lived experiences of queer and trans individuals of any background, chosen families, and nontraditional relationship structures. This section critically examines BFST through a queer lens and reimagines its concepts to be more inclusive, affirming, and applicable to diverse relational systems.

A Critical and Recontextual Approach to Bowen Family Systems Theory

Bowen's ultimate goal was to develop a theory of natural systems—a way of explaining the patterns of not only human systems but all living systems. In his early writings, he criticized the human species for believing itself to be separate and above all other life, when, in fact, we share many of the same drives and instincts as other life forms. He allowed us one exception—the prefrontal cortex, which gives us the ability to look inward and make meaning of what we see, a unique feature among species on this planet (Kerr & Bowen, 1988; Papero, 1990). But Bowen believed that humans make too much meaning, and this makes it difficult for us to observe and understand our own behavior (Papero, 1990). Perhaps the reason Bowen never reached his goal of developing a true theory of natural systems is that he spent most of his career focused on the abilities of the prefrontal cortex, namely reflection and rational thought, thereby focusing on things that were uniquely human. In a way, Bowen fell into the very trap he was trying to avoid. What is more human than that?

Rethinking Differentiation

Let us start with the best known BFST concept, differentiation of self, which has been interpreted and applied in a variety of ways. Common across these interpretations is the privileging of intellect over feelings and individuality over connection. This interpretation of differentiation is rooted in the values of white supremacy, capitalism, and patriarchy (Bograd, 1986; Goldner, 1985; Lerner, 1988; Luepnitz, 1988), and despite Bowen's dislike of false dichotomies (Friedman, 1991), this interpretation of differentiation is often applied as such—differentiated versus undifferentiated, thoughts versus feelings, autonomy versus connection, masculine versus feminine, individualism versus collectivism, etc. The conflating of differentiation with rational individualism has reinforced dominant U.S. cultural norms and led to the devaluing and pathologization of a diverse range of healthy and mature ways of relating. It has also created the unattainable goal of being perfectly differentiated.

While some critics of Bowen theory have criticized the patriarchal undertones of differentiation, others have argued that the fault lies in the interpretation, not the concept. I think that it is both. Knudson-Martin (1994) argued that differentiation does account for the feminine experience and socialization. She understood Bowen to mean that it is important to value both the "feeling system" and the "intellectual system," and that reactivity is the inability to access both and know the difference. Others have expanded on this by explaining how reactivity can look different depending on gender socialization (Walters et al., 1988). In Western societies, feminine socialization focuses on seeking connection and displaying emotions, whereas masculine socialization focuses on seeking distance and masking emotions. Both positions can be reactive, according to Bowen theory, but patriarchy often focuses on the reactivity we associate with femininity. One of the most frequent misinterpretations of BFST is that emotional reactivity refers only to external displays such as crying, pleading, or yelling. Rarely do we consider shutting down, withdrawing, and stonewalling as equally reactive positions—which they are.

In queer-contextualized BFST (QC BFST), differentiation is about finding a balance that is adaptive and functional for a given person in their relational and cultural context. This includes communal and collectivist contexts, not just individualistic Western cultures. Differentiation is about being aware of our separateness *and* our connectedness, not just to other humans, but to all life. It means awareness of our instincts, bodily sensations, feelings, and thoughts and the ability to use these to guide our actions.

Equalizing Triangles

Bowen contended that the smallest stable relationship is a triad, consisting of three people. Two-person relationships are unstable and, when under stress, will triangulate a third—analogous to a stool that needs three legs to stay upright. Although a healthy triangle is a relationship between three relative equals (Titelman, 1998), the most common example Bowen offered was that of a mother, father, and child, which is a perplexing contradiction. It is hard to believe that Bowen thought there could be three equal relationships between two adults and a child. In fact, he preferred to do therapy with parents instead of children, because he believed children and adolescents were more likely to wait for their environment to change, rather than act to change it (Bowen, 1978). So, while he acknowledged that children had less agency than their parents, he seemed to frame it as a developmental deficit, rather than a lack of power and ability to influence family emotional process.

When we place the concept of triangles into a queer context, we see more than just mother-father-child shapes. We see a kaleidoscope of inter-dependent triangles: chosen family; platonic partnerships; triads, quads, and other multipartner structures; open donor and adoption relationships; friends, exes, and extended family caring for one another and raising children together. These triangles form a web of relationships that is stronger than separate monogamous couples or nuclear families. This is because there is more flexibility in how a system copes with stress when it is more widely distributed—when there are more relationships in which emotional process can be directed, bound, and resolved (Titelman, 1998). As an example, when talking about conflict in her own romantic triad, sociologist Martha Beck quipped, "How awesome is it to have a fight when there is a referee?" (Doyle et al., 2022). She illustrates the advantage of having more than two mature and caring adults to manage stress and anxiety in a family system.

In addition to distributing the burden of anxiety throughout the system, interlocking triangles also distribute the burden of oppression and economic survival. Like his peers in psychiatry, Bowen did not incorporate a structural or political analysis into his theory. However, when we place Bowen's theory in a queer-centered context, we must include the influence of systems of power into our understanding of emotional systems. The idea that social, familial, and community networks are essential to surviving and thriving under oppression is not new (Meyer, 2015); however, it is novel—and essential—to incorporate these types of stressors into a QC BFST.

Naturalizing "Homosexuality"

A queer critique of BFST would not be complete without addressing the fact that Bowen explicitly defined homosexuality as a severe symptom of an emotional system, akin to schizophrenia, alcoholism, or obsessive-compulsive neurosis (Kerr & Bowen, 1988). For such symptoms, Bowen believed that high anxiety and low differentiation must have existed in several generations before the symptom-bearer. Therefore, homosexuality would not be found in individuals or systems with higher differentiation and a higher ability to adapt to stress. It is surprising that Bowen took such a strong position on homosexuality during a time when society was highly polarized around lesbian, gay, and transgender rights, given that he viewed polarization as a sign of low differentiation at the societal level and even coined a term for this phenomenon: **societal regression** (Bowen, 1976; Friedman, 1991). Societal regression is the hot potato of anxiety passed around the masses as we entrench ourselves into opposing camps. So, while Bowen's choice of camp might not be surprising to some given his social location, the fact that he chose a camp at all exposes his own vulnerability to the forces of societal anxiety (Friedman, 1991). Call me an idealist, but I like to imagine that if Bowen had lived long enough, there might have come a day where he gave a talk reflecting on his own emotional reactivity on this matter, similar to the talks he gave about his efforts to differentiate himself within his FOO.

Box 6.3

Societal regression The phenomenon where a society collectively experiences heightened anxiety and stress, leading to polarized and reactive behaviors.

In QC BFST, the full range of gender identity, gender expression, sexual anatomy, sexual attraction, and relationship structures are seen as natural and, therefore, neither normal or abnormal. Strong feelings about any form of human expression is conceptualized as reactivity. Friedman (1991) suggested that due to societal regression humans create false dichotomies or categories. One false dichotomy is the strict separation of sex and gender into two inextricably linked categories, what we now refer to as the gender binary (Vaid-Menon, 2020). Although he did not use the language of gender binary, Friedman—a prominent Bowen therapist and scholar—believed that gender was indeed socially constructed as a way for society to handle the anxiety of these seemingly opposing forces. I would take Friedman's analysis further to integrate the history of capitalism, colonialism, and white supremacy into the process of societal regression—that societies based in these power structures have more inequity (Alexander, 2010; Oxfam International, 2024; Rodney, 1972), and therefore more societal regression. They are less differentiated, have higher anxiety, and are more likely to bind their anxiety into polarizing debates. Therefore, in QC BFST, binaries are viewed as reactive, whereas the complex, dynamic, and nuanced nature of humans and their emotional systems is viewed as healthy, which actually brings our theory closer to Bowen's original vision of a natural systems theory.

A Critical and Recontextual Approach to Therapy

Defining the Emotional Process

Genograms as a Flexible Tool. In order to define the emotional process, BFST uses two broad interventions—genograms and process questions.

Although genograms were originally narrow in scope and reinforced white, middle-class, heterosexual family norms, they have since been used with a wide range of families, including lesbian-headed families (Swainson & Tasker, 2005). They have also been used to explore culture (Hardy & Laszloffy, 1995; McGoldrick et al., 2020) and power (Kosutic et al., 2009). In my experience, therapists who feel constrained by genograms are focusing too much on using preestablished symbols and structures, and not enough on the theoretical and clinical purpose of the genogram, which is to collect and visually represent information on the emotional process of the client's relational systems.

QC BFST retains genograms while encouraging expansion and creativity in both process and structure. This means being creative in how we gather information —through clinical interviews, collaborative drawing sessions, FOO interviews—and what information we are gathering— chosen family members, experiences of privilege and oppression, points of pride and shame, ancestral legacies, etc. Genograms can be a powerful tool for tracking the history of oppression through generations, which is an essential component of healing from intergenerational and historical trauma (Brave Heart & De Bruyn, 1998; Mullan, 2023; Myhra, 2011). If we expand the use of genograms, we must also expand the structure of them, which means being creative with symbols, colors, and formatting of genograms. There are generally accepted symbols that can serve as a starting point for creating genograms (McGoldrick et al., 2020), but clinicians should not feel restricted to using only these symbols, especially if they do not represent the lived experience and family history of the client. For example, the suggested symbol for trans individuals is the symbol of their assigned gender nested within the symbol for their actual gender (McGoldrick et al., 2020). While some trans folks may feel affirmed by this symbol, for others, it reinforces a gender binary and gender essentialism in a way that does not reflect the fluidity or complexity of their gender. I have seen trans and nonbinary clients choose stars, octagons, or clouds to represent their gender. In my practice, I typically share the commonly used symbols while also inviting clients to create new symbols for gender, sexuality, relationship structures, and any other salient pieces of their sociocultural context and identities, as they see fit.

Compassionate Questioning. The process question asks clients to think about and report on their feelings, thoughts, and behaviors in anxiety-provoking interactions. Bowen encouraged a "researcher stance," in which therapists are neutral in response to the information collected, and one person's answer prompts another process question from the therapist (Papero, 1990). The goal is to gather enough data about the emotional process so that the client can begin to see it clearly. The theory does not include reflection, softening, empathizing, or expanding on what the client says. To some, this can feel cold. And for clients who are detached from their own feelings, this therapeutic approach can be unhelpful as it reinforces stuck relational patterns.

In QC BFST, the researcher stance from the original theory is transformed to a stance of curiosity and compassion. The therapist remains curious about the system's emotional process, asking questions about how each person's actions, thoughts, and feelings influence the pattern, but they also demonstrate compassion for the distress that these stuck relational patterns can cause. QC BFST integrates softening, empathizing, and normalizing in order to neutralize the shame that people often feel when examining their own reactivity. Shame is one of many ways that anxiety manifests in a system, and it is often culturally produced. That is, we learn to feel shame through implicit and explicit discourse within systems of power. For example, we are taught to feel shame when we cry or express vulnerability through patriarchy and white supremacy. We are taught to feel shame about our bodies—their shapes, urges, and abilities—through ableism, capitalism, colonization, white supremacy, and patriarchy. Therefore, offering clients compassion for the shame and distress that comes up as they observe their emotional process allows them to make more empowered choices within their different relational contexts.

Demonstrating Differentiation

Therapists Are Human. Even though Bowen therapy is not directive—in fact, the Bowen therapist does not actively try to change the system (Papero, 1990)—it can be considered hierarchical because the therapist is expected to be the most differentiated person in the room (Kerr, 1981). This can reinforce a power imbalance between those who are differentiated and those who are not. For many years, I taught an advanced theory course that focused on BFST and self-of-therapist development. I noticed that students were often striving to reach some imagined level of perfect differentiation and felt shame about their natural emotional reactions, which they took to mean they were not differentiated. I spent quite a bit of time teaching them to bring self-compassion, nuance, and complexity to Bowen's concepts. The amount of effort it took to teach BFST in a way that resisted cultural norms of perfectionism, competition, and binary thinking highlighted for me just how entrenched those norms are in the theory. In a white supremacist, capitalist, and patriarchal society, differentiation becomes something to strive for—something that can be performed, perfected, and achieved.

In QC BFST, however, the therapist is not expected to be perfectly differentiated. Mostly, because that is not possible. Therapists, just like our clients, are humans with all of the emotions and reactivity that make it difficult for us to observe ourselves. A QC BFST therapist, however, takes explicit responsibility for how their emotions influence the therapeutic process. It is our responsibility to notice and be curious about our reactions to clients, in the same way that we ask clients to observe and question their emotional process. If I notice myself feeling bored in a session, I get curious about what my boredom is in reaction to. It could be that the client is keeping their responses superficial and avoiding direct communication about anxiety-producing topics, or that I have checked out of the conversation because it is producing some anxiety for me. By reflecting on my reaction, I can prevent it from impacting therapy and instead use it to inform the next process question I ask or the next I-position I take. Responding thoughtfully is what it means to practice differentiation.

I-Position. It can be harder to practice differentiation when client issues touch on the therapist's personal wounds or core values. This can happen often when working with the relational systems of queer and trans people, whose partners and family members may be struggling with internalized dominant discourses like heterosexism and cissexism. In addition to the curiosity and compassion mentioned previously, QC BFST therapists use the I-position as a way to define themselves and their boundaries to the client system. For example, upon meeting with a child and their family, and hearing the parents using the child's birth name and assigned pronouns, the therapist might ask the child, "what do you like to be called?" And later define their position to the family: "When I spoke with your child, she said she likes to go by Nicole, so I am letting you know that is the name I will be using." An I-position is taken to define one's own position, not to change the other person's mind (although that may happen). Because of the relative power we have over clients, and because of the common narrative that therapists know how to solve people's problems, we have to be thoughtful about how we take I-positions so that the client knows we are defining our own stance and not giving a directive.

Continue Coaching Clients to Observe Process

Once anxiety was relatively well managed in the room, Bowen would teach clients the concepts of the theory and coach them in observing their own process so that they could continue to work on differentiation without a therapist. This therapeutic task stands up well to a contemporary critique.

First, teaching clients key concepts so they can continue to do the work on their own is transparent, collaborative, and nonexploitative. And second, many somatic practitioners would agree with Bowen that learning cannot happen when there is threat or anxiety present (Menakem, 2021; van der Kolk, 2014). What BFST is missing is an explicit connection to body work. Bowen theorized about how the emotional system impacted physiological processes (Kerr & Bowen, 1988), but did not explore the complementary view that physiological processes could impact our emotional system. The next section will integrate somatic exercises into the journey toward higher differentiation.

Therapeutic Goals and Progress: More Than Going Home

Once clients get to the coaching phase of BFST, they are expected to work on their differentiation in their FOO, with the assumption that this will improve functioning in their relationships with partners, children, and friends (Bowen, 1978). Bowen did not provide any other options for this phase of treatment, despite there being many reasons why someone might not be willing or able to do this, such as geographical distance, cutoff, or death. For our purposes, many queer and trans adults may be distant or cutoff from their FOO—by force or by choice—due to abuse, neglect, or rejection. Given the realities of this context, alternative ways for increasing differentiation outside of FOO are important. But first, we must talk about cutoff.

Bowen defined emotional cutoff as a reactive relationship pattern, similar to conflict or triangulation. He strongly urged clients to repair cutoffs as a way to increase their differentiation. For people who have severed family ties due to abuse or rejection, this is a nonstarter. To address this issue in QC BFST, we must first distinguish between two kinds of cutoff. Physical cutoff entails no contact, including telephone, online, or in-person communication. Emotional cutoff, as Bowen conceived of it, is physical cutoff that is maintained through emotional reactivity: "I refuse to speak to this person because I feel disrespected by them"; "I won't see this person because I am so angry"; "I try not to think about this person because it is too painful", etc. It is this reactivity of an emotional cutoff that is problematic. If we can resolve the emotions of an emotional cutoff, then we transform it into a physical cutoff that is a conscious response.

In order to understand how to resolve emotional cutoffs without going home, we must return to the basic assumptions of the theory to understand why Bowen suggested FOO work in the first place. Bowen used concepts like nuclear family emotional process, family projection process, and multigenerational transmission process to describe the patterned ways that families managed anxiety and passed these patterns and level of differentiation onto future generations. I think of the FOO as the fire in which our emotional reactivity is forged. Bowen believed that if a person could interrupt and reshape interactional patterns where they were the most automatic and held the most anxiety—in the FOO—they would be easier to reshape in less emotionally intense relationships.

While there may be benefits to reforging our relational patterns in the fire of the FOO, differentiation can be addressed in the context of any relationship. It is important to remember that the point of going home is to take responsibility for self in the context of emotional systems; it is not to confront or demand change from others as tempting as that may be. This is done by observing one's own emotional reactivity, managing one's own anxiety differently, and choosing more adaptive responses. This can be done with an intimate partner, with close friends, or with extended family. We often repeat childhood patterns with our intimate partners; while this can be a source of struggle, if recognized, it offers an opportunity to interrupt that pattern outside of the FOO. When parents are unavailable, due to death or cutoff, building one-on-one relationships with extended family—such as aunts, uncles, grandparents, and cousins—can provide access to safer relational support while also building an indirect relationship with the estranged parent (Brown, 1999).

Another alternative to going home is genogram or genealogy work. Interviewing extended family members or using online databases to create an in-depth family history can uncover significant generational patterns and hidden context, which can help resolve anxiety. A poignant example of this comes from one of my students, who gave permission to share their story. As an adolescent, this student had been sent to a conversion camp by their parents. The student had done considerable work to heal from this experience and wanted to build a better relationship with their parents. While interviewing an aunt for a genogram assignment, the student learned that their grandmother had sent their mother to live with a relative during a particularly difficult time. The student connected their mother's experience of being sent away with their own:

> I can see why sending me away made sense to my mom. She didn't feel equipped to help me…and in her family when you can't take care of your children you send them to someone who can. Obviously, that was not the right choice, but now I can see that she was doing the best she could.

Seeing their experience as part of an intergenerational pattern resolved some of the anger and hurt the student felt and gave them a new perspective of their mother.

Ideally, our differentiation efforts will focus not only on our intellectual and emotional systems but also the bodies that house these systems. Practices that target the autonomic nervous system help regulate physiological responses to stress and balance the sympathetic (fight-or-flight) and parasympathetic (rest-and-digest) systems (Chin & Kales, 2019; Goyal et al., 2014). These practices can include breathwork, progressive muscle relaxation, mindfulness, meditation, vagus nerve stimulation, yoga, forest bathing, and bilateral stimulation such as eye movement desensitization and reprocessing (EMDR) or tapping. A thorough review of these (and other) somatic practices is beyond the scope of this chapter; however, QC BFST practitioners are encouraged to explore these practices as an integral component of queer-contextualized differentiation work. Developing greater body and mind awareness through mindful practices can increase an individual's ability to observe their own thoughts, feelings, and behaviors when they are feeling activated, and improve their ability to self-regulate in those moments. Somatic practices can also help people release intergenerational trauma that is stored in the body (Menakem, 2021; Mullan, 2023). Body-based approaches focus on creating balance in the autonomic system, which aligns with the ideal of balance in the queer-contextualized version of differentiation. In QC BFST, the body is an essential component of our individual and relational systems, and to ignore it is to inhibit our ability to differentiate.

A QC BFST acknowledges the strengths of BFST while addressing its historical and contextual limitations. By centering queer and trans people and their relationships, incorporating critical analysis, and rethinking differentiation, QC BFST provides a more inclusive and affirming framework for systemic therapy. This approach empowers therapists and clients alike to navigate relationships with greater compassion. See Figure 6.1 for a comparison of assumptions in Bowen's original theory and in the queer-contextualized version. In the next section, I offer a brief case example that illustrates the tenets of QC BFST.

Case Example

Tyler is a 43-year-old bisexual, polyamorous, cisgender white man who lives in a large Midwestern city. His two children, Ava (15) and Noah (13), split their time between Tyler's house and their mother's. In the ten years since his divorce, Tyler has built a strong support network that includes partners, exes, and friends. His anchor partner of nine years, Maggie, is queer and nonbinary. Tyler credits Maggie with helping him discover and embrace these previously hidden aspects of his identity.

Tyler came to therapy shortly after the death of his stepfather, Mike, because of his challenging relationship with his mother, Carol. He described

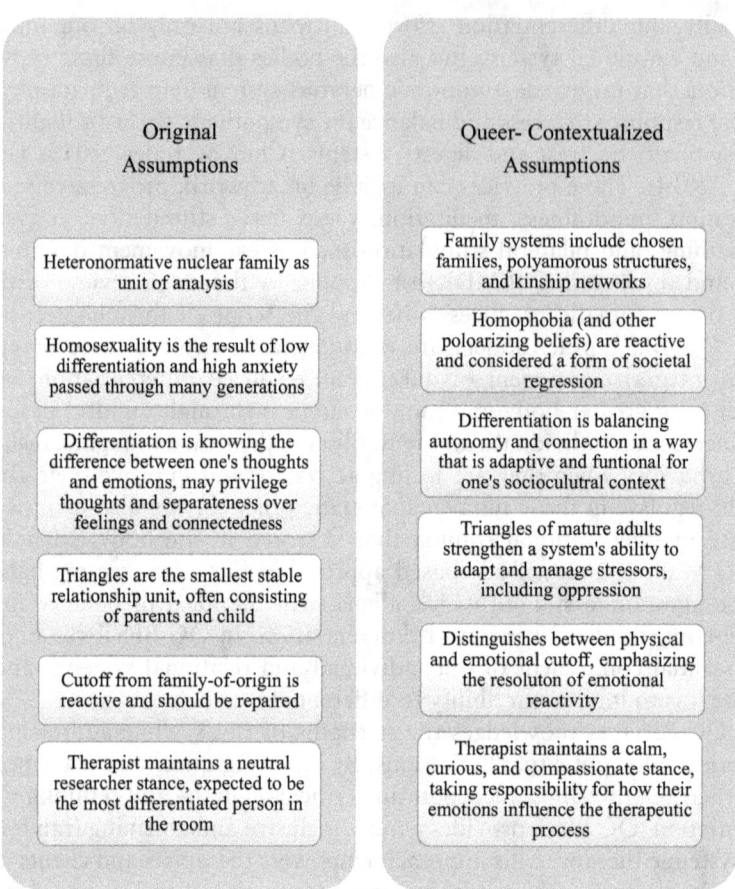

Figure 6.1 Comparison of Theoretical Assumptions in the Original and Queer-Contextualized Versions of Bowen Family Systems Theory.

his parents as deeply conservative evangelical Christians who strictly controlled many aspects of his childhood. His mother, in particular, adhered to rigid gender roles and viewed nonheteronormative relationships as sinful. After high school, Tyler and his ex-wife moved across the country, and he remained physically and emotionally cut off from his parents for two years. After having children, however, he and his ex-wife relocated back to their home state, where they resumed contact with Tyler's family.

Since Mike's death, Carol's drinking has worsened, but according to Tyler, no one in the family has addressed it. At Mike's funeral, Tyler felt dismissed by his extended family—also conservative Christians—who focused their attention on his mother while largely ignoring him, his children, and Maggie. Upon returning home, Tyler broke down in tears, which prompted Maggie to encourage him to seek therapy.

Defining the Emotional Process

The therapist began by mapping Tyler's family history with a genogram, including chosen family and relational patterns beyond traditional kinship structures. Through this process, Tyler identified long-standing dynamics of conflict avoidance, emotional cutoff, and intergenerational anxiety transmission in his biological family and patterns of connectedness and peacekeeping in his family of choice. His therapist was curious as she asked him questions to identify the stuck relational pattern between him and his mother.

Therapist: What happens between you and your mother that feels so difficult?

Tyler: She's so critical and judgmental. She has an opinion on every part of my life but never just listens to me.

Therapist: What are some things she is critical of?

Tyler: My career, my house, my relationships. She constantly tells me I need to get married again—even though I've told her I don't want to. She didn't even like Maggie when we first started dating, and now it's so important that we get married? It doesn't make sense.

Therapist: Can you make it make sense? Why do you think that is important to her?

Tyler: It comes from her church. They believe that marriage is some divine imperative, and to disobey is a sin.

Therapist: From what you've told me about your mother, she places a lot of importance on obeying God and being welcomed into an afterlife. Sounds like your mother is afraid for you and your afterlife—even though that is not important to you—and when she is afraid, she criticizes you. Does that seem right?

Tyler: Yeah, that makes sense.

Therapist: So, she gets scared and she criticizes. What do you do?

Tyler: I get angry and I leave. We usually don't talk for a while. Eventually, one of us reaches out to the other, but we never talk about the fight, and we never resolve it.

Using Tyler's genogram, the therapist asked where else in his family people were avoiding conflict or cutting off from one another. Tyler pointed out several cutoff relationships on his mother's side of the family, and noted that many of the intact relationships were superficial. After adding more relationship lines to indicate cutoff and conflict avoidance, Tyler laughed, "Wow, it's like a constellation of dysfunction." The therapist's response validated and reframed Tyler's view: "I see it as a constellation of anxiety, where everyone is using some form of distance to manage their emotional connection to each other. It's no wonder you are doing the same."

Demonstrating Differentiation

A few weeks later, Tyler came into the session upset about a recent visit with his mother. He brought his children with him for the visit, hoping that seeing her grandchildren would help his mother with her grief. Instead, Carol was critical and short with his children, like she often was with Tyler. When Carol noticed Noah was wearing fingernail polish, she raised her eyebrows and said sarcastically, "did your boyfriend get the same color?" In response, Noah shoved his hands in his pockets and went silent.

Therapist: When your mother said that to Noah, how did you feel?

Tyler: I was so angry at her! I don't want her spreading her hate to my kids. I don't want them thinking that being gay or queer or trans is a bad thing. Because what if they are? They could still be figuring that stuff out and I don't want them to feel ashamed. I don't want them to hide like I did.

Therapist: So, in that moment you felt angry and protective of your kids. What did you do? How did you respond in that moment?

Tyler: I told the kids to come out into the garage with me to sort through some of grandpa's boxes. I just wanted to get them away from her.

Therapist: You removed your kids from a possibly harmful situation. Then what?

Tyler: We stayed in the garage pretty much until we left. There is no point in saying anything to her. She doesn't listen.

At this point, the therapist noticed that her body had tensed and she was holding her breath. She felt indignation rise up when she heard that Tyler did not stand up for himself or for his children. As a QC BFST therapist, she was highly attuned to her own reactivity, and thought about how her feelings could be used thoughtfully and therapeutically. She chose to take the I-position to share part of her reaction, and then shifted to empathic questioning to see if Tyler could recognize that he was perpetuating an intergenerational pattern of conflict avoidance.

Therapist:	I am feeling angry and protective of your kids, too. I am also feeling angry and protective of you—recognizing that you also received this kind of criticism and harshness when you were young. I am wondering, in that moment when your mother made that comment to Noah, did you feel like you were also 13 years old?
Tyler:	(pauses) Yeah, I guess so. I remember feeling so angry as a kid. And helpless. Like nothing I did would change anything.
Therapist:	So, when your mother criticized Noah, 13-year-old Tyler felt angry and helpless. So, you did the only thing you could do as a teenager—you got the hell out of there. That is how you protected yourself when you were young. That kept you safe. Now, at 43, you have built a beautiful life for yourself, surrounded by people who love you for exactly who you are. I wonder if you still need to protect yourself in the same way.
Tyler:	(lets out a big exhale) No, I guess not. It's hard to realize that in the moment—I go right back to angry teenage Tyler who just wants to escape. But I have escaped, in a way. I grew up, and I've made choices that align with my values, not theirs. I guess I'm not sure what that looks like—responding to my family as adult Tyler.
Therapist:	Well, we can explore that in here and you can try on different responses out there. It will be like a series of small experiments, with you collecting data out in the field, and us analyzing it in here to see what works. Sound good?

Coaching the Client to Observe Process

Through therapy, Tyler recognized his tendency to repeat familial patterns of cutoff and criticism, believing himself to be rebellious when, in many ways, he was mirroring the same relational strategies as his FOO. The therapist helped him explore alternative ways to manage the anxiety brought up by conflict and to use distance as a thoughtful self-regulation tool rather than a reaction. When visiting or talking to his mother on the phone, he practiced engaging with her from a place of calm and curiosity.

Because she used a queer-contextualized lens, the therapist did not exclusively focus on Tyler's relationship with his mother, but encouraged him to develop differentiation outside of his FOO as well. His relationships with Maggie, his children, and his chosen family were all spaces where he could practice self-definition while maintaining meaningful connections. The therapist also introduced body-based practices to help Tyler manage

What reactions did you have as you read the chapter? Try to be curious about your reactions. Where do you feel them in your body? What thoughts or feelings come with them?

What kinds of client dynamics are more likely to trigger your own emotional reactivity?

How does your family-of-origin influence how your work with clients?

What have you discovered (or could you explore further) about your own family system that might enhance your ability to understand intergenerational processes?

How can you enhance your ability to be a calm and compassionate presence in the therapy room?

What are some polarizing debates you find yourself stuck in? What would it look like to differentiate within the context of that debate?

Bowen once said that one of the greatest diseases of mankind is to try to change another human being. As a therapist, what is your reaction to this statement?

Figure 6.2 Questions for Reflection.

anxiety in high-conflict interactions, including grounding techniques and mindful breathing, encouraging him to put his reactions on pause until he was in a calmer, more thoughtful headspace.

This case illustrates a queer-contextualized approach to BFST where classic concepts and interventions are delivered with increased care and attention to context. Genograms, process questions, and going home assignments are used to both validate and challenge relational patterns. A queer-contextualized view of differentiation affirms our full identity and relational world, reinforcing that healing doesn't have to depend solely on going home. Therapists can demonstrate differentiation in a way that centers their own humanity. By reimagining BFST in a queer-centered context, we infuse it with the compassion, curiosity, and balance that it has been missing.

References

Alexander, M. (2010). *The new Jim Crow: Mass incarceration in the age of color-blindness.* New York, NY: The New Press.

Bograd, M. (1986). A feminist examination of family systems models of violence against women in the family. In M. Ault-Riche (Ed.), *Women in family therapy* (pp. 34–50). Rockville, MD: Aspen Systems.

Bowen, M. (1976). Theory and practice in psychotherapy. In P. J. Guerin (Ed.), *Family therapy: Theory and practice* (pp. 42–90). Gardner Press.

Bowen, M. (1978). *Family therapy in clinical practice*. New York, NY: Jason Aronson.

Brave Heart, M. Y. H., & DeBruyn, L. M. (1998). The American Indian Holocaust: Healing historical unresolved grief. *American Indian and Alaska Native Mental Health Research*, 8(2), 60–82. doi: 10.5820/aian.0802.1998.60

Brown, J. (1999). Bowen family systems theory and practice: Illustration and critique. *Australian and New Zealand Journal of Family Therapy*, 20(2), 94–103.

Buckley, W. (1967). *Sociology and modern systems theory*. Englewood Cliffs, NJ: Prentice Hall, Inc.

Chin, M. S., & Kales, S. N. (2019). Understanding mind-body disciplines: A pilot study of paced breathing and dynamic muscle contraction on autonomic nervous system reactivity. *Stress Health*, 35(4), 542–548.

Doyle, G., Wambach, A., & Doyle, A. (2022, August 10). Martha Beck and Rowan Mangan: Polyamory and throuple life (No. 121) [Audio podcast episode]. In *We can do hard things*. https://momastery.com/blog/we-can-do-hard-things-ep-121/

Friedman, E. H. (1991). Bowen family systems theory and societal regression. In P. J. Guerin (Ed.), *Family therapy: Theory and practice* (pp. 42–90). Gardner Press.

Goldner, V. (1985). Feminism and family therapy. *Family Process*, 24, 31–47.

Goyal, M., Singh, S., Sibinga, E. M., Gould, N. F., Rowland-Seymour, A., Sharma, R., ... & Haythornthwaite, J. A. (2014). Meditation programs for psychological stress and well-being: A systematic review and meta-analysis. *JAMA Internal Medicine*, 174(3), 357–368.

Guerin, P. J., & Hubbard, I. M. (1987). Impact of therapist's personal family system on clinical work. *Journal of Psychotherapy & The Family*, 3(2), 47–60. https://doi.org/10.1300/J287v03n02_06

Hardy, K. V. (1989). The theoretical myth of sameness: A critical issue in family therapy training and treatment. *Journal of Psychotherapy & the Family*, 6(1–2), 17–33.

Hardy, K. V., & Laszloffy, T. A. (1995). The cultural genogram: Key to training culturally competent family therapists. *Journal of Marital and Family Therapy*, 21(3), 227–237.

Hare-Mustin, R. T. (1987). The problem of gender in family therapy theory. *Family Process*, 26(1), 15–27.

Kerr, M. E. (1981). Family systems theory and therapy. In A. S. Gurman & D. P. Kniskern (Eds.), *Handbook of family therapy*. Brunner/Mazel.

Kerr, M. E. (1984). Theoretical base for differentiation of self in one's family of origin. *Clinical Supervisor*, 2, 3–36.

Kerr, M. E., & Bowen, M. (1988). *Family evaluation*. WW Norton & Company.

Knudson-Martin, C. (1994). The female voice: Applications to Bowen's family systems theory. *Journal of Marital and Family Therapy*, 20, 35–46.

Kosutic, I., Garcia, M., Graves, T., Barnett, F., Hall, J., Haley, E., ... & Kaiser, B. (2009). The critical genogram: A tool for promoting critical consciousness. *Journal of Feminist Family Therapy*, 21(3), 151–176.

Lerner, H. G. (1988). Is family systems theory really systemic? A feminist communication. *Journal of Psychotherapy and the Family, 3* 47–63.

Luepnitz, D. A. (1988). *The family interpreted: Feminist theory in clinical practice.* New York, NY: Basic Books.

McGoldrick, M. (1995). *You can go home again: Reconnecting with your family.* WW Norton & Company.

McGoldrick, M., Gerson, R., & Petry, S. (2020). *Genograms: Assessment and treatment* (4th ed.). New York, NY: W.W. Norton & Company, Inc.

Menakem, R. (2021). *My grandmother's hands: Racialized trauma and the pathway to mending our hearts and bodies.* Penguin UK.

Meyer, I. H. (2015). Resilience in the study of minority stress and health of sexual and gender minorities. *Psychology of sexual orientation and gender diversity, 2*(3), 209.

Mullan, J. (2023). *Decolonizing therapy: Oppression, historical trauma, and politicizing your practice.* WW Norton & Company.

Myhra, L. L. (2011). " It runs in the family": Intergenerational transmission of historical trauma among urban American Indians and Alaska Natives in culturally specific sobriety maintenance programs. *American Indian and Alaska native mental health research (Online), 18*(2), 17.

Oxfam International. (2024). *Inequality Inc.* Oxfam. Retrieved from www.oxfam.org/en/research/inequality-inc

Papero, D. V. (1990). *Bowen family systems theory.* Prentice Hall.

Rodney, W. (1972). *How Europe underdeveloped Africa.* London: Bogle-L'Ouverture Publications.

Smith, K. (2019). *Everything isn't terrible: Conquer your insecurities, interrupt your anxiety, and finally calm down.* New York, NY: Hachette Books.

Stryker, S. (2017). *Transgender history: The roots of today's revolution.* Seal Press.

Swainson, M., & Tasker, F. (2005). Genograms redrawn: Lesbian couples define their families. *Journal of GLBT Family Studies, 1*(2), 3–27.

Titelman, P. (1998). *Clinical applications of Bowen family systems theory.* New York, NY: Haworth Press.

Vaid-Menon, A. (2020). *Beyond the gender binary.* Penguin House.

van der Kolk, B. A. (2014). *The body keeps the score: Brain, mind, and body in the healing of trauma.* Viking.

Walters, M., Carter, B., Papp, P., & Silverstein, O. (1988). *The invisible web: Gender patterns in family relationships.* New York, NY: Guilford Press.

Chapter 7

Queer-Contextualized Contextual Family Therapy

Rashmi Gangamma and Anh-Khoi Le

Theoretical Assumptions of Contextual Family Therapy

As an intergenerational, integrative family systems approach, contextual therapy theory is one of the few foundational theories explicitly examining justice and balance of fairness in relational systems (Boszormenyi-Nagy & Krasner, 1986). Using four dimensions of facts, individual psychology, systemic transactions, and relational ethics, contextual therapy theory allows for consideration of intrapsychic and interpersonal factors. A fifth dimension of the ontic was articulated later by Catherine DuCommun-Nagy (2002) to highlight the importance of the self in relation to others. Drawing philosophically from Martin Buber's I-Thou dialogue (Friedman, 1989), contextual therapy theory's development was influenced by ideas from object relations theory (Glebova & Gangamma, 2017; Goff, 2001), Bowenian theory (Kerr & Bowen, 1988), and Satir's model of therapy (Satir & Baldwin, 1983). The basic underlying assumption is that individuals thrive in the context of a balanced relational network where they feel seen and validated. When individuals are given their due credit, they can see and validate others in their life and continue a legacy of justice in relationships. Conversely, when individuals do not receive fair consideration in relationships, they do not feel seen or validated, which depletes their ability to further promote balance. Imbalance in relationships is manifested through a lack of trust, loyalty conflicts, and destructive entitlement. It is vital to consider, however, that how one experiences fairness and balance are relative to one's context, "facts" such as one's social identities, health status, and life events, as well as patterns across generations. Thus, examining and unpacking the revolving intergenerational ledger of fairness (Hargrave & Pfitzer, 2003) is an integral part of therapy. Ultimately, the theory proposes that the goal of therapy is relational repair (**rejunction**) and **relational accountability** in order to **rebalance** current relationships and limit the future transmission of injustice.

DOI: 10.4324/9781003308188-7

Box 7.1

Rebalance Actions of acknowledging one's experiences of unfairness, offering support to make relationships fair, and preventing future perpetuation of injustice.

Rejunction The process of restoring responsible concerns among couple/family/community members for justice and balance.

Relational Accountability The maintenance of caring efforts and behavioral integrity to counterbalance past injustice and improve current fairness dynamics.

A major technique to address processes of unfairness or imbalance in relationships is acknowledgment. **Acknowledgment** is an active process of listening and validating; the therapist adopts a multilateral stance (or **multidirected partiality**), which allows clients to feel heard and their experiences validated while simultaneously allowing them to explore and hold another's perspective. The therapist's multidirected partiality provides space for acknowledging hurt and harmful interactions, as well as moving toward an I-Thou stance. The I-Thou stance is where they can see the people who may have hurt them through a more compassionate, multidimensional lens. Central to this work is the therapist's own belief in the importance of justice and fairness in relationships and their own ability to hold a multilateral stance in their lives. Can they move to a place of **exoneration**, where they see the people who hurt them as not only perpetrators but also individuals struggling with relational resources and fairness? Therapists who work on their own understanding of what it means to have a balance in relationships, meaning-making of pain and relational suffering, and the ability to move to an expansive view of people in their lives are better prepared to assist their clients in doing the same.

This is a challenging work. Beginning students of contextual therapy often ask – how do I exonerate someone who will not even acknowledge the hurt they perpetuate? More crucially, for those of us who occupy multiple intersecting identities that are minoritized and subject to relational *and* structural injustice, how do we move to an expansive stance of considering another's perspective when we know we could easily be the target of their hate and fear? The developers of the theory and early applications

Box 7.2

Acknowledgment An active listening process in which the therapist highlights and validates both the injustice clients have faced and the support they received from and offered to others.

Multidirected Partiality The therapist's multilateral stance provides space for each person expressing their sides while encouraging them to hold others' perspectives compassionately.

Exoneration The process in which clients explore the historical struggles of people who hurt them and eventually perceive those as not just perpetrators but individuals experiencing unfairness and relational stagnation.

did not address these concerns. Like other foundational family therapy theories, contextual therapy's assumptions are rooted in a cisnormative, heteronormative, White-European perspective of relational structures. Early discussions of experiences of fairness and justice in relationships were also rooted in binary notions of sex and gender, with little room for an inclusive framework that fully considers systemic factors of oppression. We propose that through our revision centering queer experiences, we may (a) expand the "**context**" to better conceptualize how systemic factors of injustice influence relational justice and (b) reimagine contextual therapy techniques to acknowledge ethical violations and promote balance in our clients' relational systems more fully.

Box 7.3

Context Contextual therapy theory describes "context" as the background in which relationships exist. Often discussed in terms of the five dimensions of facts, individual psychology, systemic transactions, and the ontic.

This queer-centered contextual therapy ultimately is more inclusive and better equips therapists to bring third-order change in family therapy (McDowell et al., 2019). Additionally, drawing from contextual therapy's core assumption that healing is rooted in uncovering individual and relational resources, centering queer experiences allows for highlighting strengths, resilience, and power that are inherent in queer lives. Much of our current literature on LGBTQ+ experiences emphasize mental health vulnerabilities, and what is often lost in this dominant perspective is that living and loving outside of "the norm" takes extraordinary courage and strength. Through this centering and revisioning, we push toward a decolonizing, liberatory framework (Almeida et al., 2017) where we do not continue to pathologize but provide space to truly acknowledge and embrace our diverse lives.

Queer-Contextualized Contextual Therapy

The original writings of contextual therapy did not mention the unique experiences and challenges faced by those who identify as LGBTQ+. An attempt is made in early writings to acknowledge societal injustices faced by ethno-racially minoritized populations, later amplified by some feminist family therapy scholars (Dankoski & Deacon, 2000; Grunebaum, 1990). More recently, family therapists have applied central constructs of the theory to work with queer couples and families (Belous, 2015; Heiden-Rootes, 2013). However, a recontextualization of contextual therapy that centers and celebrates LGBTQ+ lives has not yet been established. It is imperative to do so since the complexity of coming into one's identities and the relational and social consequences of identifying as LGBTQ+ occur within the larger oppressive social systems of heteronormativity, cis-sexism, homophobia, biphobia, and transphobia, to name a few (Meyer, 2003). This is further compounded when LGBTQ+ individuals also occupy minoritized ethno-racial identities (Cyrus, 2017).

A main revision in queer-contextualized contextual therapy is expanding the original conception of "context" beyond family systems. The cisnormative, heteronormative, White-Eurocentric definitions of families are not inclusive for queer and trans lives. We radically change what we bring to our therapeutic dialogue on justice and balance when we expand those definitions to intentionally include macro systemic factors such as cultural norms, laws, and policies governing queer identities and relationships, neighborhood factors of safety (or lack of safety), and various ways of building community. Additionally, for those who might also identify with a racially minoritized group, including racial dynamics (Kavanaugh et al., 2020; Sadika et al., 2020), immigration (Allen & Leslie, 2020), and transnationality (Falicov, 2005, 2007) allows therapists to capture spaces where clients might feel seen or not seen, invisible or hypervisible, included or excluded, and to intentionally bring them into therapeutic conversations. Studies on microaggressions (Nadal,

2019) and everyday experiences of discrimination (Bauerband et al., 2019; Nadal et al., 2010) provide clues on the impact of harmful interpersonal interactions on one's physical, mental, and relational health. We can help foster genuine dialogue by allowing clients to explore how social indicators of injustice may be influencing how they perceive balance in relationships.

We propose that integrating the frameworks of minority stress (Brooks, 1981; Hendricks & Testa, 2012; Meyer, 2003) and intersectionality (Crenshaw, 1991) allows the contextual therapist to expand the "context" for conceptualizing fairness and developing interventions. The framework of minority stress, which acknowledges the systemic factors of discrimination, prejudice, and stigma related to one's identity in creating a hostile environment (Meyer, 2003), provides a basis for examining societal injustice in relational balance. Specifically, discrimination and prejudice can exacerbate self-doubt and rumination in those who belong to multiple minoritized groups (Cyrus, 2017). That is, from a queer-contextual perspective, how one views their self as a person deserving of love, care, and trust can be negatively impacted by society's views of who deserves this love, care, and trust. It is not uncommon to encounter clients who have not experienced adequate care and consideration in their lives and are unable to recognize and receive care as well. Sometimes, the act of receiving or accepting care from people outside of their family may exacerbate loyalty conflicts with their families of origin.

Let's consider, Barbara,[1] a 45-year-old transwoman of color who presented to therapy with symptoms of depression, reported not having anyone who "cared enough for her." As she began her gender-affirming transitions a few years ago, she experienced several hardships, including losing employment, losing a custody battle with her ex-partner, and facing eviction from her current home. These experiences reflected systemic factors of discrimination that transwomen, and particularly transwomen of color, face (Nadal et al., 2012). In her childhood, Barbara had been placed at multiple foster homes and did not develop close relationships with anyone. With this information, the therapist was able to clearly conceptualize Barbara's struggles as related to a lack of validation at multiple levels. These experiences overshadowed any instances of care that Barbara did receive in her life. The therapist began by acknowledging the larger context of Barbara's experiences of justice. Simply naming and validating the hostility she experienced in the workplace, and the discrimination she had experienced in the judicial systems as a transwoman, provided a foundation for Barbara to begin re-evaluating her claim to validation and due care. Reframing her decisions to pursue gender affirmation as a way of resisting dominant narratives and providing a model for her child's own development opened space for Barbara to consider her own strengths in relationships. Looking further for relational resources and microaffirmations (Coppola et al., 2021), the therapist highlighted the important role that her biological mother had started to play in her life, the advocates and lawyers who helped her in her legal battles, and her former mentor, who still stayed connected to her. It was crucial, though, that the therapist first begin by acknowledging pain before probing for resources. For Barbara, the acknowledgment of pain had to include racism and transphobia, along with the pain of abandonment and rejection in childhood. In this instance, a multilateral stance allowed her to see her biological mother in a different light (from a rejecting parent to someone who also experienced racism, sexism, and challenges as a single mother) and to better appreciate the fact that she was still there, in her own way, supporting Barbara. Working through this allowed her to consider her lawyers and mentor as her allies – those who were invested in helping her – without feeling disloyal to her mother. This is the expansion of context in our revision where we name and acknowledge systemic oppression and intentionally search for relational resources in the larger social network.

Barbara's example also allows us to see how the therapist can use intersectionality to widen the assumption of within-family fairness, an assumption in the original development of contextual therapy to consider its societal and institutional contexts, making it a queer-contextualized assumption. Intersectionality, which considers overlapping societal processes of oppression and subjugation, is particularly useful in working with clients with multiple minoritized identities. An extension of this framework, transnational intersectionality (Anthias, 2012; Gangamma & Shipman, 2018), allows for a comprehensive examination in the lives of LGBTQ+ individuals who also have a migration experience. For instance, I (RG), as an immigrant of color with a queer identity, must navigate my relationships with family and community differently when I am here in the United States and when I am in India. Existing laws, cultural norms, and institutional definitions of my identities in both countries influence how I see myself and my expressions in relationships.

While working with LGBTQ+ people with a migration experience and/or with transnational experiences, the context in contextual therapy must expand further to include transnational contexts. What are the clients' experiences of loyalty when navigating their relationships in different contexts? If they feel freer to be in a queer-identified relationship in their host country, but not in their home country, how does this impact their experience of loyalty conflicts? Traditionally, loyalty conflicts have been written as an expression of struggle within family contexts (for example, having to choose between divorcing parents – **split loyalty**; or taking on the traits of an estranged parent – **invisible loyalty**). However, if we center a transnational, intersectional, queer experience in contextual theory, we also need to explore loyalty conflicts within clients' cultures, communities, and ultimately their sense of "home." What aspects of their identity are celebrated and what are denied (Gangamma, 2018)? Moreover, how do these struggles influence their sense of fairness in relationships?

Box 7.4

Split Loyalty Loyalty conflicts emerge when a client has to choose one side between conflicting parents or one identity aspect over others, which damages their sense of relational fairness.

Invisible Loyalty A deep sense of loyalty to a parent, an identity aspect, a community, or so on, unconsciously expressed in seemingly unrelated ways.

Consider, for instance, a couple where one partner, Nimi, has not disclosed her sexual identity to her family of origin for fear of ostracization, and the other partner, Sara, is more "out." Sara may experience that the relationship is unfair because she feels like she must hide her true self in certain circumstances for Nimi's sake. A traditional conceptualization would merely focus on the couple's relational patterns and patterns of balance in their family of origin and provide a perspective based on a family-level conceptualization of fairness. Queer-contextualizing this conceptualization would include a more intentional examination of the systemic levels of fairness. Besides their familial patterns, what do their cultural systems look like? Does Nimi feel a sense of obligation to protect her family because her family is already minoritized in other ways in the community? Does she feel that Sara's privilege as a person belonging to a dominant racial group prevents her from seeing her family's struggles? Has this created resentment not yet voiced? Is there a sense in the couple that there is only one way of being queer – which is out and proud – and anything less is being disloyal to their LGBTQ+ community? Where do these assumptions and thoughts come from? These questions based on minority stress (Ramirez & Paz Galupo, 2019; Valentine & Shipherd, 2018) and intersectionality (Crenshaw, 1991; Ocampo & Soodjinda, 2016) can help therapists expand the concepts of interpersonal trust *to community trust*, loyalty conflicts with family *to loyalty conflicts with communities/ identities*, and destructive entitlement in relationships where one believes they are owed something because of past hurt *to destructive entitlement manifested in communities that have been historically oppressed and take actions that are exclusionary and harmful.*

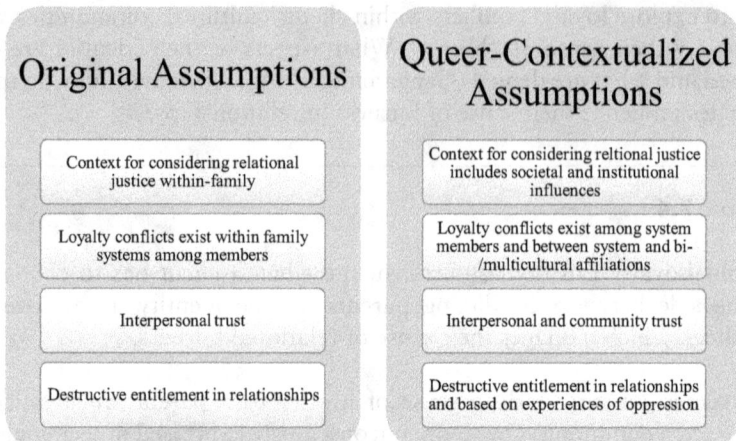

Figure 7.1 Comparison of Assumptions in the Original and the Queer-Contextualized Versions of Contextual Theory.

Figure 7.1 includes a comparison of assumptions of the original theory and the queer-contextualized version. In the final section, we present a case study to consolidate this integration and provide an example of application to practice. To protect confidentiality of client information, the case study presents a combination of work with multiple clients with similar social locations.

"You Are the Only Person in Our Lives Who Truly Sees Us": Queer-Contextualized Contextual Therapy in Practice

Kai and Jane are a queer-identified couple in their mid-30s. Kai is from a mixed cultural heritage with a mother who immigrated from South America. Kai was assigned female at birth and identifies as gender nonbinary using they/them pronouns. Jane's parents immigrated to the United States from Southeast Asia when Jane was five years old. Jane identifies as a cisgender woman and uses she/her pronouns. They started dating about ten years ago and have lived together for about eight years. Both are college-educated and in professional careers, describing their socioeconomic status as middle class.

The couple presented to therapy to explore their next steps in the relationship. They had considered becoming parents at some point but were unsure if that was the right choice for them now. Jane noted that in recent months, she had been experiencing "rage" that manifested as "screaming" and "yelling" in conflicts. Kai has become increasingly concerned that Jane's rage might turn violent, and there was no reported history of partner violence in the current relationship. Jane noted verbal abuse from a partner in a previous relationship, and Kai had been particularly sensitive to people raising their voices and intentionally stayed away from potential partners who did so. Kai was, therefore, shocked when Jane started screaming in conflict. Though Jane would immediately apologize, Kai became less convinced about staying in the relationship after each incident. Following best practices in couples therapy, individual intake sessions were conducted soon after an initial conjoint meeting. The individual sessions aimed to assess for safety and ensure that each partner had access to community resources of support in case the partner relationship became unsafe for either of them. Both appreciated the resources provided, though they were limited for those who identified within the LGBTQ+ communities.

Acknowledging and Crediting

The therapist began with centering their experiences as a queer-identified couple with multiple intersecting identities. In this case, given that both the therapist and the couple were geographically situated in a part of the country that did not have a large community of LGBTQ+ people of color, the therapist intentionally self-disclosed her own social locations in the first conjoint session. Broaching (Watts-Jones, 2010) and self-disclosure of intersectional identities (PettyJohn et al., 2020) can be powerful interventions by themselves and require the therapist's own reflection on what they might be comfortable sharing and why. For therapists who might share similar intersectional identities as clients, it is vital to work through their own loyalty conflicts in disclosing their own identities.

Box 7.5

Broaching The therapist actively includes identity-related factors in the therapeutic process and discusses their impacts on presenting problems and relationship fairness.

For instance, although the therapist had several years of clinical experience, she had only recently been comfortable sharing her social locations with clients. Part of this self-examination was coming to terms with her identity as a member of the LGBTQ+ community and disclosing her identities to her family. The experience of rejection from some family members prompted the therapist to delve deeply into the pain of not being seen and validated for who she was. At the same time, having experienced the joy of being accepted by some of her family and peers, she reflected on her own power in the therapy room, and how she could use it to promote safer spaces in her work for clients to grapple with the complexities of their identities. She decided that to signal this intention in her practice, she had to describe her work more publicly and situate her social locations. Note that each therapist must decide for themselves how open they would like to be in public domains. Assessing and deciding when and where to express oneself fully must be done thoughtfully with due consideration for one's experiences of safety in self-disclosure (Shipman & Martin, 2019).

Kai and Jane had sought to work with the therapist after reading her online profile, where she had disclosed her social identities. The couple described relief in finding someone who might be attuned to the complexities of intersecting identities in their own lives. This is one of the first points of departure from how contextual therapy was originally written by Boszormenyi-Nagy and Krasner (1986). Acknowledgment and validation, which are the foundations on which further interventions are built, were previously described as something that happens when clients share their experiences, and the therapist uses multidirected partiality to acknowledge and validate without further intensifying loyalty conflicts. However, clients can feel seen and validated even when they see their therapists representing their community's lived experiences. Of course, therapists must practice intentionality in self-disclosure, center their clients' experiences, and exercise caution not to impose their own experiences. Contextual therapy recommends that part of the therapist's own development is to understand, first and foremost, that they are not indispensable in their clients' lives (Boszormenyi-Nagy & Krasner, 1986). For example, a therapist can never replace a client's parents, however strong the therapeutic bond is. We agree and suggest that while a therapist cannot replace a parental figure or a family member, when working with communities that face multiple levels of marginalization, having access to at least one affirming person in their lives can help in validation of their experiences.

Relational Ethics/Balance of Give and Take

From a contextual therapy perspective, the presenting concern of uncertainty in the relationship's future indicates a strain in relational trust and an imbalance in give and take. The therapist explored the balance of giving and receiving in their relational contexts using their presenting concern as a starting point. Additionally, as described earlier, given the knowledge of experiences of minority stress, and based on the assumption that relational processes of justice are influenced by larger societal processes of justice, the therapist included not just the context of their relational networks (that is, partner relationship, family-of-origin relationships, peer relationships), but expanded the lens to include larger systemic factors. The therapist asked, for instance – "I am curious about your experiences of living where you are as a queer-identified, inter-racial couple. What's it like in your current neighborhood and city?". Kai said that they were always aware of how others responded to them. Their experiences of growing up in a mixed-race household as a nonbinary person made them vigilant of unwelcoming or unsafe spaces. This sense of "being on edge" did not change when they moved to their current city. Jane reflected that while she grew up in a neighborhood that was home to many immigrants from Southeast Asia, she experienced tension between feeling at home with her ethnic and cultural identity and a sense of discomfort with not being able to express her queer identity openly. There were shifts in these experiences as she moved across the country before moving to the current city, but she noted never feeling entirely at home anywhere.

As they each reflected on their individual experiences, the therapist inquired about their experiences as a couple in their neighborhood. Both Kai and Jane paused before responding that while the neighborhood itself was welcoming, they often felt "tokenized." Asked to expand on this, they noted how their neighbors had made comments such as "they were glad that people like Kai and Jane had made their home in this neighborhood" almost as a reflection of how "progressive" their neighborhood now was. While there were others from the LGBTQ+ community, Kai and Jane were the only queer people of color in that area. The therapist further deepened this conversation by prompting them to talk about the impact of these experiences on them. With the therapist's help, they recognized some comments made by their neighbors as microaggressions (Nadal et al., 2010). The therapist noted the incredible, sometimes invisible burden of recognizing and deciphering microaggressions and everyday acts of discrimination (Frost et al., 2017; Mendoza-Perez & Ortiz-Hernandez, 2021) and acknowledged the toll microaggressions must take on them. Jane said,

Now that I think of it this way, it makes more sense... I don't often talk about this with Kai because I know they experience overt hostility sometimes because of how others see their gender... and I don't want to add to it. Sometimes I think what I experience is no big deal. The other day, I overheard our neighbors make a joke about hiring an immigrant to do their yardwork because they would do it for pennies... I was shocked to hear it but brushed it off.

Kai was surprised to hear this. They said, "I wish you had talked to me about that…" This allowed the therapist to conceptualize the balance of give and take in their relationship while accounting for the invisible burdens of their interpersonal experiences of discrimination, invalidation, or not being seen by others in the community. This is an example of the expansion of context in the development of imbalanced relationships when we center queer, intersectional experiences.

This interaction in the session allowed the therapist to hypothesize and connect one of the presenting concerns of Jane's rage to the balance in the couple's relationship. Could her rage indicate building resentment around her own struggles with race and discrimination and not being seen? (Later, Jane would say how suffocated she felt and often imagined punching the sky to get out of wherever she was. The rageful screaming was cathartic for her because she felt that at least then someone would hear her. However, this came at a cost to their relationship.) By not sharing her struggles, was she replicating a pattern in her interpersonal relationship that originated in her family of origin (an indication of invisible loyalty)? Furthermore, what about Kai's own experiences made it possible for them to not connect with Jane's struggles? Could this be an indication of destructive entitlement where experiences of injustice in one's life, when unacknowledged, make it difficult to see another's pain?

The therapist asked about their experiences of not being seen, and other acts of discrimination at their places of work and in their families of origin. Both described being careful about what they shared about themselves at work. Kai had one coworker who was a "safe" person that they could discuss challenges with. Jane worked from home and had limited in-person interactions with her colleagues. She said it worked to her advantage because it was one less thing to worry about navigating. The therapist noted how the couple had to navigate not just challenges in the neighborhood and with family members but also every day in their work relationships. This acknowledgment further allowed the couple to see what else was in their "invisible suitcases" they carried around daily. Drawing from suggestions from the literature that relational microaffirmations are vital buffers against the negative impacts of microaggressions and interpersonal hostility (Coppola et al., 2021; Pulice-Farrow et al., 2019), the therapist encouraged discussions on latent strengths in the relationships – what did they each do that countered the impact of these experiences of discrimination in their everyday lives? Here we use relational resources from an action-oriented stance not only to validate struggles but also to *counter* systemic oppression – this a critical element of the queer-contextualized approach. The therapist asked about their thoughts on how the experiences of injustices outside their relationship were influencing what they did in their relationships. Over time, Kai and Jane became aware of these impacts and were able to move away from conversations that were blaming of self or other, to pausing and considering what else might be going on.

A significant part of helping clients uncover relational resources is examining intergenerational patterns. In discussions on family-of-origin relationships, Kai shared experiences of being rejected by some family members when they disclosed their identities as a young adult in their twenties. Kai had a younger sibling with whom they were once close but now were not. Kai noted that their mother was their primary source of support, who privately acknowledged their gender identity and respected their pronouns but did not actively correct others who misgendered them. Kai's father chose not to engage in a discussion or acknowledge Kai's gender identity. Jane also discussed receiving some support from her parents. Jane had disclosed her sexual identity to her parents when she and Kai had decided to live together. Jane noted that while they never explicitly talked about her experience of being queer, she said they welcomed her and Kai to their home whenever they visited. However, she was also aware that her parents did not mention her relationship with her extended family members back in her parents' native country.

As the therapist asked about the couple's family of origin, she also continued the *expansion of context*, asking about Kai and Jane's family experiences with race, gender, and immigration. Therapists' acknowledgment of, for instance, differences in cultural norms around gender, gender roles, and expression, the prevailing protections or lack of protections for people with minoritized racial identities allows for understanding individual responses in relationships. Tools for intergenerational exploration, such as the cultural genogram (Hardy & Laszloffy, 1995) and critical genogram (Kosutic et al., 2009), can help provide structure for this exploration. In addition, given family experiences of immigration in both partners, queer-contextualized contextual therapists can include additional questions to explore their parents' transnational experiences (Falicov, 2007).

Jane noted that her parents were still in contact with some of their extended family and visited them once every two or three years. Jane travelled with them until she came out to her parents as queer. She remarked that while this was not openly discussed, she inferred that her parents were more comfortable when they did not have to discuss Jane's relationship status with their extended family members in her presence. The therapist inquired about what it was like for queer-identified people in her parents' home country. This opened a discussion on different ways in which people choose to self-disclose or not in different contexts, prompting an acknowledgment that the Western-centric models of coming out often miss these cultural nuances. This also allowed for therapeutic conversations to include differences in acceptance of nonbinary expressions of gender identities. Kai was curious to learn more about what it might have been like in their mother's home country in South America.

While Jane's parents' experiences of immigration had been salient in her upbringing, Kai's mother's experiences were not discussed openly. Drawing from discussions in therapy, Kai was able to engage in a conversation with their mother about her own experiences. It took some time, but Kai was surprised and later proud to hear that their mother had fled an abusive relationship in her home country. She did not want her past to affect her children's lives and had not shared this with them. As Kai was processing what they had learned from their mother, they realized the burden that their mother had been carrying around, and how even though their mother had been strong enough to start a different life in a new country, her struggles as an immigrant woman of color may have depleted her as well. Was this why Kai's mother did not take more of an advocate role as Kai had hoped?

Rejunction and Uncovering Relational Resources

In all these conversations, the therapist worked using multidirected partiality, a major technique in contextual therapy. Here the therapist is not neutral, but sides with each person while not colluding against someone else. This allows clients to explore loyalty and loyalty conflicts and validate their own experiences while creating room for them to arrive at a place of dialogue without the pull of burdens from the "invisible suitcases" being carried around. As insight developed through therapeutic conversations, the therapist prompted both Kai and Jane to examine what they might do differently to better access their relational resources to allow them to rebuild a more balanced relationship. By centering their queer and intersectional experiences, discussions on how LBGTQ+ communities, and specifically LGBTQ+ communities of color, form "family" and "community" allowed the couple to explore these options more freely. It was essential to acknowledge that wanting to build a family of choice was a way of building relational resources, an act of resistance, and not disloyalty to their families-of-origin. This is another example of defining "family" and "community" from an inclusive lens, while allowing for the complexities of how these redefinitions impact loyalty conflicts. This was crystallized when Jane said she often heard from her parents that they could not trust anyone but themselves as they rebuilt their lives in the United States. She had inadvertently internalized this message and had not ventured to explore other friendships. The therapist noted how systemic challenges of injustice could be so overwhelming that sometimes you do need an army of allies to counter them. Toward the end of the sessions, Kai acknowledged the therapist's role by saying, "you were the only person in our lives who truly saw us." Queer-contextualized contextual therapy had provided a space for the couple to experience being seen and imagine a different world for themselves.

Next Steps for the Queer-Contextualized Contextual Therapist

We have expanded contextual theory with the integration of minority stress and intersectionality frameworks to acknowledge systemic injustice while building relational resources to counter them intentionally and actively. We acknowledge that there is room for further expansion. Boszormenyi-Nagy and others discuss the therapist's self-work as crucial in making space for the development of a multilateral stance, rejunction, and relational accountability in clients' lives. We propose that the therapist's role in limiting the perpetuation of relational injustice cannot be contained in the therapist's office. A queer-contextualized contextual therapist collaborates with community agencies serving the needs of LGBTQ+ people (especially those with multiple intersecting identities) to colocate services, builds bridges between community leaders and providers, and advocates on behalf of clients at the social-institutional level. These are highlighted in Figure 7.2.

Conclusion

In this chapter, we centered queer experiences and lives to critically expand the contexts in which we conceptualize and work toward healing relationships and alleviating distress. We invite you, the reader, to reflect on the themes and issues raised here as a beginning work to better align our theory of change with both our own and our clients' lived experiences. We acknowledge that the expansion to considering systemic injustices and including community relational resources in healing may seem daunting at first. However, if we do not, we as therapists run the risk of alienating our queer clients and further perpetrating injustice in clinical spaces.

What does a queer-centered contextual therapist do to promote justice and equity in LGBTQ+ and ethno-racially minoritized communities?

What does relational accountability look like at the institutional level?

What does multidirected partiality look like in a conversation about race and racism?

What steps can be taken to build and repair trust within queer and/or racialized communities where LGBTQ+ people with intersecting identities may have experienced injustice?

What does a queer- centered contextual therapist do to promote LGBTQ+ identities in agencies serving racially minoritized communities?

Figure 7.2 Questions for Reflection.

Note

1 Details drawn from multiple cases to protect confidentiality.

References

Allen, S. H., & Leslie, L. A. (2020). Considering queer heterogeneity: Do immigrant Latinx sexual and gender minorities have poorer health outcomes than their U.S.-born counterparts? *Journal of Gay & Lesbian Social Services*, 32(4), 479–501. https://doi.org/10.1080/10538720.2020.1762821

Almeida, R. V., Dressner, L., & Tolliver, W. (2017). Decolonizing couples and family therapy: Social justice praxis in liberatory healing community practice. In J. Lebow, A. Chambers, & D. Breunlin (Eds.), *Encyclopedia of couple and family therapy*, 10, 978–3. Springer International Publishing.

Anthias, F. (2012). Transnational mobilities, migration research and intersectionality. *Nordic Journal of Migration Research*, 2(2), 102–110. http://dx.doi.org/10.2478/v10202-011-0032-y

Bauerband, L. A., Teti, M., & Velicer, W. F. (2019). Measuring minority stress: Invariance of a discrimination and vigilance scale across transgender and cisgender LGBQ individuals. *Psychology & Sexuality*, 10(1), 17–30. https://doi.org/10.1080/19419899.2018.1520143

Belous, C. K. (2015). Couple therapy with lesbian partners using an affirmative-contextual approach. *The American Journal of Family Therapy*, 43(3), 269–281. https://doi.org/10.1080/01926187.2015.1012234

Boszormenyi-Nagy, I., & Krasner, B. R. (1986). *Between give and take: A clinical guide to contextual therapy*. Brunner/Mazel.

Brooks V.R. (1981). *Minority Stress and Lesbian Women.* Lexington, MA: Lexington Books.

Coppola, J., Gangamma, R., & Hartwell, E. (2021). "We're just two people in a relationship": A qualitative exploration of emotional bond and fairness experiences between transgender women and their cisgender partners. *Journal of Marital and Family Therapy, 47*(3), 648–663. https://doi.org/10.1111/jmft.12467

Crenshaw, K. (1991). Mapping the margins: Intersectionality, identity politics, and violence against women of color. *Stanford Law Review, 43*(6), 1241. https://doi.org/10.2307/1229039

Cyrus, K. (2017). Multiple minorities as multiply marginalized: Applying the minority stress theory to LGBTQ people of color. *Journal of Gay & Lesbian Mental Health, 21*(3), 194–202. https://doi.org/10.1080/19359705.2017.1320739

Dankoski, M. E., & Deacon, S. A. (2000). Using a feminist lens in contextual therapy. *Family Process, 39*(1), 51–66. https://doi.org/10.1111/j.1545-5300.2000.39107.x

Ducommun-Nagy, C. (2002). *Contextual Therapy.* In F. W. Kaslow, J. J. Magnavita, T. Patterson, R. F. Massey, S. D. Massey, & J. Lebow (Eds.), *Comprehensive handbook of psychotherapy Vol. III* (pp. 463–487). Wiley.

Falicov, C. J. (2005). Emotional transnationalism and family identities. *Family Process, 44*(4), 399–406. https://doi.org/10.1111/j.1545-5300.2005.00068.x

Falicov, C. J. (2007). Working with transnational immigrants: Expanding meanings of family, community, and culture. *Family Process, 46*(2), 157–171. https://doi.org/10.1111/j.1545-5300.2007.00201.x

Friedman, M. (1989). Martin Buber and Ivan Boszormenyi-Nagy: The role of dialogue in contextual therapy. *Psychotherapy: Theory, Research, Practice, Training, 26*(3), 402–409. https://doi.org/10.1037/h0085452

Frost, D. M., LeBlanc, A. J., de Vries, B., Alston-Stepnitz, E., Stephenson, R., & Woodyatt, C. (2017). Couple-level minority stress: An examination of same-sex couples' unique experiences. *Journal of Health and Social Behavior, 58*(4), 455–472. https://doi.org/10.1177/0022146517736754

Gangamma, R. (2018). A phenomenological study of family experiences of resettled Iraqi refugees. *Journal of Marital and Family Therapy, 44*(2), 323–335. https://doi.org/10.1111/jmft.12251

Gangamma, R., & Shipman, D. (2018). Transnational intersectionality in family therapy with resettled refugees. *Journal of Marital and Family Therapy, 44*(2), 206–219. https://doi.org/10.1111/jmft.12267

Glebova, T., & Gangamma, R. (2017). Contextual family therapy. In J. Carlson & S. B. Dermer (Eds.), *The SAGE encyclopedia of marriage, family, and couples counseling.* SAGE Publications, Inc. https://doi.org/10.4135/9781483369532.n110

Goff, J. F. L. (2001). Fundamentals of theory and practice revisited: Boszormenyi-Nagy and Contextual Therapy: An overview. *Australian and New Zealand Journal of Family Therapy, 22*(3), 147–157. https://doi.org/10.1002/j.1467-8438.2001.tb00469.x

Grunebaum, J. (1990). From discourse to dialogue. In R. Chasin, H. Grunebaum, & M. Herzig (Eds.), *One couple, four realities: Multiple perspectives on couple therapy* (pp. 191–228). Guilford Press.

Hardy, K. V., & Laszloffy, T. A. (1995). The cultural genogram: Key to training culturally competent family therapists. *Journal of Marital and Family Therapy, 21*(3), 227–237. https://doi.org/10.1111/j.1752-0606.1995.tb00158.x

Hargrave, T. D., & Pfitzer, F. (2003). *The new contextual therapy: Guiding the power of give and take.* Brunner-Routledge.

Heiden-Rootes, K. M. (2013). Wanted fathers: Understanding gay father families through contextual family therapy. *Journal of GLBT Family Studies, 9(1),* 43–64. https://doi.org/10.1080/1550428X.2013.746055

Hendricks, M. L., & Testa, R. J. (2012). A conceptual framework for clinical work with transgender and gender nonconforming clients: An adaptation of the minority stress model. *Professional psychology: Research and practice, 43*(5), 460–467. https://doi.org/10.1037/a0029597

Kavanaugh, S. A., Taylor, A. B., Stuhlsatz, G. L., Neppl, T. K., & Lohman, B. J. (2020). Family and community support among sexual minorities of color: The role of sexual minority identity prominence and outness on psychological well-being. *Journal of GLBT Family Studies, 16*(1), 1–17. https://doi.org/10.1080/1550428X.2019.1593279

Kerr, M. E., & Bowen, M. (1988). *Family evaluation: An approach based on Bowen theory* (1st ed). Norton.

Kosutic, I., Garcia, M., Graves, T., Barnett, F., Hall, J., Haley, E., Rock, J., Bathon, A., & Kaiser, B. (2009). The critical genogram: A tool for promoting critical consciousness. *Journal of Feminist Family Therapy, 21*(3), 151–176. https://doi.org/10.1080/08952830903079037

McDowell, T., Knudson-Martin, C., & Bermudez, J. M. (2019). Third-order thinking in family therapy: Addressing social justice across family therapy practice. *Family Process, 58*(1), 9–22. https://doi.org/10.1111/famp.12383

Mendoza-Perez, J. C., & Ortiz-Hernandez, L. (2021). Association between overt and subtle experiences of discrimination and violence and mental health in homosexual and bisexual men in Mexico. *Journal of Interpersonal Violence, 36*(23–24), NP12686–NP12707. https://doi.org/10.1177/0886260519898423

Meyer, I. H. (2003). Prejudice, social stress, and mental health in lesbian, gay, and bisexual populations: Conceptual issues and research evidence. *Psychological Bulletin, 129*(5), 674–697. https://doi.org/10.1037/0033-2909.129.5.674

Nadal, K. L. (2019). A decade of microaggression research and LGBTQ communities: An introduction to the Special Issue. *Journal of Homosexuality, 66*(10), 1309–1316. https://doi.org/10.1080/00918369.2018.1539582

Nadal, K. L., Rivera, D. P., & Corpus, M. J. (2010). Sexual orientation and transgender microaggressions in everyday life: Implications for mental health and counseling. In D. W. Sue (Ed.), *Microaggressions and marginality: Manifestation, dynamics, and impact,* (pp. 217–240). Wiley

Nadal, K. L., Skolnik, A., & Wong, Y. (2012). Interpersonal and systemic microaggressions toward transgender people: Implications for counseling. *Journal of LGBT Issues in Counseling, 6*(1), 55–82. https://doi.org/10.1080/15538605.2012.648583

Ocampo, A. C., & Soodjinda, D. (2016). Invisible Asian Americans: The intersection of sexuality, race, and education among gay Asian Americans. *Race*

Ethnicity and Education, *19*(3), 480–499. https://doi.org/10.1080/13613 324.2015.1095169

PettyJohn, M. E., Tseng, C., & Blow, A. J. (2020). Therapeutic utility of discussing therapist/client intersectionality in treatment: When and how? *Family Process*, *59*(2), 313–327. https://doi.org/10.1111/famp.12471

Pulice-Farrow, L., Bravo, A., & Galupo, M. P. (2019). "Your gender is valid": Microaffirmations in the romantic relationships of transgender individuals. *Journal of LGBT Issues in Counseling*, *13*(1), 45–66. https://doi.org/10.1080/15538605.2019.1565799

Ramirez, J. L., & Paz Galupo, M. (2019). Multiple minority stress: The role of proximal and distal stress on mental health outcomes among lesbian, gay, and bisexual people of color. *Journal of Gay & Lesbian Mental Health*, *23*(2), 145–167. https://doi.org/10.1080/19359705.2019.1568946

Sadika, B., Wiebe, E., Morrison, M. A., & Morrison, T. G. (2020). Intersectional microaggressions and social support for LGBTQ persons of color: A systematic review of the Canadian-based empirical literature. *Journal of GLBT Family Studies*, *16*(2), 111–147. https://doi.org/10.1080/1550428X.2020.1724125

Satir, V., & Baldwin, M. (1983). *Satir step by step: A guide to creating change in families*. Science and Behavior Books.

Shipman, D., & Martin, T. (2019). Clinical and supervisory considerations for transgender therapists: Implications for working with clients. *Journal of Marital and Family Therapy*, *45*(1), 92–105. https://doi.org/10.1111/jmft.12300

Valentine, S. E., & Shipherd, J. C. (2018). A systematic review of social stress and mental health among transgender and gender non-conforming people in the United States. *Clinical Psychology Review*, *66*, 24–38. https://doi.org/10.1016/j.cpr.2018.03.003

Watts-Jones, T. D. (2010). Location of self: Opening the door to dialogue on intersectionality in the therapy process. *Family Process*, *49*(3), 405–420. https://doi.org/10.1111/j.1545-5300.2010.01330.x

Chapter 8

Queer-Contextualized Gottman Method Couple Therapy

Sheila M. Addison and Christopher K. Belous

In the world of relationship therapy, there is a common approach to LGBTQ+ relationships that we call "just file the pronouns off." Pointing out cis/hetero/mononormativity is met with responses like, *"just ignore names in the case examples," "skip over the gendered parts," "take what works and leave the rest,"* or the assertion *"this is applicable to all couples!"* which is rarely backed up with evidence. We wonder how often cishet people are given advice based on LGBTQ+ experiences and expected to file the pronouns off and assume it applies to them.[1] Even today, relational resources are centered on cishet clients. LGBTQ+ people and their therapists are still expected to engage in a kind of personal fanfic: writing ourselves into texts that make no effort to include us.

LGBTQ+ people expect this treatment and are extremely skilled at looking for clues to hostility or inclusivity. Clients are often skeptical of Gottman Method Couple Therapy (GMCT) and wonder if the therapy is religiously based or queer-antagonistic. Some have encountered religiously based counselors who apply GMCT (accurately or not) in ways that reinforce patriarchy, traditional gender roles, or heterocentrism. In order to navigate a heteronormative, cisnormative (and racist, sexist, ableist, etc.) world, LGBTQ+ people learn to read the room – to interpret overt and covert messages about who is centered, who is welcomed, and who is excluded (Oswald & Adams, 2023). We see this as an adaptive technique, necessary for surviving and thriving at the margins.

In practice, we have found that GMCT is more accommodating than it might appear. The model's views on healthy relationships are supported by research that includes evidence of applicability to same-gender couples (e.g., Garanzini et al., 2017; Gottman, 1989, 2002; Gottman et al., 2003a, 2003b, 2019). Unfortunately, many of its assessment tools (see Table 8.1) require adaptation or explanation to LGBTQ+ and nonmonogamous clients. However, its techniques (see Table 8.2) are sufficiently flexible and process-oriented such that an LGBTQ+ affirming clinician can practice a queer-contextualized version of GMCT with confidence.

DOI: 10.4324/9781003308188-8

A Survey of Gottman Method Couple Therapy

GMCT emerged from decades of process and outcome research on non-clinical couples (Gottman, 1999). The Gottman Love Lab interviewed couples in the office but also filmed couples overnight in mock apartments in order to understand dyadic interactions. Their analyses identified patterns separating the **masters** from the **disasters** of marriage and partnership (Gottman, 2011) – those who had happy, long-lasting relationships versus those that broke up or unhappily coexisted. These patterns led to the development of a model of healthy relationships, the **Sound Relationship House** (SRH). The SRH uses the visual metaphor of a house with seven levels, shored up on either side by walls of trust, the degree to which each partner believes the other will put the mutual good of the relationship before their own self-interest (Gottman, 2011), and commitment, the degree to which each partner believes that staying in the relationship provides a better option than exiting it (Gottman & Gottman, 2018).

Box 8.1

Masters Those couples who have long-lasting, happy, and satisfied relationships.

Disasters Those couples who experience dissatisfaction, destructive conflict, and either end the relationship or remain together unhappily.

Sound Relationship House A visual metaphor incorporating concepts from Gottman Method Couples Therapy's description of healthy couples. The house has seven levels, with two outside walls, a roof, and a chimney. The seven levels align with the seven key elements of successful couple relationships, and the two outside walls are two additional elements, trust and commitment.

The Seven Levels of the Sound Relationship House

The Foundational Friendship

The first four levels are an essential foundation for a thriving relationship; the adage "marry your best friend" appears to have truth to it. The interventions for this domain are focused on enhancing friendship, improving connection between partners, and encouraging attunement and responsiveness. This creates a reservoir of good feelings within the relationship, which aids the couple when dealing with conflict.

Love Maps. Developing intimacy with a partner includes getting to know their internal world – their likes and dislikes, stories from their past, their sensitive or tender areas such as past hurts or traumas. But these love maps can get outdated, and as a relationship matures, the challenges of daily life can take precedence over continuing to approach one another with curiosity and interest. Refreshing and deepening love maps can happen during everyday conversations or as part of regular Rituals of Connection by asking questions whether mundane (such as a partner's favorite movie) or serious (such as discussing a memory of feeling unloved).

Fondness and Admiration. As relationships become more settled, partners often stop verbalizing their affection for one another. Couples who have happy relationships frequently appreciate one another's good qualities and kind acts, while resisting the temptation of brusqueness and complaints. Partners can incorporate appreciations into a Ritual of Connection, or share them spontaneously in the moment.

Bids and Turns. Gottman and Silver (2015) described the bid for connection as a kind of reach toward the other partner. Regardless of the significance of the bid – asking "are we out of coffee?" or initiating sex – the other can respond by turning toward (acknowledging the bid in an open and curious way, even if the answer is "no"), turning away (passively deflecting the bid through inattention or nonengagement), or turning against (responding with harshness, contempt, or other negativity).

Turns toward one another act as a deposit into a reserve of goodwill that supports the relationship when conflict inevitably arises. Conversely, turns away or against one another subtract from that reserve and weaken a couple's ability to manage conflict effectively. This resource is regularly topped off in healthy relationships, which on average have five small positive interactions (e.g., a turn toward a bid for connection) for every negative (e.g., a turn away or against), creating a surplus to draw on when there is friction.

The Positive Perspective. Partners' perception of the relationship, or its emotional valence, is largely a gestalt of the first three levels. In my (SA) practice, I call this "the rose-colored glasses vs. the poo-colored glasses."

If a client is "wearing the rose-colored glasses," even a seemingly negative event like a harsh interaction can be received with curiosity and concern for their partner. But when "wearing the poo-colored glasses," even an apparently positive incident, like an unexpected gift, may be viewed with suspicion, even hostility.

The Conflict at the Center

Manage Conflict. Most couples seek out therapy because of chronic, unresolved conflict, which GMCT calls **gridlock**. Research suggests about two-thirds of these issues are perpetual problems – issues of preference, values, or style that are not amenable to a permanent compromise of some kind (Gottman, 1999). Moving into dialogue with these problems requires skills for handling conflict productively, rather than escalation or avoidance.

Box 8.2

Gridlock A dysfunctional kind of ongoing conflict in which repeated attempts to solve the problem fail to provide improvement or resolution, and instead each partner becomes more entrenched in defending their own position. Neither partner can compromise or let the issue go, and neither feels that their perspective is understood by the other. There is usually a deeply held symbolic life dream, goal, or identity piece underneath the content of the conflict, which may not be easily apparent to either partner.

Process research shows that the early exchanges at the start of a conflict strongly predict the rest of the interaction (Gottman, 1999; Gottman & Gottman, 2018). Identifiable behavior patterns, colloquially known as **The Four Horsemen of the Apocalypse** (4H), are signs of trouble on the horizon: criticism, defensiveness, contempt, and stonewalling. Happy couples sometimes display criticism, defensiveness, and stonewalling, but they very rarely show contempt for one another and can successfully repair after a troubled exchange. Struggling couples often appear like an inexperienced driver who doesn't know how to stop a skid, piling mistake on mistake until they crash through the guardrails; their conflict ends with explosions, an abrupt cutoff, or some other disaster.

Box 8.3

The Four Horsemen of the Apocalypse Behaviors which tend to predict and escalate unproductive conflict as observed in the relationship "Disasters" observed in the Gottmans' research: Criticism (finding fault with the other partner and laying blame on them), contempt (behaviors such as ridicule, dismissiveness, sarcasm, mocking, and hostility), defensiveness (e.g., justifying one's behavior, making excuses, playing the victim, turning and attacking), and stonewalling (e.g., numbing out, ignoring the other partner, shutting down, suddenly withdrawing). Contempt is strongly correlated with the eventual decision to separate or divorce.

GMCT offers antidotes or skills for countering each Horseman. The antidote to criticism is gentle start-up, a complaint or need expressed by describing one's own feelings and thoughts, rather than labeling one's partner or resorting to accusations and attacks. Defensiveness can be countered by taking responsibility for some part of the problem before describing one's own position, or validating some part of the other partner's perspective. Stonewalling, a sign of flooding with strong emotion, can be addressed via self-soothing or coregulation: for example, taking a break and using relaxation or self-coaching techniques to address the physiological "fight, flight, or freeze" response to a perceived threat. Contempt can be avoided in the short term by remembering to "keep it in your skin"[2] – describe one's own feelings, perceptions, and needs – and in the longer term by building a kind, gentle, relational friendship. This also helps partners accept influence from one another rather than becoming increasingly polarized.

The Attic of Aspirations

Making Life Dreams Come True. TGI's research suggests that perpetual problems are typically attached to some sort of life dream for one or both partners – a vision for the future that they want to create, recreate, or avoid recreating in their adult life. A relationship in which one partner gives up their life dreams for the sake of harmony is unlikely to be remain fulfilling in the long term.

Shared Meaning. This level houses the symbols, rituals, roles, and goals that answer questions like "who are we together?" "what are we trying to create?" and "how do we honor what we are creating?" Lasting relationships have a robust "culture of us" that is unique to them and is reinforced by regularly referencing that culture: observing significant dates, displaying favorite photos, even using pet names or inside jokes with one another.

The Process of Gottman Method Couples Therapy

The goal of GMCT is to help distressed couples interact more like the masters of relationships. The approach integrates behavioral elements like structured conversations and replacing the 4H with their antidotes, but also emphasizes fostering an emotionally intimate context during therapy sessions. GMCT clinicians direct the couple into dyadic enactments while the therapist coaches from the sidelines, prompting the clients to name and experience feelings while also experiencing empathy for their partner. This emphasis on vulnerable, direct emotional contact is common to other approaches, such as Emotionally Focused Therapy (Johnson, 2004) and Integrative Behavioral Couple Therapy (Christensen, Dimidjian, & Martell, 2015), and is a key change mechanism in GMCT.

GMCT is an assessment-heavy approach, relying on oral and written, conjoint and individual methods to develop a clinical picture of the couple. Therapy begins with several assessment meetings, one with the couple and one with each individual. Clients fill out multiple questionnaires, either on paper or online, and information from the in-session and out-of-session assessments is synthesized by the therapist into a feedback session where they introduce the SRH, identify the couple's strengths and growth edges using the SRH model, and incorporate the couple's responses into a look ahead at how therapy can help them toward their goals.

Once therapy begins, interventions are largely driven by the couple. GMCT focuses on helping clients to slow down their interactions and take a more curious, open approach to one another; the Level 1 training handbook describes taking a "what is this?" attitude when encountering difficulty or novelty, rather than the "what the HELL is this!" reaction (as if to a perceived threat). Behavioral interventions integrate accessing deeper emotions and are anchored in the love and friendship underpinning the relationship. GMCT does incorporate elements of psychoeducation in early sessions as clients are oriented to structured interventions and the research behind them. The dyadic focus of sessions, by keeping the couple in interactions similar to those they might have at home rather than reporting out to the therapist, offers opportunities for state-dependent learning as clients immediately practice new skills when they experience distress or get stuck in unhelpful patterns.

GMCT therapists act as process coaches and use a warm, attuned, humanistic-experiential stance to keep clients in dyadic interactions while supporting them in changing how they approach one another. At times the therapist offers emotion coaching or feelings-based reframes that are similar to the empathic conjecture intervention from Emotionally Focused Couples Therapy (Johnson, 2004).

Queer-Contextualized Gottman Method Couple Therapy

Even though many of the changes needed to make GMCT truly inclusive of LGBTQ+ clients would need to come directly from TGI due to the top-down nature of certification and training, clinicians working with LGBTQ+ clients can take steps to queer-contextualize GMCT in their own practice. Some of these adaptations may take the form of content warnings or advance apologies[3] – preparing clients for the microaggressions and microinvalidations they will encounter in the assessments and the self-help materials meant to supplement therapy. Clinicians working with LGBTQ+ couples under the heteronormative constraints of the marriage-industrial complex have given such disclaimers for decades, but it can be critical for marginalized clients to know that their therapist recognizes that a recommended resource may be a poor fit.

Assessment in Queer-Contextualized Gottman Method Couples Therapy

Another way of queer-contextualizing GMCT involves adapting its materials for different clients. TGI has encouraged clinicians to adopt the online version of its assessment battery via the Gottman Connect website, but some LGBTQ+ clients (and those in CNM relationships, queer or otherwise) may have a better experience using paper or pdf versions of the assessments instead. Nearly all relational assessments were developed for dyadic heterosexual cisgender relationships, but at a minimum, paper assessments allow clients to write notes in the margins, create their own responses when a yes/no or Likert scale response feels inadequate, and otherwise personalize their responses in a way that is not possible with an online tool. The technology-savvy therapist could potentially create new electronic versions of forms to provide more flexibility though they would still lack the scoring features of Gottman Connect. We recommend that any therapist using GMCT with LGBTQ+ clients and nonmonogamous relationships be extremely familiar with both the paper and online versions of the assessment battery, and carefully consider how they might compensate for its existing shortcomings. Table 8.1 describes the assessments required for GMCT, their purpose, their limitations, and suggestions for revision or alternate tools for use in queer-contextualized therapy.

The Queer-Contextualized Sound Relationship House

The iconic image of the SRH, a multilevel home with walls of trust and commitment and a decorative chimney, remains the basis for our queer-contextualized version. When placed in a queer context, however, the house requires some small renovations. Since GMCT began as an attempt to understand the dyadic processes that support successful marriages, it makes sense that the original theorist focused on the inside of the house for their metaphor. We suggest it is necessary for a queer-contextualized perspective to also look out the windows and into the yard to think about the social and political context of relationships. Our queer-contextualized SRH (QC-SRH) includes the concepts of openness or contact with the world outside the relationship (the door of the house), resilience in the face of devaluation and oppression (the tree shading the house), and advocacy for one's community/ies as a source of identity and support (the Progressive Pride flag flying in front of the house). These contextual elements are all associated with improved functioning and satisfaction in the face of minority stress. The QC-SRH also incorporates a smoking chimney as a metaphor for sexual relationships. Although the GMCT assessment packet asks questions about sex, romance, and passion, it is not named as an element of the SRH and does not clearly fit into any one the three existing domains of relational friendship, conflict, or shared meaning.

Openness: The Door that Regulates Contact

Healthy relationships have a flexible but clear boundary around them that regulates contact between the world of the relationship and the larger context of their families and communities. This boundary should be neither too permeable, allowing too much contact and failing to protect the relationship from outside intrusion, nor too rigid, cutting the relationship off from others outside it. Relationships of all kinds present with struggles in this area, such as partners with different ideas about contact or resource-sharing with families of origin, but as LaSala (2013) has noted, rejecting families may present "an obstacle to gay and lesbian happiness" and cutoffs are sometimes necessary for LGBTQ+ people to ensure safety (p. 268). With greater social acceptance, family therapists have learned to help families navigate differences while maintaining their relationships, an outcome associated with better mental health for sexual minority adults (Heiden-Rootes et al., 2019; Ryan et al., 2010).

LGBTQ+ relationships often encounter boundary struggles. For example, they may present with a too-rigid boundary if one or both are reluctant to go public with the relationship or a too-permeable boundary if nonmonogamous partners have conflict over how much time, resources, and information should be shared with others. And yet, cishet relationships sometimes have analogous struggles – whether to be public about a cross-cultural or cross-generational relationship, for example, or how much time, resources, and information to share with friends. LGBTQ+ relationships help highlight the need to create and maintain healthy boundaries. A queer-contextualized version of GMCT could include prompts for building love maps, creating Rituals of Connection, and exploring Dreams Within Conflict that relate to how the partners co-navigate the world outside their relationship house.

Resilience: The Tree that Provides Shade and Stability

Living with prejudice and devaluation sets LGBTQ+ people up for higher rates of poor mental and physical health (Meyer & Frost, 2013), referred to as "minority stress." This stress can be mitigated in part by resiliency, "adaptive functioning in the face of stress" (Meyer, 2015, p. 210). Research suggests "a communal orientation toward stress" encourages people to build and maintain a network of supportive relationships (Afifi et al., 2016, p. 665), which then serves as a buffer against stress and is associated with relational satisfaction and commitment (Haas & Lannutti, 2022; Lev, 2015). Like a tree that both provides shade and holds together the soil, cultivating community resilience provides relief from the weathering elements of the outside world (e.g., racism, heterosexism, transphobia, income inequality, lack of support for families) and assists the relationship house in maintaining a stable foundation.

One factor contributing to resilience in some LGBTQ+ relationships is resistance to the heteronormative model of monogamous marriage, compulsory child-rearing, and the reification of the nuclear family. Addison and Clason (2022) point out that creating relationship structures that work for the participants can be part of "a more radical critique of inequality of all kinds" (p. 316) and in fact can provide additional support for those who live at the margins by widening their networks of intimacy and resources. The spreading roots and branches of the tree represent these multiple connections. Adapting GMCT, a fundamentally dyadic therapy, for triads, quads, and beyond is challenging, but the principles of a fundamental friendship, constructive conflict, and shared meaning are relevant regardless.

In GMCT, this part of the landscape outside the house could be assessed by adapting question 9 of the Oral History Interview (OHI). It currently reads:

Looking back over the years, what moments stand out as the really hard times in your relationship? Why do you think you stayed together? How did you get through these difficult times? What is your philosophy about how to get through difficult times?

An adapted version could read:

Looking back over the years, what moments stand out as the really hard times in your relationship? Who or what has helped you stay together? Do you see your relationship as a particularly resilient one? What is your philosophy about relationships and resilience?

The clinician could encourage clients to fill in their love maps about how their partner experiences connection and resilience, and invite clients to discuss how they might incorporate symbols of resilience into their home and life together.

Community and Advocacy: The Progressive Pride Flag

For many LGBTQ+ people, advocacy and activism are important parts of their identities. The fight for LGBTQ+ civil rights has led to legal and social victories that in turn have supported acceptance of gender and sexual minorities.[4] In the QC-SRH, we want to honor this aspect of LGBTQ+ life and suggest that all kinds of relationships would benefit from a shared commitment to improving the well-being of diverse groups in their communities.

LGBTQ+ relationships are more likely to involve partners from different racial/ethnic backgrounds, socioeconomic groups, and significantly different age brackets (Addison & Coolhart, 2015). The intersection of multiple identities requires exploring how power and privilege influence the relationship. Partners must develop a way to honor their many different identities and influences via life dreams, symbols, rituals, roles, and goals.

Community and advocacy are represented in the QC-SRH by the Progressive Pride Flag, an adaptation of the original gay pride flag created in 1978 by Baker, Segerblom, and McNamara. Developed by Quasar in 2018, the Progressive Pride Flag incorporates the black and brown stripes added to the Philly Pride Flag in 2017 (to draw attention to the issues of LGBTQ+ people of color) and includes the white, pink, and blue stripes of the transgender flag in a chevron. At a time when racial and gender differences are being exploited to try to divide marginalized groups from one another (Grant, 2022), the Progressive Pride Flag represents a commitment to unity and well-being for all of the disparate groups who make up the LGBTQ+ community.

Sex: The Smoking Chimney

The QC-SRH uses the symbol of the smoking chimney to represent the sexual "heat" of a relationship. Sex and sexual issues regularly rank among the most common presenting issues in relational therapy, and for LGBTQ+ clients, a therapist's willingness to discuss sex in a nonanxious, direct, and affirming manner is one way clients evaluate whether a clinician is trustworthy.

Although GMCT assessments ask about sex, the Individual Interview only asks about experiences of sexual violence or abuse, and the OHI does not include a question about when and how the couple introduced sex into their relationship. The Feedback Session also does not prescribe that the therapist shares any concepts or research regarding relational sex; it might be mentioned in passing while identifying gridlocked issues, but it is the only portion of the SRH assessment that is not explicitly represented in the feedback talk or the SRH drawing. It is possible to go through the entire intake process and never have the clinician bring up sex, depriving clients the chance to evaluate the therapist's comfort and knowledge in this area, and depriving the clinician the opportunity to evaluate how the partners discuss this important part of their relationship.

Chimney-related assessments might ask clients when they began to understand their own gender and sexuality, how this fits with the timeline of the relationship, and how the couple has navigated any changes. Individually, it could be helpful to ask questions such as: "What words do you use to talk about your body? Your partner's(') body/ies?" "Do you feel able to ask your partner(s) to adjust their touch or to change activities when you are having sex?" and "What kinds of sexual activities are you hesitant to suggest to your partner(s)?" Feedback should include research on the sexual skills and habits that contribute to successful relationships, and opportunities for the relationship to grow in this area.

Queer-Contextualized Adaptations of GMCT Interventions

In adapting interventions to a queer context, it is tempting to just "file off the pronouns." One strength of GMCT is that its interventions focus largely on dyadic processes, rather than on specific content, and thus are readily adaptable based on clients' concerns. Each level of the SRH model can be addressed with specific GMCT interventions to help strengthen that part of the relationship house. However, the QC-SRH model shows where there are opportunities for expanding the conversation based on a queer-contextualized view of relational health (see Table 8.2).

An Example of Queer-Contextualized Gottman Method Couple Therapy

Just after I (SA) became a Certified Gottman Therapist, I accepted a referral for a client system that made it clear I would have to significantly adapt the tools of GMCT. My new client was a closed triad: two bisexual women and one heterosexual man, all cisgender, all sexually and romantically engaged with one another.[5] The man (Patrick) and the older woman (Sharon) were a married dyad for almost two decades before Sharon began a relationship with a younger woman (Mia). Mia met Patrick and found herself interested in him as well. They eventually formed a household together.

I realized quickly that I would have to go back to using paper versions of the assessments because the Gottman Connect website only accommodated dyads. But the measures themselves were not developed for triadic use, so even giving directions and interpreting scores would require estimation and educated integration. I adapted my "assessment speech" to familiarize the triad with the process, but also to acknowledge the tools' limitations. We discussed options for the relational assessment tools, either answering twice or considering an average answer for both. I decided to ask the clients to complete the measures in whatever way they felt most comfortable and to make notes to let me know how they chose to answer.

Even this adaptation proved inadequate: one responded by filling out the PDFs, one put responses in an Excel spreadsheet, and one typed them out in a Google Doc. Scoring the instruments was more confusing than insightful, so I focused on the relationship processes suggested by the answers. I used the Individual Interviews to clarify responses, then took that information to the feedback session to collaborate with the triad on how to put their answers in the SRH context. This also allowed me to ask questions about elements of the QC-SRH such as the triad's boundary management, resilience, engagement with LGBTQ+ or nonmonogamous communities, and sexual satisfaction or concerns.

Some assessments asked about specific conflicts, such as with extended family, and the clients wrote notes like "which part of the family?" and "right now, or before we all got together?" Of course, there were different "extended families" across the timeline of their different relationships.

Patrick and Sharon had separated from abusive families while still caring for vulnerable family members. Patrick's relatives were skeptical of non-monogamy, but he got respect as a man who could "attract two women." At the same time, Sharon's relatives criticized her for "turning lesbian." Mia hid her relationship with the married couple from her family as she thought they would "accept the gay thing but not the married thing," telling them her older roommates were mentors.

The triad's care for its boundaries showed their skill at managing their openness to the world. Navigating these difficult relationships without resorting to a cutoff is a kind of resilience common to many LGBTQ+ people (Addison & Coolhart, 2015). The clients' struggles with distilling these relationships down to a few yes/no answers on an assessment makes sense, given the complexity of their context.

Looking at their forms spread across my floor, I formed a clinical impression of the triad. The GMCT assessment packet, even if mononormative, did help me estimate how committed they were to each dyad, and to the triad itself. I contextualized the demand-withdraw patterns of the "hard times" in their OHI via comments on the 19 Areas instrument, which identified the gridlocked issue of how "out" to be about the relationship. The SRH tool tracked their overall friendship and their mismatched dreams and goals, while the conflict scales illuminated individual perspectives on their friction. I made informed guesses about the elements unique to the QC-SRH using questions I added to the OHI.

A truly queer-contextualized GMCT would eliminate this extra work, but even with existing limitations, I believe beginning therapy with a comprehensive assessment process is better for clients than jumping into clinical work and then getting bogged down in information-gathering just as clients want to address their clinical goals. I combined the assessment information with my clinical experience to conceptualize the triad using queer-contextualized GMCT. For example, I know that due to heteronormativity, the trio might privilege the mixed-gender relationships at the expense of the women's dyad. Combining that knowledge with the SRH and 19 Areas assessments suggested that Mia tried to preserve harmony by silencing herself when Sharon gave advice about handling Patrick. Mia's silence was perceived as stonewalling, while Sharon's advice landed as criticism. The Detouring Scales suggested Mia and Patrick both felt uncomfortable with strong emotions; this explained the gendered demand-withdraw pattern of Patrick and Sharon and explained how Mia got triangled into the middle, flooded due to Sharon's expressiveness, but protective of her closer relationship with Sharon and reluctant to trust her relationship with Patrick. The SRH model also gave me a way to broach the topic of building a "culture of us" that included all three of them, rather than privileging Patrick and Sharon's existing culture and expecting Mia to adapt. This case illuminated how using queer-contextualized GMCT with the QC-SRH addresses the dynamics of privilege and power that thread their way through every relationship, even cishet monogamous ones.

As we moved into the working phases of therapy, I coached them in dyadic enactments, a cornerstone of the GMCT process, while adapting to the needs of the triad on the fly. Each intervention designed for two was potentially another microaggression, leaving an odd person out no matter how I tried to engage the third person. I knew I needed to cycle through each intervention once or even twice more to let each dyad have a turn, though this pace was frustrating for the clients at times.

Engaging all three while slowing down their cycle of conflict required careful structuring of each intervention. Important strategies included *orchestrating direct connection* and *activating the triad*. The triad tended to sit facing me in a line, which made it hard to help them connect with one another. Meeting via telehealth meant I couldn't reconfigure the seating, so I frequently had to coach dyads to sit face-to-face. We found that dining chairs in a small circle were more practical, if less comfortable, than their couch. My view wasn't always ideal, but their connection was more important. During a dyadic intervention, I coached the third partner to observe the process; otherwise they intellectualized and took sides (triangulation) or checked out. I used names as a cue to focus others' words, to attend to their body language or expression, or to show that I was tracking their perspective as well. The triad slowly explored the benefits of direct communication on their interactions and well-being – particularly increased understanding and empathy – and they began to exhibit signs of improved stability and belongingness. This relational connection had the beneficial effect of pulling the triad together in times of difficulty rather than pushing them apart.

Conclusion

Queer-contextualizing a body of work as long-standing and entrenched in research, pop culture, and the professional zeitgeist as Gottman Method Couples Therapy is challenging, but not impossible. The first major problem was assessment. It quickly became apparent that not only did assessing a triad require substantially more work, but the process increased the clients' anxiety. Second, GMCT interventions need options to include polycules and respond to emerging issues such as gender, power, and nontraditional partnered systems. Third, GMCT acknowledges that clients from devalued identities need therapists who understand their experience, but current trainings offer no examples of this in therapy. The certification process does not assess therapists' ability to address these needs, even though it may be essential to client outcomes. The certification process encouraged deferring to clients' content rather than actively reframing their struggles in terms of social forces. A queer-contextualized GMCT, with the QC-SRH landscape of resilience and advocacy, offers built-in tools to help clients in devalued relationships talk about how their conflict and gridlocked problems are informed by their context. Fourth, TGI as a brand lacks visible LGBTQ+ inclusion. As an affirming clinician, therapists advertise inclusivity, but when incorporating Gottman products into their work, they risk contradicting that message.

One of the ways in which clinicians can work toward being more helpful for their clients is through the use of self-supervision – reflecting on challenging or novel clinical situations and making a plan to increase skills and counteract biases as needed. To help with this growth process, we encourage clinicians to consider the following reflective questions, based on our own clinical experience and informed by the theoretical discussion posed in this chapter.

In what ways do your current paperwork, documentation, environmental, and/or advertising reflect a hetero/mononormative ideal?

●How do your current assessment practices gather information about boundary management, resilience, community/advocacy, and sex?

●What would you do if your clients objected to an assessment or intervention you rely on in your work?

●By what standard(s) do you evaluate relationships as healthy, resilient, and a positive influence on those involved? What values inform that yardstick?

●How do multiple forms of oppression influence the clients in your practice?

●What challenges or frustrations have you anticipated or encountered using GMCT with LGBTQ+ clients? How have you considered addressing these barriers?

When we state that it is unhelpful - and in fact potentially harmful - to simply "file the pronouns off" of hetero/mononormative relationship resources, what reactions do you notice inside yourself?

Figure 8.1 Questions for Reflection.

Notes

1 We don't actually wonder this.
2 Thanks to Carrie Cole for this phrase.
3 One could call these "pre-emptive repairs" as well, just as GMCT encourages couples to use.
4 The irony of writing this at a time of unprecedented efforts to criminalize trans-affirming care and eliminate discussion of LGBTQ+ identities in public life is not lost on us.
5 The case study in this chapter is a composite case study based on several clients.

References

Addison, S. M., & Clason, N. (2022). "I will always come home to you": Affirmative therapy with clients practicing consensual non-monogamy. In R. G. Harvey, M. J. Murphy, J. J. Bigner, & J. L. Wetchler (Eds.), *Handbook of LGBTQ-affirmative couple and family therapy* (pp. 297–323). Routledge, Taylor & Francis Group.

Addison, S. M., & Coolhart, D. (2015). Expanding the therapy paradigm with queer couples: A relational intersectional lens. *Family Process, 54*(3), 435–453. https://doi.org/10.1111/famp.12171

Afifi, T. D., Merrill, A. F., & Davis, S. (2016). The theory of resilience and relational load. *Personal Relationships, 23*(4), 663–683. https://doi.org/10.1111/pere.12159

Belous, C. K., & Wampler, R. S. (2016). Development of the gay and lesbian relationship satisfaction scale. *Journal of Marital and Family Therapy, 42*(3), 451–465. https://doi.org/10.1111/jmft.12158

Buehlman, K. T., Gottman, J. M., & Katz, L. F. (1992). How a couple views their past predicts their future: Predicting divorce from an oral history interview. *Journal of family psychology, 5*(3–4), 295.

Christensen, A., Dimidjian, S., & Martell, C. R. (2015). Integrative behavioral couple therapy. In A. S. Gurman, J. L. Lebow, & D. K. Snyder (Eds.), *Clinical handbook of couple therapy* (pp. 61–96). Guilford Press.

Garanzini, S., Yee, A., Gottman, J., Gottman, J., Cole, C., Preciado, M., & Jasculca, C. (2017). Results of Gottman Method Couples Therapy with gay and lesbian couples. *Journal of Marital and Family Therapy, 43*(4), 674–684. https://doi.org/10.1111/jmft.12276

Gottman, J. M. (1989). Children of gay and lesbian parents. *Marriage & Family Review, 14*(3–4), 177–196. https://doi.org/10.1300/J002v14n03_09

Gottman, J. M. (1999). *The marriage clinic: A scientifically based marital therapy.* Norton.

Gottman, J. M. (2011). *The science of trust: Emotional attunement for couples.* Norton.

Gottman, J. M., Driver, J., Yoshimoto, D., & Rushe, R. (2002). Approaches to the study of power in violent and nonviolent marriages, and in gay male and lesbian cohabiting relationships. In P. Noller & J. A. Feeney (Eds.), *Understanding marriage: Developments in the study of couple interaction.* Cambridge.

Gottman, J. M., & Gottman, J. S. (2018). *The science of couple and family therapy: Behind teh scenes at the love lab*. Norton.

Gottman, J. M., Gottman, J. S., Cole, C., & Preciado, M. (2019). Gay, lesbian, and heterosexual couples about to begin couples therapy: An online relationship assessment of 40,681 couples. *Journal of Marital and Family Therapy, 46*(2), 218–239. https://doi.org/10.1111/jmft.12395

Gottman, J. M., Levenson, R. W., Gross, J., Frederickson, B. L., McCoy, K., Rosenthal, L., Ruef, A., & Yoshimoto, D. (2003a). Correlates of gay and lesbian couples' relationship satisfaction and relationship dissolution. *Journal of Homosexuality, 45*(1), 23–43. https://doi.org/10.1300/J082v45n01_02

Gottman, J. M., Levenson, R. W., Swanson, C., Swanson, K., Tyson, R., Yoshimoto, D. (2003b). Observing gay, lesbian and heterosexual couples' relationships: Mathematical modeling of conflict interaction. *Journal of Homosexuality, 45*(1), 65–91. https://doi.org/10.1300/J082v45n01_04

Gottman, J. M., & Silver, N. (2015). *The seven principles for making marriage work: A practical guide from the country's foremost relationship expert*. Revised edition. Harmony.

Grant, M. G. (2022, February 17). *The groups pushing anti-trans laws want to divide the LGBTQ movement*. The New Republic. https://newrepublic.com/article/165403/groups-pushing-anti-trans-laws-want-divide-lgbtq-movement

Haas, S. M., & Lannutti, P. J. (2022). Relationship maintenance behaviors, resilience, and relational quality in romantic relationships of LGBTQ+ people. *Couple and Family Psychology: Research and Practice, 11*(2), 117–131. https://doi.org/10.1037/cfp0000186

Heiden-Rootes, K., Wiegand, A., & Bono, D. (2019). Sexual minority adults: A national survey on depression, religious fundamentalism, parent relationship quality & acceptance. *Journal of marital and family therapy, 45*(1), 106–119. https://doi.org/10.1111/jmft.12323

Johnson, S. M. (2004). *The practice of emotionally focused couples therapy: Creating connection*. 2nd ed. Routledge.

LaSala, M. C. (2013). Out of the darkness: Three waves of family research and the emergence of family therapy for lesbian and gay people. *Clinical Social Work Journal, 41*(3), 267–276. https://doi.org/10.1007/s10615-012-0434-x.

Lev, A. I. (2015). Resilience in lesbian and gay couples. In K. Skerrett & K. Fergus (Eds), *Couple resilience*. Dordrecht: Springer. https://doi.org/10.1007/978-94-017-9909-6_3

Mastroianni, B. (2022, June 21). How mindfulness can support the transgender experience. *Healthline*. www.healthline.com/health/mind-body/embracing-the-trans-and-non-binary-body-through-mindfulness.

Meyer, I. H. (2015). Resilience in the study of minority stress and health of sexual and gender minorities. *Psychology of Sexual Orientation and Gender Diversity, 2*(3), 209–213. https://doi.org/10.1037/sgd0000132

Meyer, I. H., & Frost, D. M. (2013). Minority stress and the health of sexual minorities. In C. J. Patterson & A. R. D'Augelli (Eds.), *Handbook of psychology and sexual orientation* (pp. 252–266). New York, NY: Oxford University Press.

Oswald, F., & Adams, R. B. (2023). Feminist social vision: Seeing through the lens of marginalized perceivers. *Personality and Social Psychology Review*, 27(3), 332–356. https://doi.org/10.1177/10888683221126582

Ryan, C., Russell, S., Huebner, D., Diaz, R., & Sanchez, J. (2010). Family acceptance in adolescence and the health of LGBT young adults. *Journal of Child and Adolescent Psychiatric Nursing*, 23(4), 205–213. https://doi.org/10.1111/j.1744-6171.2010.00246.x

Chapter 9

Queer-Contextualized Solution-Focused Brief Family Therapy

Benjamin T. Finlayson and Sara Smock Jordan

Overview of Solution-Focused Brief Therapy

Solution-focused brief therapy (SFBT) is future-focused, goal-directed, and requires the therapist attend to the client's words for solutions (de Shazer & Dolan, 2007). The premise of solution-focused therapy is simple, but the practice can be difficult. SFBT was developed through the careful observation of therapists, particularly Insoo Kim Berg, as they practiced therapy and made notes about *what worked*. Steve de Shazer, Insoo Kim Berg, and their team at the Brief Family Therapy Center (BFTC) in Milwaukee watched sessions behind one-way mirrors and realized that the therapist is just as much a part of the system as the family in the room, that is, therapist system + family system = new system of interaction (de Shazer, 1992; de Shazer, p. xvi, 1994; de Shazer, personal communication, January 1999). This insight is the foundation for the therapist's involvement in the co-creation of solutions *within* the therapeutic context (de Shazer, 1992). As the team observed Insoo, the only prominent Asian American woman therapist in the field at the time, they saw her relate to the family system as equal to the therapist. This was a first step in dismantling the patriarchal power that underpinned other clinical models.

So why do we say SFBT is difficult to practice? SFBT is not based on causality or directionality like models based on attachment theory or hierarchy. SFBT does not make assumptions about the cause of the symptomology or direction of treatment (de Shazer, 1982). This may leave some therapists wondering where to go in session and sliding into "problem-solving" in order to find a direction. Instead of problem-solving, SFBT constructs solutions within the specific contextual conversation between the clients and the therapist (Korman et al., 2020). The therapist is listening for what is meaningful to the client through language they use to describe the problem. By doing so, the therapist does not claim an "expert" role of understanding and predicting the lived experience of clients in a

DOI: 10.4324/9781003308188-9

system. When the client says, "Goodness, I haven't been able to eat popsicles on Tuesdays!" the therapist's response isn't "go eat a popsicle." The solution-focused therapist might say, "And being able to eat popsicles is important to you. It says that you don't feel judged. Do I understand that correctly? What difference would that create for you, to eat popsicles again on Tuesdays?"

Box 9.1

Post-structural An open view of the meaning of language and human behavior. A post-structural lens rejects binary interpretations and avoids presuming the world within pre-established, socially constructed structures.

Looking back, what was it that was so impactful at the BFTC? What were these therapists doing differently that made this model of therapy unique and effective across populations? Essentially, they were co-creating reality through conversation that was focused on the co-construction of meaning. SFBT therapists believe *language* holds significant power within the context of the therapeutic conversation because meaning is co-constructed through dialogue. SFBT uses a **post-structural** view of language, meaning words and meaning are negotiated within the immediate context of interaction (de Shazer, 1991, 1994; de Shazer & Berg, 1992; Knudsen, 1988). When a client says they are depressed, the meaning of depression is negotiated through the conversation. This differs from other structural approaches where words, like depression, have universal meanings. When we use the word "family" to describe family therapy, you, the reader, may begin to visualize your interpretation of that word. If we introduce the word "family" before you offer your experience of the word "family," we might mistakenly *speak* you into the assumptive, structuralist definition of family that could be biological, parents, spouse, siblings, heterosexual, monogamous, cisgender relationships – and that may not be for you. It is critical to note that even though SFBT is post-structural, it is not post-systemic since it values the complexity of multiple levels of influence. SFBT is an ecological model of therapy that creates a canvas to observe sequential and simultaneous actions of people (de Shazer, 1982). This systemic approach grasps the nuances and complexity of relational systems that are continually in flux and often consistently negotiate new meaning. Hopefully you are coming to see how SFBT is simple – yet difficult!

Box 9.2

Tenets Many models have assumptions or directionality. Since SFBT does not offer a structure of causality, the tenets were introduced as a helpful guide for the therapist to learn what to listen for as the client shares their story.

The model and practice of SFBT is influenced by seven **tenets:** *if it isn't broken, don't fix it; if it works, do more of it; if it's not working, do something different; small steps can lead to big changes; the solution is not necessarily directly related to the problem; the language of solution development is different from the language used to describe a problem; no problems happen all the time; and, the future is both created and negotiable* (de Shazer & Dolan, 2007). These tenets reflect SFBT's assumption about how change occurs – through the subtle infusion of solution and strength-focused language into the dialogue of a session. Starting with the client's problem-talk, a solution-focused brief therapist inspires clients to speak solutions and strengths into being by inquiring about exceptions, what has worked in the past, and what clients hope for in their future. The tenets of the model were introduced later in its development, and we would argue that the tenets better serve the model as assumptions of solution-talk within therapy than a "checklist" of techniques the therapist must perform as an SFBT therapist. SFBT assumes people are currently doing the best they know how to do at any given moment, and that even misguided attempts at solutions among family members *are* attempts at solutions, rather than defiant resistance to change (Korman et al., 2020). In fact, the assumption that the solution is not necessarily related to the problem carries the notion that clients have within them the resources and strengths to solve their problems.

Box 9.3

SFBT Conversations This term is a signal for therapists using SFBT that remaining in solution-talk requires something different than staying in a saturated space of problem-talk with the client. Though client's may not have the language "SFBT," they should experience something different by just the way the therapist holds conversation.

To help facilitate **SFBT conversations,** Berg and de Jong (1996) developed the process of *listen, select, build.* Through this process, the therapist actively *listens* for moments of difference. The therapist then *selects* this moment to *build* into the preferred future. Therapists learning the model may miss the nuance of language and attempt to solution-*force* their clients away from problem-talk. This can result in frustration with the seemingly surface-level SFBT conversations and client's feeling unheard or deprioritized in the therapeutic process. By going slow, listening intently to each client, and utilizing the process of listen, select, build, therapists can improve the utility and alliance of a single session (Perkins & Scarlett, 2008).

Dominant Critique of SFBT

Marriage and family therapy models in general have been critiqued as hegemonic and framed through a pathologizing Western, white, cisgender, and heteronormative culture. SFBT has been questioned for its lack of systematic integration of social structures of oppression and gender and sexuality dynamics (Dermer et al., 1998). The feminist critique of SFBT highlights an overall lack of attention in the SFBT literature to the influence of individual or family development and the influence of larger systems of oppression and power (Dermer et al., 1998). Further, SFBT may fail to address insight and the etiology of a concern because of its focus on behavior change and preferred future (Dermer et al., 1998). SFBT does not provide a mechanism for challenging stereotyped behavior and demonstrates less awareness of issues of hierarchy, power, and abuse of professional privilege than feminist approaches (Dermer et al., 1998). We argue, however, that this is not a failure of the model, but a misunderstanding of how the model articulates change and the purpose of solution-talk. Perhaps if written accounts of the model could better articulate how a therapist maintains consciousness of systems of oppression in order to avoid pathologizing clients' experiences, these critiques might be less prevalent. In essence, the aim of SFBT is (at times) fantastical in its desire for an apolitical conversation, so it is the work of the therapist to understand how their own biased use of language clouds the experience of those seeking change in therapy. It is important to note, however, that the model does not claim discussion of politics, and oppression will *never* occur. It is under the direction of the client that the therapist pursues discussion of macro systems of oppression based on what is real and workable for the client. We are reminded of one of Insoo's clients – a woman dying of AIDs-related illness. To our surprise, Insoo asked the **miracle question** and naturally the client said, "I wouldn't be sick." Insoo, understanding this isn't a workable goal but a very real feeling, sat silently. As Insoo sat in silence, the client remarked that not being sick wasn't real and probably not what she [Insoo] was asking, so she stated, "I guess I would die well…". Our response to critiques of this model is that people most often get stuck when they think of goals. Goals suggest specific types of solutions – solutions that are realistic and obtainable. Life circumstances, like death and illness, are not "fixable," thus, a solution of curing a disease or having a deceased person come back to life are not "workable goals." Similarly, a goal that hinges on the abolishment of oppressive systems in the U.S. would also be improbable given how omnipresent and enduring these forces are. This is why we ask clients to tell us [the therapist] what their *realistic*, preferred future is. Asking clients about their preferred future centers the meaning *they* give to their cultural identit[ies] and allows them to decide how relevant experiences of oppression are for discovering their solutions.

Box 9.4

Miracle Question This is a hallmark of SFBT; however, not every SFBT therapist utilizes the miracle question in similar ways. The "takeaway" concept of the miracle question is the ability to help the client see themselves in a place where they are not immediately bound by problems. Some therapists say, "If I could wave a magic wand" to help the couple imagine a space where change is actualized.

Wait! Before you continue reading, you may benefit from reading the introduction again. The model and practice of SFBT are built around using language *as intervention*. When people get frustrated with SFBT, it often comes from misunderstanding the pragmatics of the model. Thus, frustration results from rushing past the discovery process where therapists uncover the magic within the words that client uses. As the title of the classic text indicates, SFBT is "more than miracles" and not a last resort when you are unsure of what to ask your clients next (de Shazer & Dolan, 2007). It is not simply finding solutions to problems. The words your clients use should "sparkle" in your mind as if you just received a beautiful gift to unwrap and ask, "Why did my client gift me with this word? Let's ask!" SFBT is an intentional dedication to understanding the language your client uses and attuning to what is important to them – even if they say, "I'd wake up in my home and I would be able to eat a popsicle in my underwear and not feel judged!" In this example, the dedication to language *is* the intervention. By taking the client at their word, the therapist can animate solutions within the client's reality through subtle adjustments in language, asking questions like "and what would be different *when...?*"

Queer-Contextualized Solution-Focused Brief Therapy

The founders of SFBT discovered that *what worked* in therapy was a negotiation of language between the therapist and client, with the client bringing their worldview and experiences and the therapist bringing the language of solutions. The language of solutions might involve speaking about exceptions, strengths, and hopes that contribute to a shared meaning between the client and therapist. For example, a therapist might say, "Math can be very hard to some people but you say you are good at it. What did you do to become so good at something that others find difficult?" The importance of language remains for a queer-contextualized version of SFBT, which attempts to hold both macro and micro views as essential elements of client difference and uniqueness (Berg & Miller, 1992). In work with Asian American clients in the BFTC in Milwaukee, Insoo noted that problem resolution must be considered in the cultural context of the client, which also sets the course of therapy in accordance with the client's identity (Berg & Miller, 1992). In order to queer-contextualize SFBT, we need to state this aspect of the model more plainly, because it is currently only implied. What was not published is how Insoo Kim Berg began her clinical work with Asian Americans by negotiating the meaning of "problems" and their cultural relevance to the clients (Ho, 1990). In other words, SFBT had elements of client-centered cultural humility through its post-structuralist roots, but seldom is that written in founding texts. In alignment with these origins, queer-contextualized SFBT is slow-moving and first asks what it means for the clients to be in therapy. In doing this, we suspend the implicit assumption that clients are coming to therapy viewing their experiences as problematic. I (BF) typically begin a session by asking, "What will have happened here that would indicate to you this has been worth your time being here?" This question suspends the assumption that the clients have a problem and demonstrates that I value the client's direction and insight into what is meaningful for their therapeutic work.

Assessment

When reviewing intake paperwork and formal assessments, it is important that therapists consider the cultural context of language and how language is used in systems of power and control to reinforce dominant culture (Allen & Mendez, 2018; Oswald et al., 2005). Frequency-based assessments are typically used to measure how often a problem is occurring or how severe it is. In queer-contextualized SFBT, we flip this on its head and use formal assessment tools to support the tenet that "no problem happens all the time." As we review assessments, we note a response like "a few times a week" as a potential moment for exceptions in SFBT. A post-structuralist conceptualization emphasizes the importance of viewing assessments as a spectrum of human experience, rather than as definite truth. For example, the DSM assessment criteria of gender dysphoria states that the client has a "strong desire to be of the other gender..."(American Psychiatric Association, 2013, p. 452). A queer-contextualized use of SFBT avoids assessments that simplify or dichotomize experiences of being queer, allowing for expansive experiences of gender and sexuality. An SFBT assessment of gender identity experiences would instead focus on the client's own descriptions of their experience in their body and any dissonance they perceive between their current gendered state and their desired gendered state. SFBT takes an expanded approach to assessment, viewing it as one of many lenses into the client's reality but never assuming that what is found reflects a subjective truth to the client's experience or pathology.

Intervention

Box 9.5

Meaning-Making The active process of taking the client's words literally and then asking for more information. For example, when the client states they would be happier as a result of therapy, we believe that! Then, we ask what is different about "happier" than the happy they may be feeling in some capacity now.

Structuralist A worldview that believes human behavior is understood through discovering the underlying structures that drive thought perception and feeling.

SFBT intervention is focused on the bidirectional process of **meaning-making** that occurs through language. This is markedly different than intervention strategies that stem from **structuralist** notions of human behavior, experience, and development. Though conversation in SFBT might involve discussion of behavior and emotions, such dialogue is rooted in post-structuralist assumptions of reality. In contrast to the original version of SFBT, queer-contextualized SFBT actively involves the therapist in the generation of solutions as a resource for client growth. This involvement includes the therapist sharing their knowledge of community resources like networking groups with clients. Most importantly though, queer-contextualized SFBT interventions should be tailored to each client based on what they say is their preferred future (de Shazer & Molnar, 1984). Queer-contextualized SBFT, like the original SFBT, is not problem-solving, nor is it solution-*forcing*. Through interventions, solution-focused therapy is an exploration of multiple solutions that may or may not be directly related to the problem and are often entirely unrelated to the problem. With this understanding as the guiding principle, a queer-contextualized SFBT practice encourages clients to go deeper into their relationships and experiences to build more meaningful futures. In the following sections, we will illustrate how queer-contextualized SFBT therapists can more explicitly help clients situate themselves in their social location and solution-building mindset.

Between Session Change

Box 9.6

Pre-Session Change Highlights that something is already happening between the time that the family booked the therapy appointment and the time that they show up for session one. Soliciting pre-session change may sound like, "Using that same scale that we just used, where would you place yourself looking back on the day that you scheduled the appointment?"

Between-session changes, like the utilization of **pre-session change** (what happens between scheduling and intake), disrupt the notion that the problem is happening *all the time* and disrupt the stability of the problem pattern. Despite being a core feature of SFBT, this model is commonly practiced in a way that dismisses or downplays between session change by asking clients what they would like to focus on in session, as though change can only happen in that hour. This often-overlooked aspect of SFBT is *central* to the queer-contextualized version of SFBT since it prioritizes client autonomy and recognizes that the time between sessions is often filled with stories of resilience. Therapists can facilitate this in many unique ways, but a common question may sound like, "What has been better since the last time we've seen each other?" That being said, we recognize that for many queer and transgender clients, survival is critical, life is endured, and enjoyment is often overlooked. The propensity for therapists to see a client as resistant because "nothing was better" between sessions might increase frustration and jeopardize the working alliance.

Alternatively, the queer-contextualized SFBT model recognizes that *seeing problems* like discrimination and retaliation for queer and trans clients can be a matter of life or death. Contextualizing the client in the macro system, I (BF) explore ways the client has utilized coping between sessions that kept the problem from getting worse. Noting that somehow, despite how difficult their situation, the clients have managed to come back to session. This is an important place of exploration for the client and therapist – what the clients have tapped into to "keep going."

Listen for What Is Meaningful

Listening for what is meaningful for clients is essential since what is important to the client may not be directly related to their solution. I (BF) am reminded of my beginning work as a solution-focused therapist. I was so impassioned by the model. It was and is how I see the world and it is, in many ways, how I want my clients to experience the world. How many times have we thought, "If only you [the client] could see what I see for you!" By focusing on this, however, I started by listening for what was meaningful to me instead of the client. When I did this in the past, I overlooked the strong negative feelings my client had toward their trauma history and did not help them to accept or normalize the functions of these strong emotions (Lipchik, 2002). I fell prey to the critique that SFBT quickly passes by intense, negative, problem-focused stories of the past. Talking with clients in their language of emotion can help them feel more understood and to see how these feelings (though perhaps intense through the therapist's lens) have served as positive protection for them (Lipchik, 2002). The emotion associated with language is a vehicle for change and the first small step is for the therapist to learn the language of suffering *and* resilience. In a queer-contextualized SFBT conversation, however, the therapist should deliberately explore how the client relates to words like "resilience," which are assumed to be positive but might not always be positive for each person. In fact, using the word resilience to refer to something positive can reinforce dominance, since resilience is commonly defined as the ability to withstand or endure difficulty – in this case, the difficulty stemming from living in a society centered around white cisgender heterosexuality. Praising resilience could imply acceptance of dominant cultural norms, without which queer resilience would not be needed.

The Miracle Question

Insoo Kim Berg was inspired to ask the miracle question, one of the most recognizable interventions of SFBT practice, after one of her clients said,

"Maybe only a miracle would help" (Berg & de Jong, 1996). Using future-oriented language, Insoo would ask clients to speak about what it would be like if their miracle happened. In doing so, she dismantled the implicit assumption that miracles are elusive and extraneous to the system. The **miracle question** has helped therapists and their client systems land just on the other side of the problem ever since. A queer-contextualized use of the miracle question includes client context in the miracle, involves collaboration, and requires check-in with the client in order to intentionally incorporate the client's cultural values. Through a queer-contextualized lens, we suggest ditching the use of the word "miracle" with clients. Speaking from my own experience as a gay male, I (BF) prayed through much of my life for a miracle that I would not be gay. *Miracle* may imply a religiosity and may center on experiences within marginalized communities to rid themselves of the othering identity. *Miracles*, in other words, may be for the privileged that can make dreams a reality. Some suggested alternatives include, "a shift happens," "a vision question," or "an energy change." The important thing is that whatever term is used (1) should be culturally appropriate for the client, and (2) the alternative miracle label needs to be defined (Jordan, 2017). For instance, a therapist might say, "Imagine something shifts. That 'something' is whatever brought you here and now it's gone..." The therapist works to understand the language, values, and cultural identities that are meaningful to the client, before situating that information within the broader treatment context of external systems, (e.g., income, parenting, unemployment, etc.). Doing so requires a slower and more deliberate use of the miracle question, meaning that a queer-contextualized SFBT therapist might not attempt to ask the miracle question until at least three sessions into therapy. This is different than the original practice of SFBT where the question was most utilized in session one. Waiting to use the miracle question allows the therapist time to understand more clearly what is meaningful to the client, and what language may perpetuate marginalization to the client. Here is a brief example of a queer-contextualized use of the miracle question:

Client A: The joy is just gone. I just feel hurt, sad, and as though the energy has changed between us.

Therapist: Now, I would like to ask you a kind of strange question, but some have found it very helpful. Do you mind if I ask you?

Clients: Sure.

Therapist: You both have told me about the hurt and sadness in the relationship. You also told me stories of great joy, connection, and romance. And right now, it sounds difficult to see that place of joy. Is that correct?

Client B: Yes, I know it was there but right now I just don't know what I feel.

Therapist: You just don't know what to feel right now. Will you imagine with me? What would it be like for you both to go home today, fall asleep, and as you sleep, the energy changes and what brought you both into therapy is suddenly no longer present.

When you awake tomorrow, what would be the first thing you notice that would indicate that the energy has changed?

In this example of the miracle question, we use the client's language as closely as possible. The question needs to feel real and obtainable for the client, and to do so, we stay within their metaphor – and life! We intentionally infuse the language of a miracle into the problem-focused language that they used to describe their concern. This use of the miracle question should not wish away systemic oppression. In fact, it is important to be explicit that oppression exists as a real problem for the client. The point of the miracle question is to help clients find ways of being and thriving despite larger social oppressive forces that the client may not be able to directly control.

A Case Study in Listening, Selecting, and Building

Solution-focused therapy is a pragmatic, language-driven model that rests on the understanding of the client and their cultural context(s) at the micro and macro level. A queer-contextualization (QC) of SFBT emphasizes *what works* in solution-focused practice and incorporates small changes that create greater outcomes for clients through the exploration of power, privilege, and oppression. See Figure 9.1 for a comparison between the original SFBT and the queer-contextualized version. The fictionalized case study below shows a queer-recontextualized version of SFBT that offers the therapist a stronger voice in the collaborative process.

Greg (30) and Jeff (34) are seeking counseling for an affair in their relationship. Greg (white, gay, male) and Jeff (Black, gay, male) have been together for five years and share a consensual open relationship with boundaries that are clear to both of them. They plan to marry within the next year. The couple was working through the hurt from Greg's affair, when Jeff then acted outside of the rules of their relationship. The clients' presence in therapy and shared participation during session indicate hope and engagement in the therapeutic process. Individually, both partners enjoy their work and their life together. Both clients state that the

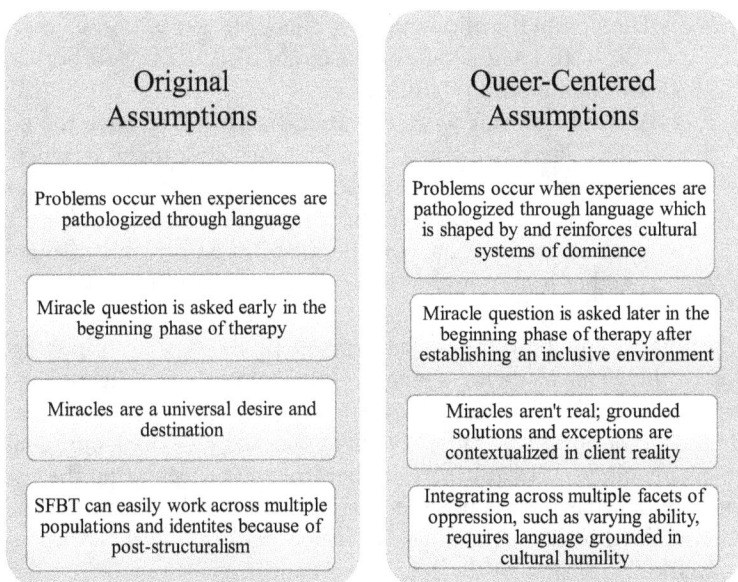

Original Assumptions	Queer-Centered Assumptions
Problems occur when experiences are pathologized through language	Problems occur when experiences are pathologized through language which is shaped by and reinforces cultural systems of dominence
Miracle question is asked early in the beginning phase of therapy	Miracle question is asked later in the beginning phase of therapy after establishing an inclusive environment
Miracles are a universal desire and destination	Miracles aren't real; grounded solutions and exceptions are contextualized in client reality
SFBT can easily work across multiple populations and identites because of post-structuralism	Integrating across multiple facets of oppression, such as varying ability, requires language grounded in cultural humility

Figure 9.1 Comparison of Theoretical Assumptions.

current openness of their relationship is important to them. Guided by the QC SFBT framework, the therapist began initial sessions with a strengths-based foundation. QC SFBT encourages the therapist to draw attention to strengths though diversity, such as the couple's ability to work through difficult romantic challenges, when larger queer culture is pushed into patterns of heterosexual performance (Wallace, 2002). This framework differs from standard SFBT practice in that QC SFTs do not wait for clients to express moments of exception, instead, actively note the elements of resilience in oppression and highlight strengths and resources that have yet to be unearthed for the clients.

Session One

QC SFBT begins at the first interaction. Before stepping into traditional questions of what brought clients to therapy, the therapist is first focused on the client's lives beyond the problem. This explicit conversation is different than assumed conversations one may have as a SFBT therapist. Such a conversation is distinct from a typical SFBT introductory conversation in that it uses language to expand the clients' identities beyond what has brought them to therapy: it is empowering!

Therapist: Thank you for allowing me a chance to get to know you both. You both have a supportive circle of friends. You both value community and relationships.

As we begin our work together, I also like to have the end in mind. There will come a point in our work together when you leave session, look at each other, and decide that you both have done the work you were hoping to do and you will not need to come back. What will be different as a result of our time together in therapy? What will we have addressed?

Asking what might be different as a result of therapy gives power and agency to the client to define change. Though some SFBT therapists may already ask a similar first session question, the QC SFBT framework uses this language because it is radically client focused by (1) encouraging the clients to imagine successful work in therapy and (2) centering the clients' perspective of what is or is not the problem. In this circumstance, the clients define the direction of change, and the therapist actively encourages a non-pathologizing view of the presenting concern.

Session Three

Though one may assume SFBT avoids it, QC SFBT is not afraid of problem-talk! Between session one and three, it is likely that problem-talk occupies about fifty percent of the conversation. Remember that within problem-talk lies the language of solutions! During the first three sessions, the therapist asked Greg and Jeff questions around the affairs, and the couple used words like "fair" and "right" and "equal." Considering the words "fair" and "right" and "equal" within the broader cultural system, the therapist was conscious of how each person has a different experience of fair, right, and equal. Their use of the same words with seemingly different meanings provided the therapist an opportunity to facilitate a discussion in which solutions would emerge.

Greg: When he met up with him, it didn't feel like I was seen as an equal. It's not that I particularly care that he met with him, it's the conditions under which they met. I just feel like I have atoned for what I did and yet, I am being punished with expectations that aren't held equally.

Therapist: Greg, you said that Jeff meeting with that guy, created a feeling that *you are not seen as equal.* That you are *punished with expectations* that are not *equal* for you. Did I hear that right?

Before moving on, the therapist matched, exactly, the words the client used without any transformation or interpretation. Then, the therapist asked for confirmation.

Greg: Yeah. There are just different expectations for me, and I feel punished. I don't understand how long I have to sit in this crap.

Therapist: Okay, we will certainly come back to some of that. Right now, I am hearing that having different expectations creates a feeling of punishment. I bet that makes it hard to see the good sometimes.

The therapist summarized it being hard, carefully using the client's language, but did not dig deeper into the "problem." At this point, the therapist feels ready to ask the miracle question having taken the time to understand what needs to occur during this shift.

Therapist: I am going to ask you both an interesting question, that other clients have found helpful. You both have told me about the hurt and sadness in the relationship. You also told me stories of great joy, connection, and romance in our first session. Do you remember that?

Greg: Yes.

Jeff: (looking away) Yes, I do remember that.

Therapist: Imagine with me. Let's say tonight, when we are done with session, you both go home as you normally would. You will see those men as you both planned together. And when they leave, you both will have dinner, finish up any work, and then you will get ready for bed as you normally do. You both exchange a kiss, turn in for bed, and fall asleep. As you sleep, though, a shift in energy occurs. During this shift, everything that brought you in to therapy is gone away. The sadness and the hurt are gone away, and because of this shift, togetherness, romance, and fairness are all back within your relationship. Because it happens while you both are sleeping, you aren't aware this shift in energy has taken place. When you awake the next day, what is the first thing you notice that is different because of this shift?

Jeff: Wow. Uhm. I am not sure...but honestly, I don't think I would have the need to be in control.

Therapist: Ah, you would not need to be in control. I have not heard you mention control, I am surprised. Tell me more about what would take the space of control?

Jeff: hmm well...as we've talked today I think I have noticed that part of my acting out and breaking rules also comes from me needing to control what Greg does. I would view him more as an equal participant in our relationship.

Therapist: Greg, Jeff mentions that after this shift, he'd see you as more of an equal participant, can you tell me what that means to you? How would you experience this shift in Jeff?

Greg: I think I would see him as less protective of me. When we first started dating, it's something we never talked about, but as a bottom, I think he viewed me as more effeminate or more in need of protection. And I know there are some cultural pieces to that, but I think that has really seeped into our dynamic after the affair. So, I guess I would notice him letting me have just as much freedom to ask for what I want and it being a discussion, not a dismissal.

Therapist: Mmm so cultural influences of power/control in sex would be less present again? And, you would notice him discussing this with you? What might this look like when the day begins, after the shift?

Greg: Morning breakfast. Jeff would make us breakfast and he'd ask me about my day. The dogs would be around the table. Jeff would be singing some of his music as he cooks. The morning would feel like home again.

It is not uncommon for clients to describe what will be gone instead of what would be newly present. Clients may also skip forward in the shift too, like when Jeff and Greg start discussing control. This is something the therapist plans to revisit, but for now, the focus is on holding Greg's response and then gently moves them back to the start of the day after the shift.

Therapist: I can see by both of your faces this has you both thinking again about those times when elements of the shift were present. If I were to put on a scale where 10 is the day after the shift as you have described, and 0 is just the opposite of that, where would you both say you are?

Self-of-the Therapist

If it isn't working, do something different. The original version of solution-focused therapy is a client-centered approach, but it does not explicitly attend to the influences of marginalizing cultural forces. As a result, SFBT therapists from dominant cultural backgrounds are inclined to use solution-talk without addressing the impact of oppression and marginalization on client systems. This implementation of SFBT is contrary to the culturally attuned model that the founders inductively created alongside their clients. SFBTs are reminded of the origins of the model, when Steve, Insoo, and the team at the Milwaukee center realized that the therapist and the clients form a new subsystem as soon as the family system enters the room. Given that SFBT therapists believe small steps can lead to big changes, it is important that individual therapists consider what it would take for them to do one small thing that would create a more inclusive and affirming practice for their clients. It is also important that queer-contextualized SFBT therapists reflect on their own practice and what self-of-the-therapists concerns are impacting them. Figure 9.2 presents a list of questions for you to consider as you evolve alongside your clients.

What are moments that I may *push* clients into solutions because of my own discomfort with emotional responses in therapy? What would it require of me to be aware that this is happening in session?

SFBT requires a therapist to "stay" in solution-talk for long durations of time, even when client's circle back into problem saturation. What is your own orientation toward solutions in and outside of therapy? To what extent does your language reflect an orientation toward confinement and problems, or toward expansion and solutions?

Though client-centered, in what circumstances should I use my own agency as a therapist to present questions that may be meaningful for the client to explore (i.e., "I have heard that others in similar experiences struggle with their partner...but that does not seem to be the case for you...")

In practice, do I spend more time listening to understand than listening to respond? In other words, if you were asked to "repeat back" what you heard your client say that was meaningful, could you do so?

How can I utilize the DSM to highlight client strengths surrounding the client through their diagnoses?

How can you use the post-structuralist roots of SFBT to capture the influence of systems of dominance and the effects of oppression in conversation?

Figure 9.2 Questions for Reflection.

References

Allan, S. H., & Mendez, S. N. (2018). Hegemonic heteronormativity: Toward a new era of queer family therapy. *Journal of Family Theory & Review, 10(1)*, 70–86. https://doi.org/10.1111/jftr.12241

American Psychiatric Association. (2013). *Diagnostic and statistical manual of mental disorders* (5th ed.). https://doi.org/10.1176/appi.books.978089 0425596

Berg, I. K., & de Jong, P. (1996). Solution-building conversations: Co-constructing a sense of competence with clients. *Families in Society: The Journal of Contemporary Human Services, 77(6)*, 376–391. https://doi.org/10.1606/1044-3894.934

Berg, I. K., & Miller, S. D. (1992). Working with Asian American clients: One person at a time. *Families in Society: The Journal of Contemporary Human Services*, (1), 356–363.

de Shazer, S. (1982). *Patterns of brief family therapy*. The Guilford Press.

de Shazer, S. (1991). Here we go again: Maps, territories, interpretations, and the distinction between "the" and "a" or "an." *Journal of Marital and Family Therapy, 17(2)*, 179–181. https://doi.org/10.1111/j.1752-0606.1991.tb00882.x

de Shazer, S. (1992). What question is being asked? *American Family Therapy Association Newsletter, 47*, 31–32.

de Shazer, S. (1994). *Words were originally magic*. WW Norton & Co.

de Shazer, S., & Berg, I. K. (1992). Doing therapy: A post-structural revision. *Journal of Marital and Family Therapy, 18(1)*, 71–81. https://doi.org/10.1111/j.1752-0606.1992.tb00916.x

de Shazer, S., & Dolan, Y. (2007). *More than miracles: The state of the art of solution-focused brief therapy*. Routledge. https://doi.org/10.4324/978020 3836484

de Shazer, S., & Molnar, A. (1984). Four useful interventions in brief family therapy. *Journal of Marital and Family Therapy, 10(3)*, 297–304. https://doi.org/10.1111/j.1752-0606.1984.tb00020.x

Dermer, S. B., Hemesath, C. W., & Russell C. S. (1998). A feminist critique of solution-focused therapy. *The American Journal of Family Therapy, 26(1)*, 239–250. https://doi.org/10.1080/01926189808251103

Ho, M. K. (1990). *Intermarried Couples in Therapy*. Springer.

Jordan, S. S. (Ed.) (2017). Solution-focused brief therapy. *The SAGE encyclopedia of marriage, family, and couples counseling* (pp. 1576–1580). SAGE Publications, Inc. http://dx.doi.org/10.4135/9781483369532.n475

Knudsen, T. L. (1988). [Review of *superstructuralism: The philosophy of structuralism and post-structuralism*, by R. Harland]. *Journal of Peace Research, 25(1)*, 103–104. www.jstor.org/stable/423989

Korman, H., de Jong, P., & Jordan, S. S. (2020). Steve de Shazer's Theory Development. *Journal of Solution Focused Practices, 4(2)*. https://digitalscholarship.unlv.edu/journalsfp/vol4/iss2/5

Lipchik, E. (2002). *Beyond technique in solution-focused therapy: Working with emotions and the therapeutic relationship*. Guilford Press.

Oswald, R., Blume, L., & Marks., S. (2005). Decentering heteronormativity: A proposal for family studies. In Bengston, V., Acock, A., Allen, K., Dilworth-Anderson, P., & Klein, D. (Eds.), *Sourcebook of family theories and methods: An interactive approach* (pp. 143–165). Sage. https://doi.org/10.4135/9781412990172.d32

Perkins, R., & Scarlett, G. (2008). The effectiveness of single session therapy in child and adolescent mental health. Part 2: An 18-month follow-up study. *Psychology and Psychotherapy: Theory, Research and Practice, 81*(1), 143–156. https://doi.org/10.1348/147608308X280995

Wallace, D. L. (2002). Out in the academy: Heterosexism, invisibility, and double consciousness. *College English, 65*(1), pp. 53–66. https://doi.org/10.2307/3250730

Chapter 10

Queer-Contextualized Collaborative Family Therapy

Brooks Bull and Justine D'Arrigo

As a postmodern theory of therapy, collaborative language systems (CLS), now more broadly referred to as collaborative therapy (CT), shares the philosophical foundations of many other postmodern family therapy models by honoring a multiplicity of truths, emphasizing the relational nature of knowledge, and an overall emphasis on the importance of lived experience over expert therapist knowledge (Anderson, 1997). Founding theorists Harlene Anderson and Harold Goolishian identified postmodernism, hermeneutics, and social constructionism as the theoretical foundations of CLS, each remaining influential to CT today. **Postmodernism** encourages us to see truth as local and subjective rather than universal and objective, honoring client knowledge; this was, and remains, a radical departure from traditional family therapy theories that impose meaning, privilege therapist expertise, and value professional knowledge over local/client knowledge (Chenail et al., 2020). CLS assumes, given its roots in **hermeneutics,** that interpretation is not an objective science but subjective and dependent on who is doing the interpreting (Anderson & Goolishian, 1992). Finally, **social constructionism** emphasizes the relational nature of knowledge; together we create our worlds, we don't discover them (Gergen, 2009).

Norms and Assumptions of Collaborative Therapy

Drawing on these postmodern foundations, Anderson was able to articulate a radically different way of thinking about and showing up to the work of therapy. CT challenges basic assumptions about both health and change and shifts dramatically away from modernist notions of what a problem is, what a therapy session should sound like, and who should attend. For example, whereas a modernist family therapist might have in mind some notion of optimal family structure or functioning and see the work of therapy as getting the client closer to that ideal, a collaborative

DOI: 10.4324/9781003308188-10

Box 10.1

Postmodernism A critique of modernism; emphasizes departing from notions of absolute truth and understanding the world through grand theories and metanarratives to instead embrace the coexistence of a multiplicity and a variety of situation-dependent ways of life (Burr, 1995).

Hermeneutics A philosophical discipline concerned with understanding and interpretation; it acknowledges that understanding of a text, discourse, human behavior, and emotion is a process that is influenced by the beliefs, assumptions, and intentions of the interpreter, therefore, suggesting that all understanding is interpretive rather than categorically correct (Anderson, 1997).

Social constructionism Emphasizing that reality is created and constructed through language and relationships rather than discovered through scientific inquiry. There is no "real" world to discover, but worlds that we can make together (Gergen, 2009).

---

therapist simply does not. Collaborative therapists recognize the restrictive concept of "family" as the determinant of who should be present in the room and shift instead to thinking in terms of **problem-determined systems**. Collaborative therapists see it as more helpful to think of people as "part of a system that has coalesced around a problem" (Anderson, 1997, p. 66), and therefore hold sessions with those who are in conversation about the problem with one another, or in other words, with the problem-determined system rather than the family-determined system.

Box 10.2

Problem-determined systems A group of people who form a system connected through conversations about a shared problem (Anderson, 1997).

CT also follows the postmodern turn in family therapy by rejecting the notion that the therapist is or should be the arbiter of what is healthy and optimal for their clients. Indeed Anderson (1997) challenges the simple meaning of the "problem" in therapy: "I do not believe there is such a thing as a problem, that is, consensus around a definition that reflects an objective pathology" (p. 73). Instead, Anderson (1997) maintains the belief that "problems emerge as linguistic events or positions which are often interpreted and described in conflicting ways" (p. 74), and that ultimately, problems become rooted in and sustained by monological (dominated by one voice or perspective) interactions. Therefore, CT does not have a stated set of assumptions about health, ideal family structure, or an optimal developmental trajectory for people or families. Instead, Anderson invites us to facilitate a therapeutic process that focuses more on generative dialogue and a way of being rather than focusing on solving a problem. The mechanism of change in CT is language itself, and conversation is the intervention. Anderson suggests that orienting to our work in this way allows us to participate in problem dissolving conversations, conversations where, eventually, the complaint no longer exists.

Evaluation and Recontextualization of Collaborative Therapy

Because CT does not have established values for how people should live or how families should be configured, there is already ample space for queerness to be articulated, and made visible in therapeutic conversation (McDowell et al., 2018). CT is well positioned to make room for queerness by its lack of restrictive values and the spaciousness it cultivates. The refusal to privilege the nuclear or biological family above other social structures also makes it well suited to center queerness and the alternative family structures queerness invite. The overall value on non-pathologizing, using client language, and being curious also makes CT a good fit for working with queer people. That said, the theory was created in a context of pervasive whiteness, dominant heterosexuality, and cisgender privilege. Making space for queer experiences or not actively oppressing minoritized people is not the same as centering. As a result, there are ways this theory of therapy could be used to harm queer people and communities. Therefore, we identify below places the theory falls short of centering and supporting the natural development of queer people and offer a re-visioning of some of the core tenets of the theory.

CT, as articulated by Anderson (1997), assumes problems dissolve through language and therapeutic conversation. There is a lack of attention to material context that plainly does not meet the needs of people living outside the dominant identity categories whose lives are marked by minority stress (McDowell et al., 2018). For example, a highly trained collaborative therapist could facilitate beautiful and nuanced conversations that change the way a client's problem is talked about, and perhaps even ease relational tension within a couple or family and provide some relief without ever naming that the actual culprit, the origin of the mental health concern, is racism, xenophobia, transphobia, or sexism. The fact that the model does not require practitioners to identify the cultural source of stress is evidence of its origin in the soup of white supremacy and gender binarism. Put simply, the model could be employed in a way that completely elides the topics of identity and power. One place the theory engages with the concept of power is in the therapy room; in that way, CT provides a robust map for how therapists can be aware of their own power, cognizant of the weight of their own words, and work to bring forth the client's expertise and self-knowledge (Anderson, 1997). As is, however, the model does not extend that critique and deconstruction of power outside the session room (D'Arrigo-Patrick et al., 2016).

One core tenet of CT that fits with a recontextualized queer approach is the concept of **not-knowing**. Because the spirit of not-knowing has so often been misunderstood, and is such an integral foundation to collaborative practice, it is important to clarify a few things. First, it is critical to understand that not-knowing does not mean therapists know nothing, or that the knowledge therapists accrue over many years of training and practice ought to be discarded. The point here is not to feign ignorance. Instead, not-knowing is about intentionally and continually shifting our relationship to what we know or think we know. Just as the role of the therapist is about shifting our way of being in relationship with clients, not-knowing is about shifting our way of being in relationship with knowledge. Choosing to allow oneself to be in a position of not-knowing means employing humility, tentativity, and transparency. It also means looking for ways to draw forth client knowledge and meaning-making, often privileging this over how professional discourses might seduce us to impose meaning on the client. This requires a capacity to sit with uncertainty and ambiguity, given that from this stance, we avail ourselves to the risky position of learner rather than expert. It requires us to hold our professional knowledge as one possible way to understand and allows us to become **conversational partners** who make room for uncertainty, mutual puzzling, and not understanding too quickly. If we listen from a not-knowing position, we are more apt to believe and be curious to deepen our understanding of what a client says, rather than position ourselves to evaluate and assess.

Box 10.3

Not-knowing refers to a therapist's position – an attitude and belief – that a therapist does not have access to privileged information, can never fully understand another person, always needs to be in a state of *being informed* by the other, and always needs to learn more about what has been said or may not have been said (Anderson, 1997, p. 134).

Conversational partners "..a mutual relationship, in the telling, inquiring, interpreting, and shaping of the narrative.." (Anderson, 1997, p. 113).

When we queer-contextualize not-knowing, we must reconcile this posture with the power dynamics in both the therapy room as well as the larger social context. Not-knowing gets complicated in situations where one family member is voicing queerphobic remarks, negating another person's identity, or espousing white supremacist values. The question becomes how do we assume a posture of not-knowing while also deeply knowing things, and holding strong values and opinions? As trans therapists and teachers ourselves, this issue has been enacted many times in our session rooms and classrooms. The case study that follows will illustrate using a revised not-knowing stance that allows the therapist to be open and curious while also never losing touch with the need to be the advocate and conspirator of the queer person in the system. Taken further to a truly queer-centered place, a not-knowing stance can grow into a decolonizing approach where self-determination is the bedrock value, and queerness, transness, and all other words used to describe identity are taken as true and worthy because they are claimed by the person speaking them (binao-han, 2014). Queerness itself defies categories, is ever-shifting, and eschews assumptions; it therefore fits well for collaborative therapists working from not-knowing positions.

Being public, another core tenet of CT, is another place where the theory already makes space for work with queer clients. Being public is a practice that emerged from collaborative therapists' experience working in therapy teams, where co-therapists began encouraging one another to share their thoughts, questions, and even disagreements in the presence of clients as a way to remain committed to the not-knowing spirit. Being public with inner therapist knowledge allows clients access to what previously remained a veiled and protected world. Revealing out loud those inner private thoughts, prejudices, wonderings, speculations, and questions has become a common way that collaborative therapists remain in the position of conversational partner and open to both client feedback and influence. However, this is another aspect of the model that needs to be more finely articulated to truly center queer people. Being public, as is true with any therapeutic intervention, should be done with judiciousness, and to support the most vulnerable members of the system. That means going public when it benefits the development and self-actualization of the queer client in whatever form that queerness is taking: the genderqueer kid, the two-spirit adolescent, the transpinay partner, the newly emigrated bakla, the cross-dressing elder.

Box 10.4

Being public

> Related to reflecting (and to sharing one's work in general) is the notion of being public – more readily revealing, more readily sharing out loud my private inner dialogues and monologues: my thoughts, prejudices, wonderings, speculations, questions, opinions, and fears. And, in doing so, opening myself to feedback, evaluation, and critique. Consequently, I expose myself more as a person to all those with whom I work.
>
> (Anderson, 1997, pp. 102–103)

CT queers the notion of therapist as expert who speaks only in curated, polished interpretations and rather invites a more emergent process of creation.

Multipartiality

> A therapist wants each person in the conversation to feel that his or her version is as important as any other. It is a position of *multipartiality*, one in which a therapist takes all sides simultaneously. This is in contrast to neutrality, in which a therapist strives not to take any one person's side.
>
> (Anderson, 1997, p. 95)

Lastly, there is one important concept from CT that deserves special attention, both because it is so central to the theory and also because it is the most troubling aspect to square with a recontextualized queer approach. **Multipartiality**, Anderson's (1997) concept for how a therapist orients to all people in the system, suggests that all voices ought to hold equitable space and value, and that each participant in the conversation be invited to both share from their particular vantage point and that each contribution be held with deep regard. Anderson (1997) contends that it is the therapist's main task to facilitate the creation of a dialogic process, and multipartiality is seen as a way for therapists to keep all voices in motion and take all sides simultaneously. While we can appreciate this as a valuable departure from the modern idea of neutrality (a concept that plainly refuses to acknowledge power differentials and avoids taking sides at all), it still does not do enough to account for power. A queer-contextualized collaborative therapist must advocate openly and publicly ally with the queer people in the client system. This is especially evident when working with queer and trans children who are less powerful on account of age and family position, as well as queer and trans people of color, immigrants, and other people directly impacted by white supremacy. We certainly value the sincerity with which a multipartial stance seeks to engage everyone in the conversation as an equal and contributing member, though feel strongly that when the well-being of clients with targeted identities is at stake, different rules apply. To invite each voice and perspective equally, such as the perspective of, for instance, a transphobic parent, could result in damaging effects for queer clients. In these clinical contexts, there are immense imbalances of power, and making room for, actively inviting, or holding as valuable the potentially harmful narratives and discourses about queer identities violates our duty of care to the most vulnerable in the system. We take this seriously as we are aware of the potentially life-threatening consequences these narratives can hold for queer people, especially youth. The case study below illustrates a radically revised version of multipartiality, where the potentially harmful remarks from an adult in the system are interrupted and redirected by the therapist before inviting the child into the therapy conversations.

In order to center queerness, CT must be supplemented with a more articulated and robust set of values to guide the therapist. Where the original theory beautifully clears away pathologizing assumptions and makes ample room, the queer-contextualized theory provides signposts, value-driven markers for the therapist to use to position themselves in alignment with the queer people in the system. A summary of these enhancements is provided in Figure 10.1.

Case Study: Queer-Contextualized Collaborative Therapy with a Trans Family

In this composite case vignette, we move from a theoretical queer-recontextualization of CT to a specific example of therapy with queer people. In this instance, we will illustrate the concepts explored above in

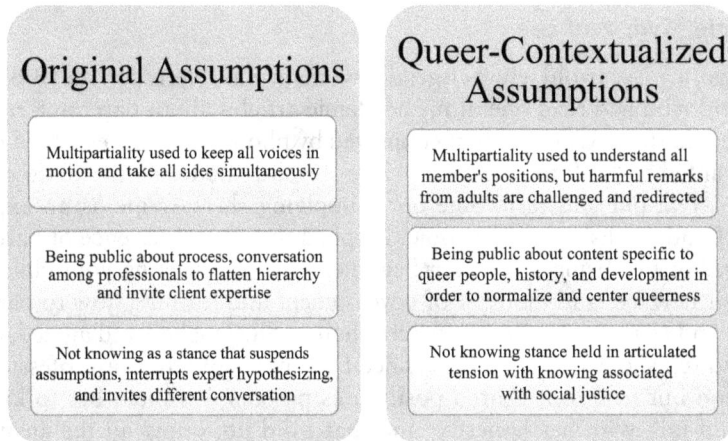

Original Assumptions	Queer-Contextualized Assumptions
Multipartiality used to keep all voices in motion and take all sides simultaneously	Multipartiality used to understand all member's positions, but harmful remarks from adults are challenged and redirected
Being public about process, conversation among professionals to flatten hierarchy and invite client expertise	Being public about content specific to queer people, history, and development in order to normalize and center queerness
Not knowing as a stance that suspends assumptions, interrupts expert hypothesizing, and invites different conversation	Not knowing stance held in articulated tension with knowing associated with social justice

Figure 10.1 Comparison of Assumptions in the Original and the Queer-Contextualized Versions of Collaborative Therapy Theory.

our work with a transgender child and his two cisgender parents. As we move from a broader level to a specific, personal level, our language will need to change to match the circumstance, and so we use the words trans instead of queer since that is how the client identified. Mirroring client language is a core principle of CT.

Overall, the task of a queer-contextualized collaborative therapist is to create conversations that ultimately support the queer person in the system above all, and to continually square this with the concept of not-knowing. To have a stake in the outcome of therapy and remain committed to a collaborative practice is not mutually exclusive but does produce moments of tension for the therapist. For many students of this theory of therapy, there can be an invitation to let go of outcome, to prioritize above all the expertise of the client, and to trust the collaborative process to lead to helpful therapeutic outcomes regardless of content. In the case of work with families with transgender children, therapists are faced with a starkly uneven power differential in which the child is less powerful due to both age and the oppression associated with gender nonconformity. For that reason, the therapist is the advocate of the child no matter what, even if the child happens not to be in the room, or never attends a single session of therapy. How to be an advocate for a transgender child depends on the family, and in particular the parents sitting in the session room. What does this parent need in order to be the most supportive person to their child? What experiences have the parents had that create blocks to support, and how can conversation open space for parents to find their way through those blocks? This is the general aim of the work.

Maggie, Syd, and Lee

Maggie, a 55-year-old white cisgender woman, was referred to me (B.B.) by a friend who had read one of my academic articles about parenting transgender children. When we first connected by phone, Maggie remarked that she wanted to "talk to an expert" since she had "no idea what to do since her 14-year-old had just come out," implying she saw me as an expert since I had published on the topic. I replied that my experience of parenting was one of being a constant beginner – always meeting your children at their new age and moment of development and learning how to parent again and again as the circumstances change. She laughed and agreed, and I could tell she was taken aback since I did not reply from a professional position but from our shared position as parents. I wanted her to know I would talk with her honestly, and that I did not know all the answers even though I've devoted much of my life to understanding the experiences of families with transgender children. I was practicing *being public* from our first contact, hoping it would help facilitate more rich, generative conversations once therapy began in earnest.

During our first session, I learned Maggie adopted her child Lee from China when Lee was a baby. She described her journey of becoming a parent as long and winding a story about enduring disappointments and emotional hardship to ultimately be redeemed in receiving her beloved child. She mentioned she met Syd, her now husband, during the process of adopting Lee, that he moved in when Lee was 18 months old, and that they married soon after. I reflected that she seemed to have arrived exactly where she wanted to be all those years. She agreed that it did feel that way, that she was meant to be a parent, and that Lee was the child she was meant to have. I noticed her narrative centered on Lee and herself, and I wondered where Syd was in all of this but decided not to ask quite yet. I kept that wondering private for the moment, instead following where it seemed she wanted to go. I asked her to tell me more about Lee, and what she hoped for in this new conversation with me. I chose not to follow my curiosity about Syd because I was still determining who was in fact a member of the problem-determined system. CT allows therapists to configure the right group for each specific conversation, so I trusted that if Syd needed to be involved, it would become clear as I got closer to Maggie's experience.

Having the Right Conversation

Clients often take a minute to answer this question: "what are you hoping for in this conversation"? My sense is they are not used to thinking of therapy as merely conversation, and, in some cases, it is uncomfortable to think of it in these terms since it moves therapy farther away from a medical model of seeking services from an expert behavioral health provider. It is a crucial question for me as a collaborative therapist, however, since it invites the client to also be responsible for agenda-setting. Rather than receiving expert information from me as a "pediatric gender specialist" (which often leads to conversations about either (1) the veracity of their child's gender or (2) what to do, interventions for the parents to implement), I invite clients to identify hopes and goals for the process – agenda items that are invariably more closely linked to their actual lives. Readers may wonder why I am not apt to begin therapy with investigations into the child's gender identity, or why I do not want to go straight to interventions for the parents to implement at home. These conversations may indeed happen over the course of therapy, but at the beginning I am careful not to position myself this way since my power as a therapist can so easily sweep the conversation into well-worn ruts of assumptions about what the clients are experiencing.

Maggie paused and replied that what she hoped for most was to leave the session feeling hopeful. She explained she felt confused and scared about what to do, desperate to be supportive to Lee. "I don't want to waste any more time!" I asked questions to deepen her description of how she felt like she had already lost time in her life, or had to wait for things to happen, and how she didn't want to replicate that in Lee's adolescence. "What might you miss out on, I wonder?" I asked aloud. Another pause, and then she replied

> I don't want to miss any more time with my son. All these years I've been relating to Lee as a daughter, and that didn't feel right to him – now I understand that – and I don't want to miss any more time with him where we aren't actually connecting.

There is a prominent discourse in therapy literature on the experience of grief for family members of transgender people (Bull & D'Arrigo-Patrick, 2018), and many therapists come to these sessions primed to excavate and help clients describe their grief (languaged sometimes as grief about losing the daughter they thought they had, etc.). CT provides a map for how to resist assumptions and getting pulled into dominant discourses, and therefore remain more closely engaged with the client's reality. Therefore, a queer-contextualized collaborative therapist would know that the grief discourse looms large in the zeitgeist, is widely accessible to both clients and therapists alike, and be vigilant not to participate in inviting the client into it before they even mention it themselves.

As this session with Maggie unfolded, I realized, however, that she was expressing a type of grief – sadness about losing out on time when she did not understand who Lee really was. She explained

> I always put it in the framework of adoption – that Lee struggled with social scenarios, our life in a rural New England town because he was (almost always) the only adopted, only Chinese American person in the room. I always thought about it in those terms first, and what I now realize is that it obscured me from seeing anything else about Lee's experience – gender was not on my radar in any way, even though as I think back on it now there were lots of gender-related moments of distress throughout the years.

I felt moved by Maggie's insightful sharing and told her as much. "I can easily see how much you love your child, and how committed you are to being a loving, present Mom." When a truly collaborative, authentic conversation is unfolding in therapy, it becomes easy to validate the parent for what they are doing well. "It is moving to see you working so hard to learn and show up for your kid like this." This moment illustrates maintaining a not-knowing stance in two ways: first by not assuming Maggie was experiencing grief about "losing the daughter she thought she had," and then again when Maggie did actually express grief, thereby upending (or perhaps more accurately adding another level of nuance) to my belief that the grief discourse is foisted on parents by oppressive professional literature and therapists who unwittingly reproduce that discourse in their sessions rooms. Not-knowing is about being in relationship with knowledge, with humility, tentativity, and remaining open to revision.

Beginning therapy with Maggie in this way, curiously, open to her experience and goals, but vigilant not to replicate harmful discourses or speak too soon from an expert position set the stage for a series of conversations that centered Lee's well-being and Maggie's development as a parent. This is in contrast to a therapy that would have centered investigating Lee's gender identity (perhaps creating a timeline of gender nonconforming behaviors) and testing it for veracity and consistency. Conversations like that may satisfy some need that a parent has to get their child's gender "checked out" by an expert, or to do their due diligence in some way, but the message it sends to the child (explicitly or implicitly) is that they are not the arbiters of their own identity, cannot be trusted to know themself, and that their transness is itself at best a curiosity or at worst a pathology.

Problem Systems, or Who Attends Sessions

Although Maggie presented to therapy as an individual client, it quickly became clear that these conversations would likely include other people, and that Lee would benefit from more family members being present. This came to mind when Maggie described Lee's apparent isolation and loneliness. Anderson (1997) explains that in collaborative practice

> therapy system membership cannot be predicted by the first session's membership. Each session determines who participates in the next. Each therapy conversation is a platform for and influences the next. The participants in the conversation mutually decide who should attend the next session and when it should occur.
>
> (p. 89)

I asked Maggie at the end of our first session: "What do you think it would be like for Lee to have you bring more people into the conversation? Is there anyone you wish were here right now?" Maggie quickly answered she wished Syd were present, and that although he is supportive "in his way," she and Syd were experiencing some conflict about Lee being trans. I asked if it would be helpful for Syd to talk to me alone first, or if she would prefer to meet together next time. Maggie answered that she would run it by Syd and get back to me, and laughed as she said "it will help that you have that on your wall," as she pointed to my professional credentials. "He wants a professional, yes?" I asked, not sure if I understood her meaning. "Yes, he actually asked me what degrees you have." It was an end-of-session conversation that let me know that Syd would be expecting expert assessment and validation if he were to attend therapy. I thanked Maggie for sharing all of this with me and we set a date for a second session with just Maggie, Syd, and me.

Lee would not attend a therapy session with me for 6 weeks, after his parents had thoroughly talked through their initial questions and vetted me as a "real expert" (Syd's words) and "someone they can trust" (Maggie's words). It worked well that Syd needed time to get to know me since I also wanted to make sure our conversations would not harm Lee in the early stages. Sometimes even the most well-meaning, supportive cisgender parents say things that deeply wound their queer and trans children, and it's the therapist's job to minimize this experience as much as possible. Collaborative therapists work with parents ahead of time to unearth any roots of transphobia that can flower into comments like what Syd voiced early on: "I see a lot of kids coming out as trans on the internet and wonder if there is some social contagion going on here. I wonder if Lee is trying to fit in by trying this out." Moments like this can be devastating for queer family members who reasonably feel dismissed, minimized, and pathologized. Allowing cisgender parents space to work through these questions about their child's identity without the child present is a crucial part of queer-contextualized CT. My response to Syd's comment illustrates the concepts of both multipartiality and being public (the conceptual anti-dote to taking the side of a transphobic family member).

Contending with Multipartiality

When Syd began to express his fear that Lee had fallen prey to what he called "Rapid-Onset Gender Dysphoria" (a term deployed to discredit transgender identities, especially in young people; for a thorough critique of the term's harmfulness, see Serano, 2018), I felt a familiar moment of tension inside. Collaborative practice invites therapists to take all sides simultaneously, not to be neutral but rather to align with all versions and all members at once. It is a liberatory move that can create dynamic conversational spaces and deep veins of curiosity for everyone. However, when a power differential and a bludgeoning cultural discourse oppresses one family member more than another, it is impossible to align with that and remain committed to centering queer people.

CT provides (at least) two different ways to respond to this type of com-munication, both of which preserve the values of respectful, collaborative practice. *Shared inquiry* and *being public* (discussed more fully below) became my guiding principles as I talked with Syd; I hewed closely to the collaborative value of "suspending preknowledge and focusing instead on client expertise" (Anderson, 1997, p. 63) when I asked Syd genuinely what the words social contagion and rapid-onset gender dysphoria meant to him. My exact words were something like

> I've heard those words before, social contagion and ROGD, they keep coming up in conversations like this one and on my computer screen, and it seems like they mean so many different things depending on who is speaking. Syd, I am wondering what those words mean for you, what they bring up?

I tried to align not with Syd's content, but to remain in my curious, open pos-ition in order to align with his emotional experience. My hunch was he was scared, and that the words he was repeating soothed some part of him that wanted to feel like there was an understandable origin to Lee's trans-ness, and that it could be intervened upon before it took hold. I held these hunches tentatively and steadied myself to remain open to Syd's actual experience.

Being Public

Syd explained that he felt uncomfortable with what seemed to him a new trend: "this wasn't going on in my high school!" I used *being public*, CT's commitment to being known and open with clients as the guiding principle in my next set of responses.

> Syd, I hear the worry, and I see the distress this is causing. It brings up for me a whole bunch of experiences I've had – as a researcher, as a therapist, as a parent, and as a trans person myself. Can I speak from a few different positions with you right now?

I wanted his consent to bring more parts of myself to the conversation, and I wanted to invite more parts of him as well. Anderson (1997):

> Reflecting and showing myself to the other permit me and the other to have more flexibility in dealing with the only natural, multiple, and sometimes conflicting opinions about the complex predicaments clients present. They allow me to have or assert a strong opinion and to participate in controversial situations without polarizing or freezing positions. Everything said is provisional grist for the mill.
>
> (p. 103)

From this position, I shared my knowledge of the role parental support plays in decreasing suicide risk for trans and queer youth (Ryan et al., 2010; Weinhardt et al., 2019), as well as my experience as a parent who frequently felt unsure what the right course of action was at any given moment.

> In moments like this, when I don't feel sure, I return to what is for sure. It is for sure that trans and gender nonconforming kids suffer more bullying and stigma. This is not a way to get into the popular crowd. And it is for sure that having even one caregiver who is not just quietly OK with it but giving full-throated support makes a huge difference in terms of mental health and safety.

Expanding the Unsaid

By listening to Syd's worries and being open about my professional knowledge and personal experiences, I hoped to make room for what was not yet being said in the room. I was not sure what it was, but I had a feeling there was more. "I have a feeling that there is more to talk about here, not just about Lee and his immediate needs, but perhaps more for you two to share about your own experiences thus far. Does that make sense?" I asked both parents. By using a very open-ended question, I wanted to convey that I was interested in new directions and would follow wherever they wanted to go. I have found that this usually leads to a rich vein of conversation, usually words that haven't been spoken aloud yet. "I feel afraid for Lee, and afraid for our family." Maggie said softly after a pause. She and Syd had a conversation about their (as yet unspoken) fear about having a trans child, and their shame that they wondered what other people would think. I reflected and expanded on their conversation when they looked to me. "What would it mean for you two as adoptive parents in a small community to have another way in which your family is seen as different from the norm?" I wanted to communicate that I saw their outsider position and could validate the hardship. By the end of this session, the mutually constructed understanding was that Syd and Maggie were also feeling the effects of oppression, and that as white, cisgender, financially resourced, heterosexual adults, they were unaccustomed to feeling discriminated against. Cisgender parents of trans children are also subject to scrutiny and discrimination, and the fear they feel about taking on this family-level identity is an important topic for therapy before the child enters the room.

Box 10.5

Expanding the unsaid

"...[T]houghts that are not clearly formed and those that have not been spoken. It is a resource that resides totally in the inventive and creative aspects of language and narrative, not in the psychic structure (for example, the unconscious), the biological structure (for example, the brain), nor the social structure (for example, a family). Rather, this capacity for change lies in people's ability to be in language with one another and, through the linguistic process, create and develop the realities that have meaning for them...

(Anderson, 1997, p. 118)

Expanding the unsaid centered what was most true for this particular family as opposed to conducting therapy sessions where clients are invited to rehearse well-worn cultural scripts – scripts about origin or scripts meant to investigate another person's identity, some of which may ease some surface-level anxiety felt by cisgender parents but will not actually provide any support to the transgender child. Surface-level conversations begin with questions like how do I know if my kid is really trans? and develop into professional conversations that invoke assessment of the child's gender identity: is the child persistent, insistent, and consistent in their gender nonconforming identity? If we as therapists choose to center these professional, medicalized questions, we are also endorsing the idea that each child lives in a family that consistently invites (or at least makes space for) their culturally oppressed transgender identity, and provides enough support for it to be persistently inhabited in different contexts. An example of an anti-trans therapist stance would be to put great meaning on the fact that a trans child does not "ask for or demand" their pronouns be used with every family member. In Lee's case, he was not comfortable asking his grandparents to use he/him pronouns because he was afraid they would "think it was weird and disgusting." Being aware of transphobia and the very real consequences of social rejection, isolation, and violence does not mean a child's gender identity is not real. Because our society continues to be founded on oppressive discourses that value gender conformity and binaries of all kinds, this is an unrealistic standard to which we professionals hold transgender children. To follow a professional protocol that privileges assessment of gender identity above all closes off other conversations and forecloses any possibility of expanding the unsaid.

Conclusion

Queer-contextualized CT keeps much of the theory intact – the postmodern base that invites and honors multiple truths, lived experience, uses client language, and is open to revision. It keeps the spaciousness and room for individual meaning-making and creativity to emerge. It identifies language and conversation as the mechanism of change. What is radically revised in a queer-contextualized CT is the silence inherent in the theory, the lack of guidance or talk about how social positions materially impact peoples' lives. There is a whiteness to that silence, one that makes too much room for status quo replication. In an imagined world where queer people and families are centered, there would be a default understanding that queer children follow a natural and somewhat predictable path of identity development, and similarly, that queer relationships follow a legible series of developmental markers as well. That would be floating in the air, accessible to both clinician and client, ready to be brought into the conversation. Therapists would "be public" about the knowledge they hold about queer development and offer it readily as part of the dialogue. Instead of tacitly making space for queer clients, queer-contextualized CT assumes queer clients to occupy the center. Therefore, there would be no silence about identity, social position, privilege, or oppression because that would be a fully talked about aspect of human development across the life-span. We would explicitly name the oppressive nature of heteropatriarchy and how its assumptions about how a person should live, look, and relate cause harm.

Queer-contextualized collaborative therapists use the foundational principles of CT: being public, not-knowing, expanding the unsaid, using a problem-determined system rather than family of origin, but we do so with a matrix of knowledge and understanding surrounding those principles about how queer people live and grow. We offer developmental frameworks that center queer lives, and not just in the minority stress way but in a normalized way that emphasizes the predictable, natural stages of development outside of interactions with oppressive structures. In this way we can make the world we want to live in more and more with each therapeutic conversation. For example, and as was certainly the case with Lee and his parents, trans and queer kids bestow gifts to their families in predictable and stable ways, and therefore parents of transgender kids will undergo a predictable set of experiences that deeply enhance their own personal development. Queer-contextualized collaborative therapists can organize these experiences and offer a map for families that both normalize and celebrate their queer family lives.

How does the concept of "not knowing" operate in your clinical practice? How can you hold the tension between being collaborative and "not knowing" with a commitment to practice in ways that center queerness and challenge oppressive influences?

Are there things you need to learn about queer people and the history of queerness in order to offer positive, normalized examples of queer development in therapeutic conversations?

What would "being public" about your knowledge about queerness, including your own social location and identities, mean for your practice? What would shift?

What does collaboration look like in a context where people have different access to power and resources? How can you collaborate with a parent who is stuck in oppressive discourses?

Figure 10.2 Questions for Reflection.

References

Anderson, H. (1997). *Conversation, language, and possibilities: A postmodern approach to therapy*. Basic Books.

Anderson, H., & Goolishian, H. (1992). The client is the expert: A not-knowing approach to therapy. In S. McNamee & K. J. Gergen (Eds.), *Therapy as social construction* (pp. 25–39). Sage

binaohan, b. (2014). *decolonizing trans/gender 101*. biyuti publishing.

Bull, B., & D'Arrigo-Patrick, J. (2018). Parent experiences of a child's social transition: Moving beyond the loss narrative. *Journal of Feminist Family Therapy*, *30*(3), 170–190, DOI: 10.1080/08952833.2018.1448965

Burr, V. (1995). *An introduction to social constructionism*. Taylor & Frances/ Routledge. https://doi.org/10.4324/9780203299968

Chenail, R., Reiter, M., Torres-Gregory, M., Ilic, D. (2020). Postmodern family therapy. In K. S. Wampler, R. B. Miller, & R. B. Seedall (Eds.), *The handbook of systemic family therapy* (pp. 417–442). Wiley.

D'Arrigo-Patrick, J., Hoff, C., Knudson-Martin, C., & Tuttle, A. (2016). Navigating critical theory and postmodernism: Social justice and therapist power in family therapy. *Family Process*, *56*, 574–588.

Gergen, K. (2009). *An invitation to social construction*. SAGE Publications.

McDowell, T., Knudson-Martin, C., & Bermudez, J. M. (2018). *Socioculturally attuned family therapy: Guidelines for equitable theory and practice*. Routledge.

Ryan, C., Russell, S. T., Huebner, D., Diaz, R., & Sanchez, J. (2010). Family acceptance in adolescence and the health of LGBT young adults. *Journal of Child and Adolescent Psychiatric Nursing*, *23*(4), 205–213. https://doi.org/10.1111/ j.1744-6171.2010.00246.x

Serano, J. (2018). *Everything you need to know about Rapid Onset Gender Dysphoria*. Medium. https://juliaserano.medium.com/everything-you-need-to-know-about-rapid-onset-gender-dysphoria-1940b8afdeba

Weinhardt, L. S., Xie, H., Wesp, L. M., Murray, J. R., Apchemengich, I., Kioko, D., & Cook-Daniels, L. (2019). The role of family, friend, and significant other support in well-being among transgender and non-binary youth. *Journal of GLBT Family Studies*, *15*(4), 311–325. https://doi.org/10.1080/15504 28X.2018.1522606

Glossary

This glossary includes sociocultural language used throughout the book. While many of these terms can be understood in the context in which they are used, we wanted to offer clear and simple descriptions for concepts that are often confusing or complex. We view these definitions as a starting point, and not a final answer, as language is highly contextual and changes rapidly. Definitions were created with the assistance of student consultants and generative AI.

Ableism
Ableism is discrimination or prejudice against people with disabilities. It manifests through stereotypes, marginalization, or barriers in access to resources, services, and opportunities. Ableism can be both overt (e.g., derogatory language) and subtle (e.g., structural barriers in society that make life more difficult for disabled people).

Affirmative
Affirmative refers to the act of validating, supporting, or confirming something, especially in relation to someone's identity. For example, gender-affirmative care might include using someone's pronouns, validating their identity, or supporting a medical transition. Queer-affirmative care might include exploring attraction and identity and supporting diverse relationship structures.

Assigned Sex or Gender
At or before birth, individuals are typically assigned both a sex and a gender based on the appearance of their external genitalia. For instance, a baby born with a vulva is often assigned the sex of female and the gender of girl, even though biological sex is multifaceted and gender identity is not yet known. Many people go on to identify with the sex and gender they were assigned at birth; these

individuals are referred to as cisgender. Others may not identify with these assigned categories and may instead identify as transgender, nonbinary, gender expansive, or in other ways that reflect their lived experience.

Bakla
Bakla is a term from Filipino culture that refers to a person who was assigned male at birth but identifies and lives as a woman or feminine individual. In some contexts, bakla is used as a cultural and linguistic term for transgender women, though it has different social and cultural connotations than the Western concept of being transgender.

Ballroom House
A ballroom house refers to a collective or chosen family within the LGBTQ+ ballroom culture, often centered around performance, support, and belonging. Houses are typically led by a house mother and/or house father and provide a space for marginalized LGBTQ+ people, especially those of color, to express themselves through voguing and competing in balls.

Bias
Bias refers to an inclination or preference for or against a particular group, idea, or individual, often in an unfair or prejudiced way. Bias can be implicit (unconscious) or explicit (conscious) and can affect how we perceive, treat, or make decisions about others, often based on race, gender, or other characteristics.

Biphobia
Biphobia is the fear, hatred, or prejudice against people who are bisexual. It can involve invalidation of bisexual identities (e.g., assuming bisexual people are confused or going through a phase) or discrimination that targets people attracted to more than one gender. Biphobia can occur within both heterosexual and LGBTQ+ communities.

BIPOC
BIPOC stands for Black, Indigenous, and People of Color. This term emphasizes the unique experiences of Black and Indigenous people, who often face the most severe forms of discrimination, while also acknowledging the diverse experiences of all people of color.

Bisexual
Bisexual refers to a person who experiences romantic and/or sexual attraction to more than one gender. Bisexual people can be attracted to

individuals of the same gender and different genders. It's important to note that bisexuality does not require equal attraction to all genders, and attraction can vary over time.

Capitalism Capitalism is an economic system in which private individuals or companies own and operate the means of production and distribution of goods and services. In capitalist societies, profit is the primary goal, and wealth is typically distributed based on market competition. Capitalism is often critiqued for perpetuating inequality, exploitation of workers, and environmental degradation.

Chosen Family A chosen family is a group of individuals who intentionally form deep, supportive relationships that resemble the bonds of a traditional family, regardless of biological or legal ties. This concept is especially common in LGBTQ+ communities and among people who may be estranged from or unsupported by their families of origin. Also referred to as family of choice.

Cisgender A cisgender person is someone whose gender identity aligns with the sex they were assigned at birth. For example, a person who is assigned female at birth and identifies as a woman is cisgender.

Cisheterosexual A cisheterosexual (or cishet) person is someone who is both cisgender and heterosexual — meaning their gender identity matches their sex assigned at birth, and they are romantically and/or sexually attracted to people of a different gender.

Cishetmono-normative Cishetmononormative refers to the societal assumption or expectation that being cisgender, heterosexual, and in a monogamous relationship is the default or "normal" way to live. This perspective often marginalizes or excludes those who do not fit into these categories.

Cisnormative Cisnormative describes the assumption or belief that all people are cisgender, or that being cisgender is the norm. This can lead to the erasure or invalidation of transgender and nonbinary identities in social, medical, legal, and cultural contexts.

Cissexism Cissexism is the belief that being cisgender (identifying with the gender assigned at birth) is superior or more valid than being transgender. It leads to discrimination against transgender individuals and assumes that everyone's gender identity aligns with their assigned sex at birth. Cissexism can manifest in attitudes, behaviors, and policies that invalidate or ignore the experiences of transgender people.

Collectivism
Collectivism is a cultural or social philosophy that emphasizes the importance of the group over the individual. In collectivist societies, community well-being, collaboration, and mutual support are prioritized, often over personal goals or independence. Collectivism is in contrast to individualism, which emphasizes personal autonomy and self-reliance.

Coming Out
Coming out is the process by which an individual openly shares their sexual orientation, gender identity, or another aspect of their identity that may have previously been unknown or kept private. Coming out is an ongoing decision and process for many LGBTQ+ people.

Compulsory Monogamy
Compulsory monogamy refers to the social expectation or pressure that people should form romantic and sexual relationships with only one partner at a time, usually within a long-term, committed structure like marriage. It suggests that monogamy is treated as the default or natural relationship model, often marginalizing or pathologizing non-monogamous relationships.

Consensual Nonmonogamy
Consensual nonmonogamy (CNM; also referred to as ethical nonmonogamy or ENM) describes any relationship structure in which all partners agree to engage in romantic or sexual connections with more than one person. Consent is a core principle of CNM — everyone involved is aware of and consents to the relationship dynamic. Examples include polyamory, open relationships, and swinging.

Cross-dressing
Cross-dressing is the act of wearing clothing and accessories that are traditionally associated with a different gender than the one a person is typically perceived as. People cross-dress for many reasons, including self-expression, performance (such as drag), comfort, or exploration of gender identity.

Cross-dressing does not necessarily reflect a person's gender identity or sexual orientation.

Decolonizing
Decolonizing is the process of challenging and undoing the lasting impacts of colonialism on knowledge, culture, identity, land, and power. In practice, decolonizing can involve centering Indigenous ways of knowing without appropriating, resisting systems imposed by colonization, and restoring autonomy and representation to communities historically marginalized or oppressed by colonial powers and discourse.

Discrimination
Discrimination is the unfair or unequal treatment of individuals based on characteristics such as race, gender, sexuality, ability, age, or other aspects of identity. It can occur on an individual, institutional, or systemic level, and it often leads to marginalized groups being denied equal access to resources, opportunities, or rights.

Dominant Discourse
Dominant discourse refers to the prevailing ways of thinking, speaking, and understanding the world that reflect and reinforce the values, beliefs, and interests of those in power within a society. These discourses often shape what is considered normal, truthful, or acceptable, and can marginalize or silence alternative perspectives and voices.

Egalitarian
Egalitarian describes a belief in or commitment to equality — especially social, political, and economic equality — among all people. An egalitarian perspective or system seeks to reduce or eliminate hierarchies and discrimination based on factors like gender, race, class, or ability.

Ethno-racial
Ethno-racial is a term that acknowledges the interconnected nature of both ethnicity (shared cultural traits, language, or heritage) and race (often socially constructed categories based on perceived physical differences). It's used to describe people's identities or experiences shaped by both racial and ethnic factors, especially in contexts where those aspects are difficult to separate.

Eurocentric
Eurocentric refers to a worldview or perspective that centers European culture, values, history, and experiences as the norm or superior, often

ignoring or devaluing the knowledge systems, contributions, and histories of non-European peoples. Eurocentrism can shape education, media, art, and social structures in ways that marginalize other cultures.

Gay
Gay typically refers to someone who is romantically and/or sexually attracted to people of the same gender. While it can describe people of any gender, it is often used to describe men who are attracted to other men.

Gender Binary
The gender binary is the concept that there are only two distinct and opposite genders: men and women. This framework assumes that everyone fits neatly into one of these two categories, based on the sex they were assigned at birth.

Gender Dysphoria
Gender dysphoria is the distress or discomfort that can occur when a person's gender identity does not align with the sex they were assigned at birth or with societal expectations tied to that sex. Not all transgender or gender-diverse people experience dysphoria, but for those who do, it can impact emotional, mental, and physical well-being.

Gender Euphoria
Gender euphoria is the positive, affirming emotional experience that arises when a person's gender identity is seen, validated, or expressed in ways that feel authentic and right to them. It can manifest as joy, comfort, confidence, or a deep sense of alignment between one's internal sense of self and how they are perceived or treated. Gender euphoria is often described as the counterpart to gender dysphoria and plays a vital role in the well-being of many trans, nonbinary, and gender-diverse individuals.

Gender Expansive
Gender expansive is a broad term used to describe people whose gender identity or expression extends beyond traditional ideas of the gender binary. It includes those who identify as nonbinary, genderfluid, agender, and more — anyone who moves outside expected norms of gender identity and expression. Also gender nonconforming.

Genderqueer
Genderqueer is a term used by some people whose gender identity does not fit within the conventional

categories of "man" or "woman." It can reflect fluidity, resistance to gender norms, or an identity outside of or in between genders.

Heteronormative
Heteronormative refers to the belief or social expectation that heterosexuality is the only natural, normal, or acceptable form of romantic or sexual relationship, also known as heterocentrism. This perspective enforces rigid gender roles and often assumes traditional pairings of cisgender men and women in relationships, marginalizing queer identities and relationships.

Heteropatriarchy
Heteropatriarchy is a social system in which straight men hold dominant power and where heterosexuality and patriarchy (male dominance) are reinforced together. It privileges cisgender heterosexual men while systematically disadvantaging women, LGBTQ+ people, and those who don't conform to traditional gender and sexual norms.

Heterosexuality
Heterosexuality, also referred to as being straight, is a sexual orientation in which a person is romantically and/or sexually attracted to people of a different gender — typically framed as men attracted to women and women attracted to men. It's often treated as the societal default due to heteronormativity.

Homophobia
Homophobia is fear, hatred, discomfort with, or discrimination against people who are attracted to the same gender — including gay, lesbian, bisexual, and other queer people. Homophobia can be individual (personal prejudice), institutional (laws or policies), or cultural (social norms and media).

Indigenous
Indigenous refers to the original peoples of a region who have distinct cultural, historical, spiritual, and political ties to their ancestral lands. Indigenous communities often have deep-rooted traditions, languages, and ways of life that existed long before colonization. The term can vary globally — for example, First Nations, Native American, Aboriginal, or Māori — depending on the context.

Individualism
Individualism is a belief system or cultural value that emphasizes the importance of personal

independence, self-reliance, and individual rights. In individualist societies, people are often encouraged to prioritize personal goals over collective or community needs, which contrasts with more collectivist cultures that value group harmony and shared responsibilities.

Intersectionality Intersectionality is a framework for understanding how different aspects of a person's identity — such as race, gender, sexuality, class, disability, and more — intersect and overlap, especially in relation to systems of oppression and privilege. Coined by scholar Kimberlé Crenshaw, it highlights that people can experience multiple, interconnected forms of discrimination at once.

Intersex Intersex is a term for people born with physical sex characteristics — such as chromosomes, hormones, or genitalia — that don't fit typical definitions of male or female bodies. Being intersex is a natural variation in human biology, and it is separate from gender identity or sexual orientation.

Lesbian A lesbian is typically a woman who is romantically and/or sexually attracted to other women. Some nonbinary people who have similar attractions may also identify with the term, depending on how they relate to womanhood and lesbian identity. Trans women may also identify as lesbians.

LGBTQ+ LGBTQ+ is an inclusive acronym that stands for Lesbian, Gay, Bisexual, Transgender, and Queer, with the "+" representing other sexual and gender identities (such as intersex, asexual, pansexual, and more). It's used to describe a diverse and expansive community of people whose identities fall outside of cisgender and heterosexual norms. May also be written as LGBT, LGBTQ, LGBTQIA, and more.

Liberatory Liberatory refers to anything that seeks to promote freedom, equality, and the dismantling of oppressive systems. In a liberatory context, actions, movements, or ideologies work toward the empowerment and liberation of marginalized groups. It often focuses on breaking down systems of power, such as racism, sexism, capitalism, or colonialism, and building more inclusive, just societies.

Marginalization   A systemic process of pushing individuals or groups to the edges of society and denying them full access to rights, resources, and opportunities due to their identity, background, or social status. This can include people marginalized by race, gender, sexuality, disability, class, and more.

Masc   Masc (short for masculine) is a term used to describe gender expression that aligns with or embodies traits traditionally associated with masculinity. It can be used by people of any gender and is often found in LGBTQ+ communities as a self-descriptor (e.g., "masc-presenting" or "masc-of-center").

Mixed-gender Relationship   A mixed-gender relationship is a romantic or sexual relationship involving partners of more than one gender. This term includes, but is not limited to, relationships between a man and a woman. It's inclusive of nonbinary, trans, and gender-diverse people whose relationships involve partners of different genders.

Mononormative   Mononormativity is the belief or assumption that monogamy — having one romantic or sexual partner at a time — is the only valid, natural, or moral way to have relationships and that other relationship structures (like polyamory or open relationships) are abnormal, less valid, or less committed. Also known as monogamism.

Microaffirmations   Microaffirmations are small, everyday actions or words that recognize and validate someone's identity, worth, or contributions. These can include using someone's correct pronouns, actively listening, or expressing appreciation. They help create inclusive and supportive environments, especially for marginalized groups.

Microaggressions   Microaggressions are subtle, often unintentional, comments or behaviors that communicate bias, stereotypes, or discrimination toward marginalized groups. Though "micro," these acts can have a cumulative and harmful impact over time. Examples include backhanded compliments, assumptions based on identity, or dismissive language.

Microinvalidations   Microinvalidations are a type of microaggression that subtly dismiss or negate someone's identity, experience, or feelings — often by suggesting they're overreacting or imagining things. For example, telling a person of color that "racism doesn't exist anymore" invalidates their lived experience.

Minoritized   Minoritized describes a group of people who have been pushed into a minority status through social, political, or economic power structures — regardless of their actual numbers. Unlike "minority," which can imply a fixed or numerical status, minoritized highlights that marginalization is something done to a group by systems of power.

Minority Stress   Minority stress refers to the chronic stress and mental health strain that people from marginalized groups experience due to ongoing discrimination, prejudice, and societal exclusion. It helps explain higher rates of anxiety, depression, and other health issues among LGBTQ+ people, people of color, and others who face systemic bias.

Nonbinary   Nonbinary is a gender identity for people whose gender doesn't fit within the traditional categories of man or woman. Nonbinary individuals may identify as a mix of genders, no gender, or move fluidly between genders. It's an umbrella term that can include identities like genderfluid, agender, and genderqueer.

Oppression   Oppression is the systemic and repeated mistreatment, discrimination, or denial of rights and opportunities toward a group of people based on aspects of their identity — such as race, gender, sexuality, class, or ability. It involves power imbalances that are maintained through institutions, culture, and social norms.

Patriarchy   Patriarchy is a social system in which men — especially cisgender men — hold primary power and dominate in roles of leadership, moral authority, and control over resources. It often enforces rigid gender roles, devalues femininity, and marginalizes women, trans people, and others who do not conform to traditional gender norms.

Platonic Partners   Platonic partners are people who share a deep, committed, non-romantic relationship that is often emotionally intimate and may involve cohabitation, life planning, or mutual caregiving. These partnerships challenge the idea that romantic or sexual relationships are the most meaningful kinds of bonds. Also known as queer platonic partners.

Power   Power is the ability to influence, control, or make decisions that affect others. Power exists at multiple levels — individual, interpersonal, institutional, and systemic — and can be used to maintain privilege or to challenge injustice. Power is often unequally distributed in society based on identity and social status.

Privilege   Privilege refers to unearned advantages or benefits that individuals receive based on aspects of their identity, such as race, gender, sexuality, class, or ability. People with privilege may not always be aware of it, but it can protect them from the types of discrimination and barriers that marginalized groups face.

Pronouns   Pronouns are the words we use to refer to someone when we're not using their name and may include established pronouns (e.g., she/her/hers, he/him/his, they/them/theirs) or neopronouns (e.g., ey/em/eir, ze/hir/hirs). In lieu of pronouns, some individuals prefer to be referred to by their name only.

Queer   Queer is a broad and inclusive term used by some people to describe identities or experiences that fall outside of heterosexual and/or cisgender norms. Once used as a slur, queer has been reclaimed by many in LGBTQ+ communities as a powerful, fluid, and self-affirming identity. Not everyone is comfortable with the term, so its use depends on individual preference.

Queer-contextualize   Queer-contextualize means to interpret or frame something — such as a text, experience, history, or cultural norm — through a queer lens. This approach challenges heteronormative assumptions and centers LGBTQ+ perspectives, identities, and experiences. It can reveal how power, identity, and resistance operate in ways that traditional frame-works often overlook.

Racism Racism is a system of oppression that privileges people who are socially categorized as white, while disadvantaging and discriminating against people of color. It operates at multiple levels — individual, institutional, cultural, and systemic — and is rooted in the belief that some races are inherently superior to others.

Radical Radical refers to ideas, movements, or actions that seek deep, fundamental change to existing systems, rather than just surface-level reforms. To be radical means addressing the root causes of injustice — such as racism, patriarchy, capitalism, or colonialism — and imagining alternative futures built on equity and liberation.

Recontextualize Recontextualize means to reinterpret or place something (like a word, idea, event, or image) into a new context, which can shift its meaning or significance. This is often used in critical analysis, activism, or art to challenge dominant narratives or give voice to marginalized perspectives.

Sex Sex refers to a set of physical characteristics — including chromosomes, hormone levels, internal and external reproductive organs, and secondary sex traits — that are often used to categorize individuals as male, female, or intersex at birth. These traits exist along a spectrum and do not always align neatly, especially in the case of intersex individuals. While biological sex is frequently assigned at birth based on external anatomy, it does not determine a person's gender identity.

Sexism Sexism is discrimination or prejudice based on a person's sex or gender, often rooted in the belief that men are superior to women and gender-diverse people. It operates through individual actions and institutional systems that uphold male dominance and reinforce gender-based power imbalances.

Same-gender A same-gender relationship is a romantic or sexual relationship between people of the same gender. This term is often used to describe relationships between two people of the same gender identity, such as two men or two women, though it can include relationships between trans and nonbinary people of the same gender as well.

Transgender
Transgender (often abbreviated trans) describes individuals whose gender identity differs from the sex they were assigned at birth. Transgender people may or may not choose to transition, and their gender identity can be male, female, both, neither, or somewhere in between. Trans may also be used as an umbrella term to include people who are gender expansive, nonconforming, or nonbinary.

Transnational
Transnational refers to processes, organizations, or phenomena that extend or operate across national boundaries. This term is often used to describe issues, identities, or movements that are not confined to one country or culture, such as transnational migration, economies, or social movements.

Transphobia
Transphobia is fear, hatred, discrimination, or prejudice against transgender people. It can manifest in overt actions (like violence or verbal abuse), as well as in subtler behaviors, such as misgendering or invalidating someone's gender identity. Transphobia is rooted in the gender binary.

Transpinay
Transpinay is a term used to describe a transgender woman (someone assigned male at birth but who identifies and lives as a woman) from the Philippines. It combines "trans" (for transgender) and "Pinay" (a colloquial term for Filipino women) and is used to affirm the identity of transgender women in Filipino culture.

Triadic Relationship
A triadic relationship, also triad, in the context of polyamory refers to a romantic or sexual relationship involving three people. These three individuals may all be romantically or sexually involved with each other, or two may be involved with one person while maintaining connections with each other as well. A triad is one form of a polyamorous relationship structure. Also known as a throuple.

Two-spirit Relationship
Two-spirit is a term used by some Indigenous cultures in North America to describe people who embody both masculine and feminine qualities

or have a gender role outside of the typical male/female binary. Two-spirit individuals may have special cultural, spiritual, or ceremonial roles within their communities, and the term has been reclaimed by some Indigenous people to honor their gender and sexual diversity.

White Supremacy White supremacy is both an ideology and a system that asserts that white people are superior to people of all other races and should therefore dominate society. It often manifests in racism, institutional discrimination, and social practices that uphold white privilege and the marginalization of people of color. White supremacy can exist at both individual and systemic levels.

Whiteness Whiteness refers to the social and cultural construction of the identity associated with being white. It involves the privileges, norms, and systems of power that are historically associated with white people in many societies. Whiteness can also refer to the specific social positioning of white people, often in opposition to people of color, and the ways in which these racial dynamics shape social, political, and economic systems.

Xenophobia Xenophobia is the fear, hatred, or prejudice against people from other countries or cultures. This often manifests in discriminatory behaviors, policies, or attitudes that marginalize or exclude immigrants or foreigners. Xenophobia is rooted in a fear of the "other" and can lead to racism, nationalism, and social division.

Index

For Product Safety Concerns and Information please contact our EU
representative GPSR@taylorandfrancis.com
Taylor & Francis Verlag GmbH, Kaufingerstraße 24, 80331 München, Germany